Dynamic HTML
in Action

Dynamic HTML in Action

Michele Petrovsky

Osborne McGraw-Hill

Berkeley   New York   St. Louis   San Francisco
Auckland   Bogotá   Hamburg   London   Madrid
Mexico City   Milan   Montreal   New Delhi   Panama City
Paris   São Paulo   Singapore   Sydney
Tokyo   Toronto

Osborne/**McGraw-Hill**
2600 Tenth Street
Berkeley, California 94710
U.S.A.

For information on translations or book distributors outside the U.S.A.,
or to arrange bulk purchase discounts for sales promotions, premiums, or
fund-raisers, please contact Osborne/**McGraw-Hill** at the above address.

Dynamic HTML in Action

1234567890 AGM AGM 901987654321098

ISBN 0-07-882437-0

Publisher
  Brandon A. Nordin

Editor-in-Chief
  Scott Rogers

Acquisitions Editor
  Megg Bonar

Project Editor
  Cynthia Douglas

Editorial Assistants
  Gordon Hurd
  Stephane Thomas

Technical Editor
  Rebecca Tapley

Copy Editors
  Heidi Steele
  Deborah Craig

Proofreaders
  Carroll Proffitt
  Joe Sadusky

Indexer
  Richard Shrout

Computer Designer
  Jani Beckwith

Illustrator
  Arlette Crosland

Cover Design
  Regan Honda

I'd like to dedicate this book to the many people in data processing,
like those who developed and maintain the software suites Linux and Apache,
who not only create something marvelous but then give it away for free.
Their generosity colors their work, contributing to its quality.
What's more, they've contributed to us all in another way—
by helping many who otherwise wouldn't have been able to do so
take a ride on the Information Superhighway.

About the Author . . .

Michele Petrovsky received her Master of Science in Computer/Information Science from the University of Pittsburgh in 1981, and a Bachelor of Arts in Spanish and Russian from Pitt in 1973.

Michele has worked as a freelance author and editor for the past several years; as well as being published regularly, she teaches at the university and community college levels. More recently, Michele was a contributing author for the Que title *Upgrading and Repairing Networks*, the author of *Microsoft Internet Information Server Sourcebook*, published in October 1997 by John Wiley and Sons., and the author of *Implementing CDF Channels*, to be published in January 1998 by McGraw-Hill.

Michele lives on a Christmas tree farm (really) just north of Wilmington, Delaware, with her husband, three cats, and the occasional visiting deer, hawk, owl, possum, raccoon, and skunk. When she's not reading, writing, or teaching, Michele likes to garden, do tai chi, and watch *Star Trek*—old and new. She welcomes conversations with readers at

petrovsk@voicenet.com

Contents at a Glance

Part 3 References

Contents

Part 3

References

Foreword

Hundreds of people contributed to this book; I'm just the one who's lucky enough to get her name on the cover. Designers, engineers, hackers, mathematicians, and programmers envisioned and then actualized the technologies and techniques the book discusses. Agents, editors, LAN administrators, and Webmasters moved the book from germinating outline to finished manuscript. DHL and Federal Express trucks and planes shuttled hardcopy and diskettes from Southeastern Pennsylvania to Northern California for a couple of months, and later moved thousands of volumes all over the country, so folks like you could pick one up, read it, and hopefully both learn and enjoy.

We're all interconnected. This book and the technologies it discusses and represents, and of which it is a part, are the effect; the interconnectedness is the cause, *not* the other way around. These technologies, like everything, have the greatest impact when they and some of what they produce are shared.

That's why I plan to use ten percent of my proceeds from this book to donate PCs and software to groups and organizations who might otherwise not be able to obtain them. I'd like to urge everyone who reads *Dynamic HTML in Action* to do something along the same lines.

Acknowledgments

No writer could ask for a better group of co-creators than the folks at Osborne/McGraw-Hill. Thanks to Alan, Cynthia, Lars, Megg, and Stephanie. You guys made it fun!

Nor could anyone imagine a better partner and friend than Tom Parkinson. Thanks, Big T, for all the hardware-crisis resolution. And for all the smiles.

Introduction

Everywhere you look today in data processing periodicals, you see mention of something called *Dynamic HTML*. Trouble is, not all of those who created, fleshed out, or report upon the concept define it in the same way. To some, Dynamic HTML covers any Web page that incorporates even a single simple animation. At the other end of the continuum are those who view Dynamic HTML as including only pages whose display is completely at the direction of browser-based scripts, and requires no interaction with a server beyond an initial request for information.

Explaining the term Dynamic HTML, and the concepts behind it, is the purpose of this book. In it, we've adopted the solid middle-of-the-road definition espoused by such bodies as Microsoft Corporation and the World Wide Web Consortium. That is, *Dynamic HTML in Action* considers Dynamic HTML to encompass the use of:

- style sheets
- high-resolution graphics and animation
- sound and video
- a high degree of interaction of a page with databases, whether or not that interaction involves the need for repeated calls to a server

What's in This Book

We've structured this book around a real-world project—the development of a Web page as a gift to the members of the National Writers Union. In building this page, and therefore in *Dynamic HTML in Action*, we've assumed nothing. We've attempted to make the book's content comprehensible by even the most novice Web author or designer. So, throughout the book, you'll see material that might, to those of you with a more extensive background in Web design and implementation, seem at first to pertain more nearly to other topics, such as:

- "traditional" or "static" HTML
- database programming
- development tools

The method behind our madness is this: *Dynamic HTML in Action* offers a broad enough view of Dynamic HTML and the technologies upon which it draws and is built that people with many different operating environments, programming tools, and skill levels will be able to benefit equally from it. For instance, we offer coding examples in a number of languages, such as:

- Visual Basic
- Visual Basic, Scripting Edition (VBScript)
- JavaScript
- JScript

and more. In similar fashion and for similar reasons, those coding examples do *not* present complete pages. Rather, they focus strictly on the programming principle they are intended to illustrate, as a means of focusing your attention on that principle.

Dynamic HTML in Action covers everything you need to know in order to be able to understand and use this most recent stage in the evolution of Web publishing. It offers:

- background information on the nature of, and software environments surrounding, Hypertext Markup Language (HTML)
- a review of the principles involved in Web page design
- an overview of Internet Explorer 4.0 and Netscape Communicator 4.0, the two commercial applications most likely to dominate the implementation of dynamic HTML
- step-by-step discussion of and instruction in using the major features of Dynamic HTML

How This Book Is Organized

Dynamic HTML in Action has three major parts, organized as follows.

Part 1: *Background*

Chapter 1: *Web Publishing* An overview of Web publishing (the nature of HTML; an overview of "traditional" HTML; standards for static HTML; standards for dynamic HTML; constraints and requirements imposed by dynamic HTML)

Chapter 2: *Designing Your Page* Choosing elements that will remain static; choosing elements that will become dynamic; choosing the nature of the activity of dynamic elements

Chapter 3: *Introducing Internet Explorer 4.0*

Chapter 4: *Introducing Netscape Communicator 4.0*

Part 2: *The Project*

Chapter 5: *Adding Intelligence to the Client Display* Incorporating dynamic elements

Chapter 6: *Adding Depth and Texture* Using Cascading Style Sheets (layering elements, and causing elements to appear transparent)

Chapter 7: *Animation* The X, Y, and Z coordinate positioning of elements

Chapter 8: *Moving Elements: Positioning for Optimal Functionality*

Chapter 9: *Moving Elements: Determining Positioning*

Chapter 10: *Moving Elements: Positioning at Runtime*

Chapter 11: *Preparing for Interaction with Databases: Data Binding*

Chapter 12: *Data Binding to Sort or Filter Retrieved* Scripting to define sorting or filtering parameters; scripting to permit repeated sorting or filtering

Chapter 13: *Data Binding to Update Information* Scripting to permit the user to modify or delete items; scripting to permit repeated modification or deletion

Chapter 14: *Data Binding to Create Database Records* Using scripting commands or HTML tags; creating data entry forms which incorporate data binding

Chapter 15: *Preparing for Multimedia: DHTML, Image, and Sound* CD-ROM quality sound and images; scripting to expedite downloading of multimedia material; dealing with bandwidth considerations

Chapter 16: *Using DHTML to Incorporate Sound in a Web Page*

Chapter 17: *Using DHTML to Incorporate High-Resolution Images in a Web Page*

Chapter 18: *Reviewing the Page*

Part 3: *References*

Appendix A: *HTML 3.2 Quick Reference*

Appendix B: *Dynamic HTML Quick Reference*

Appendix C: *JavaScript Quick Reference*

Appendix D: *VBScript Quick Reference*

Appendix E: *Excerpts from the HTML 4.0 Working Draft Specification*

Appendix F: *A Brief Evolutionary History of HTML*

Bibliography: Not only print, but also online sources of information

Glossary: Not only DHTML terms, but also background concepts

Who Should Read This Book

Anyone involved in the creation, maintenance, or management of a Web site of any size or complexity can benefit from *Dynamic HTML in Action*. For instance, Web authors and managers of long standing may want to forego the material in Part 1, and dive straight into Part 2. Those new to Web publishing, on the other hand, may find the background information in the book's first section helpful in establishing a context for their learning. While the book is aimed largely at Web designers and authors, its explorations of scripting and interaction with databases make it a useful tool for programmers as well. And even folks who don't know a tag from a directive need not despair. The Quick References in Part 3 are more than enough to get you started.

Because Dynamic HTML is interdisciplinary, drawing upon skills as diverse as graphics design, human/machine interface design, and Web content development and coding, anyone involved in any of these areas can use *Dynamic HTML in Action* to good effect.

Note

The project that serves as the central example of this book is one that the author conceived and developed as a contribution to the National Writers' Union, of which she is a member. Readers should not misconstrue this project as being in any way a product of the Union as an entity. The NWU did not participate in the design of this project; nor will the Union be involved in its maintenance. Both those are the responsibility of the author.

PART ONE

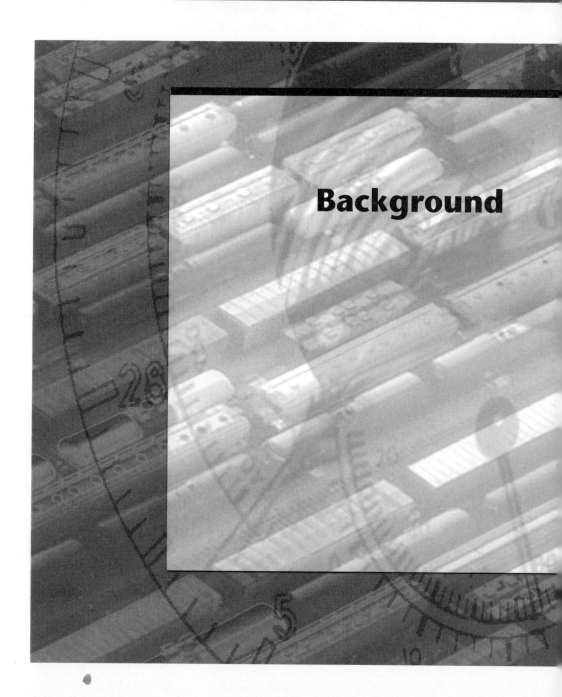

Background

Chapter One

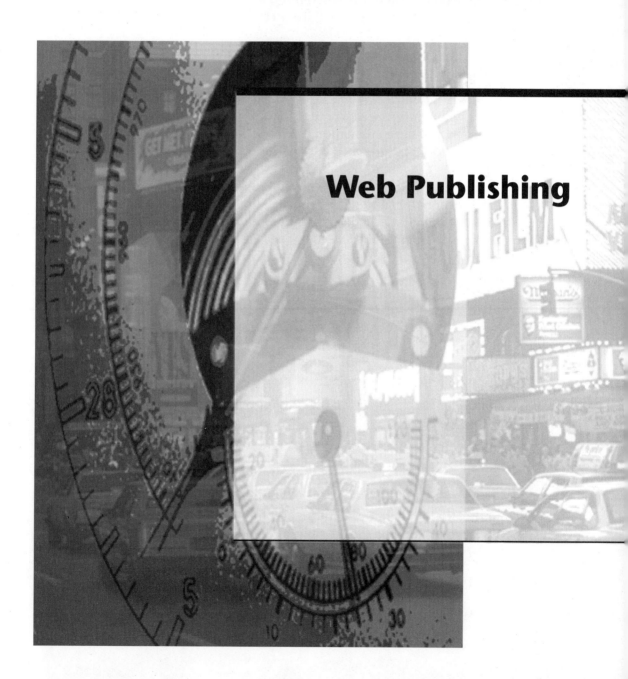

Web Publishing

For an institution that hasn't yet reached its 30th birthday, the Internet has a remarkable track record. Nowhere is that performance more evident than in the evolution of the means of transmitting and displaying information. And nowhere is that evolution more clearly showcased than in the development of Dynamic HTML from HTML.

The Evolution of Dynamic HTML

Dynamic HTML, like so much jargon, can have different meanings depending upon who's using the term. Most often, though, the phrase is used by software vendors to describe the combination of HTML, style sheets, and scripts that allows documents to be animated and interactive, and even to employ media such as sound and video.

On April 24, 1997, the World Wide Web Consortium (W3C) published a set of general functional requirements for extensions to HTML. These requirements mean that HTML has standardized around Netscape Navigator 3.0 and Microsoft Internet Explorer 3.0. The extensions, which make up Dynamic HTML as most of us understand it, are discussed in a series of W3C standards for cascading style sheets (CSS), which we'll discuss in more detail in Chapter 6.

The W3C continues to consider enhancements to traditional HTML for inclusion in future versions of the markup language:

- dynamic page change by means of scripts
- frames and subsidiary windows
- improved access to HTML features for people with disabilities
- ability of documents themselves to create other, interactive documents that will interact with databases
- better handling of specialized notations such as mathematical symbols
- more standardized access to and handling of multimedia components
- forms that are richer visually and let the user interact with a Web or a database server at a greater level of detail
- a single model for document structure and activity
- use of style sheets as the major means of controlling active displays

Let's look at some of these features more closely.

Scripting

Scripting refers to the ability to add command files or scripts, through which you can augment the capabilities of HTML and embed or otherwise associate objects such as image and music files with HTML-based documents. W3C's current work on scripting defines and describes several areas:

- a notation for scripts that is separate from standard HTML notation
- a standard event model (*Events* are any actions, usually user-initiated, to which a browser might be expected to respond. So clicking a Forward button, pulling down a menu, and simply clicking the OK button are all legitimate events.)
- implementing scripting through linked script files
- including script commands within a document
- including script commands within individual HTML components

An HTML element *identifies a basic characteristic of the document makeup, such as an image that you want to include in the document. Elements in turn carry* attributes, *which further define the characteristic. For example, the IMG element, which allows you to place a graphic image in a Web page, has, among others, the SRC (source) attribute, which defines the location and filename of the image you're including.*

Interactive Documents and Interaction with Databases

The W3C intends tomorrow's HTML to include improvements to forms and interactive documents, especially improvements that will facilitate access for people with disabilities.

Mathematics

At the time of this writing, HTML lacks an effective means of embedding mathematical expressions in documents. The W3C aims to define a method of representation that can more easily convey complex mathematical expressions. One possible vehicle for such representation is the Extensible Markup Language, or XML.

Sidebar

XML is actually not so much a language as a standard for certain aspects of hypertext document markup. Because of the historical and current fluidity of HTML and Web scripting, some industry watchers have gone so far as to designate the XML standard as the next revolution in Web publishing.

Multimedia

Most industry experts expect that the content of Web pages will come to resemble that of today's multimedia CD-ROMs and television programs. Which is to say, don't be surprised if tomorrow's Web is essentially a distribution system for interactive and real-time multimedia content.

Unfortunately, unlike the consensus approach to enhancing HTML, there are currently several different groups working independently on the integration of real-time multimedia into the Internet. These groups include:

- CD-ROM researchers and vendors
- Internet-based audio-on-demand and video-on-demand researchers and developers
- World Wide Web Consortium

Sound like a recipe for non-interoperability? It does indeed. Luckily, however, the W3C has members from all three groups, and all of the groups recently took part in a workshop on real-time multimedia and the Web. One outcome of the event is that the participants agreed to make the Consortium the forum for exchanging ideas and reaching consensus on integrating real-time multimedia into the Web.

Creating Real-Time Multimedia Content

Both the Web community in general and the individuals and organizations developing Internet-based on-demand audio and video are aware that Web and CD-ROM functionality overlap in offering more, and more dense and rich, media as part of their content. Therefore, the W3C is proceeding with the assumption that real-time multimedia will be integrated into the Web through enhancements to basic Web technologies such as HTML, images and image maps, and URLs. This assumption separates the Consortium from other groups working on real-time multimedia. For example, the Java community uses Java code-generating applications to produce real-time multimedia content and then uses low-level Java code to format the distribution of that content.

Today's Web technology is also limited in its ability to produce continuous multimedia presentations. To create this type of presentation, authors must define things such as

"Three minutes into the presentation, show image X. Keep it on the screen for 30 seconds"

In other words, we still lack a robust and reliable way to synchronize within and between media that make up a continuous presentation. Currently, you have to use a scripting language such as JavaScript or Visual Basic to synchronize media. However, script-based content has two disadvantages:

- it can be laborious to produce and maintain
- it makes it harder to use search engines and other automated tools such as conversion utilities

Controlling Audio and Video Replay

You can integrate *simple*, as opposed to *real-time* (or *continuous*) audio or video content into a Web page in several ways. For instance, you can use audio as a background to your page, in the form of a continuous loop that repeats a particular aural phrase. However, at the time of this writing, there is no standardized way to control audio or video replay in your Web page. The World Wide Web Consortium is investigating two means of solving this problem:

- defining a standard API that will allow a web-content author to explicitly control replay
- defining standard attributes for the HTML element OBJECT

Sidebar

An *object* is just what its name implies—some component of an HTML page. An object could be a clickable button or bar; a database that's associated with the page; or a sound or video file that's incorporated into the page.

Network Transmission of Real-Time Multimedia

Since multimedia Web content moves mainly over the Internet, which is still almost exclusively based on TCP/IP, the W3C's work on transmitting real-time multimedia focuses on this environment and on a new member of the TCP/IP suite: *the real-time streaming protocol* (RTSP). RTSP provides functions similar to those of a CD player, such as play, fast forward, pause, stop, and record. The RTSP version most likely to be endorsed has much in common with HTTP. This will allow Web developers to continue to use technologies and methods—such as content caching, user authentication, and traffic encryption—that were originally developed for HTTP. Figure 1-1 compares RTSP and HTTP.

HTTP:	RSTP is:
connectionless (You connect, put in a request, receive the results of the request, and disconnect. No permanent connection is maintained.)	like HTTP in providing content caching and some security
stateless (No information about a transaction is kept, once the transaction is completed.)	an enhancement of HTTP in providing streaming functionality
not always completely secure	

Figure 1-1. *RSTP and HTTP*

Real-Time Transport Protocol and Application-Level Framing

Another new protocol, the *real-time transport protocol* (RTP), is being touted as the emerging standard for moving real-time multimedia data across the Internet. RTP is based on the conviction that real-time data should be split into packets in a such a way that the receiver application can process each packet independently. This latter process, called *application-level framing* (see Figure 1-2), helps to synchronize multimedia streams when there is packet loss as a stream makes its way across the Internet. If you're sending an HTML page that is synchronized with an audio stream, RTP and application-level framing ensure that any packet loss in the HTML transmission will not cause an interruption in the real-time output. Rather, it will only result in what amounts to a hole in the displayed page. You can also use application-level framing to facilitate Web multicasting.

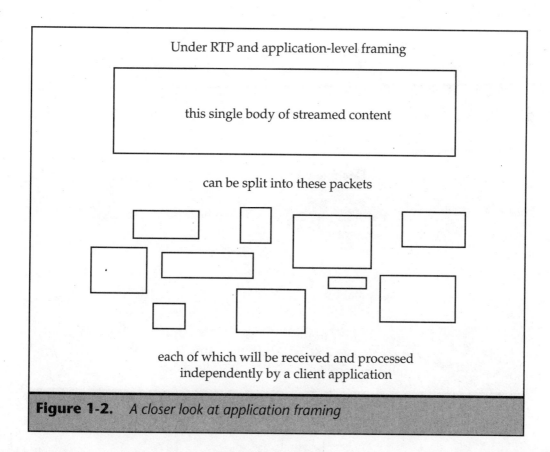

Figure 1-2.   *A closer look at application framing*

Document Modeling and Style Sheets

As a means of further standardizing the nature and structure of documents on the Web, the W3C has developed the *Document Object Model* (DOM). DOM, whose makeup is sketched in Figure 1-3, is a platform- and language-independent interface that will allow documents to be dynamically accessed, and their contents, structure, and style to be dynamically altered. Furthermore, DOM seeks to ensure that the results of any processing carried out on Web documents can be easily incorporated back into the presented page.

These are the DOM requirements that pertain most directly to our discussion of DHTML:

- general requirements
- content manipulation
- document manipulation
- document meta-information
- event modeling
- structure navigation
- style sheets

Let's take a closer look at the most important of these categories.

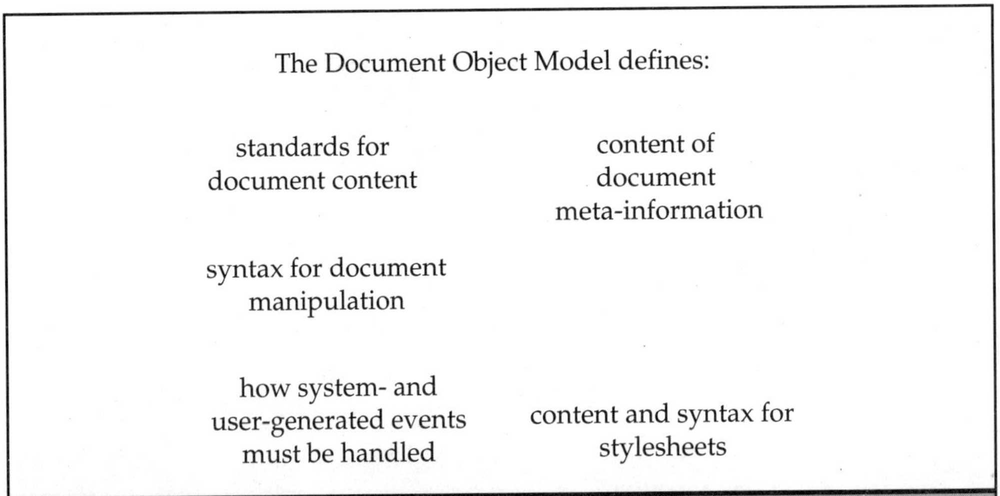

The Document Object Model defines:

standards for
document content

content of
document
meta-information

syntax for document
manipulation

how system- and
user-generated events
must be handled

content and syntax for
stylesheets

Figure 1-3. *Anatomy of DOM*

General DOM Requirements

Let's begin by taking a glance the World Wide Web Consortium's overall goals for what the DOM must accomplish.

- Consistent naming conventions must used through all levels of the DOM.

- DOM can be used both to construct and to deconstruct a Web document.

- DOM must be is language-neutral and platform-independent.

- DOM will not create problems related to security, validity, or privacy.

- DOM will not preclude the use either of tools external to the content of a Web document, or of scripts embedded within Web documents.

- There will be a core DOM that is applicable to HTML, CSS, and XML documents.

Content Manipulation

The standards published by the World Wide Web Consortium become the features presented by commercial software. That will be as true for DHTML as it has been for any software category. So, let's take a look at what abilities the W3C expects to see in any software that manipulates the contents of Web documents:

- add, change, or delete document content at runtime

- determine the containing element from any text part of the document

- navigate dynamic content

Document Manipulation

Document manipulation, as opposed to the manipulation of document content, involves messing around with the structure and characteristics of a Web document. Because the W3C's goals are pivotal in defining the shape of Web-related software, we must examine what abilities the W3C wants HTML-based document manipulation to include:

- add, remove and change elements or attributes in the document structure, if permitted by the document definition

- deliver a consistent reproducible document structure from any document acted upon by the DOM

Document Meta-Information

If software vendors adhere to W3C requirements for document meta-information, HTML documents will have to contain or reference information such as source location and creation date.

Event Modeling

The Document Object Model seeks to ensure that Dynamic HTML will provide the ability to respond to any action users may take in dealing with a Web document. We've outlined DOM's subsidiary event model in Figure 1-4, and summarized that model as follows.

- All elements on a Web page will be capable of generating events.
- Binding to events, that is, linking specific actions to particular events, will be provided for.
- Events will be categorized as interactions, updates, and changes.
- Events will be defined to be platform- and language-independent.
- Events will bubble through the structural hierarchy of the document. That is, they need only be recognized once to have an effect throughout the document, if such a global effect is appropriate.
- Responses to events will be capable of overriding default browser behavior.
- User interactions with documents will be promptly recognized and responded to.

Structure Navigation

The W3C has created a set of requirements that address problems associated with navigation around or between Web documents. Tasks such as finding the parent of a given page would be affected by the Consortium's structure navigation requirements, which include this type of criteria:

- All elements and attributes in the document can and must be able to be dealt with as programmable objects.
- Means to query all elements and attributes must be provided.
- Means for navigation from any element to any other element must be provided.

The DOM Event Model
specifies how to handle:

associating actions
with events

categorizing events

the relationship of events to
the structure of the document

how differences between event
handling and default browser
actions will be resolved

Figure 1-4. *A kaleidoscope of events*

CSS

Style sheets, and specifically cascading style sheets, constitute one of the most important of the W3C's enhancements to HTML. W3C developed CSS to meet the needs of Web designers by allowing designers to explicitly define such characteristics of a Web page's display as:

- colors
- fonts
- white space

The W3C's work on CSS began in 1994 at CERN; the set of standards referred to as CSS1 became a W3C Recommendation in December 1996. CSS1 defines the language in which style sheets must be written and the properties that designers can use to define the presentation of documents.

Note ▶ *What the W3C calls a* recommendation *can be considered a standard. What it calls a* draft *is a first stab at a recommendation.*

In addition to CSS1, you can find the text of several other CSS-based specifications on the World Wide Web Consortium's Web site at http://www.w3c.org. These two are relevant to DHTML:

- Aural Cascading Style Sheets or ACSS, which describes the CSS properties that pertain to aural output devices such as speech synthesizers

- CSS Positioning, which extends CSS to support the positioning and visibility of HTML elements

Here's most of what W3C wants to find in style sheets:

- The CSS style sheet model will be defined as the core component of an overall model; this core will also be applicable to other style languages.

- CSS style sheets will permit the embedding of styles in all categories of Web page elements.

- Selectors, rules, and properties contained in individual style sheets must be subject to being added, removed and changed. (We'll define these in Chapter 6.)

- All forms of implementing a CSS style sheet must be subject to being added, removed, and changed.

The following browsers support at least the bulk of the W3C recommendations for cascading style sheets at the time of this writing:

- Arena, W3C's own test bed browser

- Emacs-w3, also and affectionately known as Gnuscape Navigator

- Microsoft Internet Explorer 4.0

- Netscape Communicator 4.0

Style Sheets in More Detail

Web style sheets have been around for a number of years, but their power and importance went largely unnoticed for quite some time. Web authors who wanted to influence the presentation of the pages they created frequently used Netscape's proprietary extensions rather than the more powerful style sheets. But today, with more and more authoring tools and browsers implementing style sheets, the advantages of this tool are becoming apparent.

Netscape's BODY attributes have been widely accepted on the Web. But BODY attributes as they are frequently used force an author to choose between the benefits of such abilities as being able to place an image in the background of a document and the costs in time and effort needed to do so. Style sheets, on the other hand, allow an author to choose from a gallery of images controlled by different style sheets. So, for instance, you could use a 24-bit style sheet for one application, and for another use an 8-bit style sheet, depending on how many colors the target system can display. Style sheets can make your life easier in other ways. For example, style sheets let you specify such presentational details as tab settings and horizontal rulers only once. From then on, you can simply apply the relevant style sheet to most or even all of the documents to be displayed at your site. What's more, if, at some later point, you decide that you want to add an HTML directive such as

```
WIDTH="70%"
```

you only need to change this parameter once.

Style sheets also reduce download time because all of the style information related to a document, or even to a Web site, is contained in a single file.

Style sheets provide a great deal of flexibility in creating presentation effects. You can apply properties such as color, background, margin, and border to all elements. In contrast, using HTML and its sometimes-proprietary extensions forces you to rely on attributes that may be available for only a few elements.

Furthermore, style sheets let you apply a style to all units of a particular type, such as:

- all emphasized text
- all level-two headings
- all paragraphs

Some CSS-compliant authoring tools you might want to investigate are:

- *Allaire's HomeSite editor (v2.5 and above)*

■ *Harlequin's Webmaker*

■ *Sausage Software's HotDog*

CSS Positioning

In this section, we'll do a quick cook's tour of the important CSS positioning properties to get a feel for their role in the project we'll soon be starting.

Position

Position establishes one or more of the following:

■ A new clipping region for child elements that are absolute-positioned

■ A new rectangular plane for the layout of child elements that are absolute-positioned

■ A stacking order, or Z order relative to a parent element

■ An origin for the positioning of child elements

■ An x and y position for a child element relative to either its parent absolute-positioned origin (if the child element is absolute-positioned) or relative to its normally rendered position (if the child element is relative-positioned)

Parent and child? Take these terms literally. If an HTML element's presence and display depends on the presence of another element, the first element is the child of the second (parent) element.

Width and Height

You can specify percentage values for both the *width* and *height* properties. These values are implemented in terms of the height and width of the element that defines the coordinate system in which they appear, and within which you're placing the positioned element.

Clip

Clipping alters the display of an HTML document, although it does not affect how it is laid out. The clipping region defines the part of the element that is visible. The region is computed by the intersection of the parent's clip region with the value of a element's *clip* and *overflow* properties. Any part of an element that is outside a defined clipping region, including borders and padding belonging to the element, will be transparent.

Coordinates for clipping relate to the element's origin. Interestingly enough, negative clipping coordinates are permitted. And using the default value for *clip* causes the clip rectangle to cover all of the element to which you apply it.

Overflow

The *overflow* property determines what happens when an element's contents exceed its height or width. Setting *overflow* equal to *none* means that the element won't be clipped. Setting *overflow* to a value of *clip* indicates that clipping should be performed with no scrolling mechanism. Finally, setting *overflow* to a value of *scroll*, while somewhat dependent for its exact results on the nature of the client display, should cause some scrolling.

Z-index

If you want to specify the stacking order of elements, you need to use *z-index*. Doing so overrides ordinary HTML behavior, which would stack the elements bottom-to-top in the order in which they are named in the HTML document. *Z-index* allows stacking order to be given as an integer that represents the element's position in the stack relative to sibling and parent elements: Elements with negative *z-indexes* are stacked below their parent element, while elements with positive *z-indexes* are stacked above their parent. What happens if you want to stack elements that are neither siblings nor parent/child? You can determine the order in which such elements will be stacked by evaluating both elements' ancestors according to the rules we just discussed.

Visibility

The *visibility* property determines the initial display state of an element, but nothing else. Elements that are hidden take up the same physical space as they would if they were visible. You simply cannot see them. Or, in more correct Web jargon, they have been rendered *transparent*. The *visibility* property is most frequently used in scripting to dynamically display a selected one of several overlapping elements.

A Quick CSS Tutorial

A style sheet is made up of *style rules* that tell a browser how to present a document. Each rule is in turn made up of a *selector*—usually an HTML element such as BODY, P, or EM—and the style to be applied to the selector. There are numerous properties that may be defined for an element. Each property takes a value, which together with the property describes how the selector should be presented.

The correct syntax for a style rule in a CSS style sheet is:

```
selector { property: value }
```

You read that right. Those are curly braces enclosing the property value, not square brackets or parentheses. This syntax holds even if you need or want to attach multiple style declarations to a single selector. Just be sure to separate the properties involved by a semicolon, as in:

```
selector { property1: value1; property2: value2 }
```

Linking HTML Code to an External Style Sheet

You can link an external style sheet (that is, a style sheet you've stored in a physical file other than the one containing your HTML code and document) to the code and document by embedding the HTML element LINK in the document's HEAD section. You can also place the optional TYPE attribute there if you want to tell the client browser to ignore style sheet types it does not support. In similar fashion, the optional MEDIA attribute specifies the medium (or media) to which the style sheet should be applied.

 *When should you use an external style sheet? These are a good choice when you want to apply a single style to a number of pages. With an external style sheet, you can change the look of an entire site simply by changing this one external style sheet file. Another benefit is that most browsers cache external style sheets, thereby cutting down on delays in page presentation.*

Embedding a Style Sheet

To embed a style sheet within an HTML document, you must place the STYLE element in the document's HEAD section. And as was the case with linking to external style sheets, you can also use the optional attributes TYPE and MEDIA with STYLE. But bear in mind that some older browsers are oblivious to the STYLE element, and as a result may show the contents of that element to the user, rather than carrying out the instructions inherent in that content. But being the on-top-of-things author that you are, you know how to prevent this, by encasing the STYLE element within SGML comment delimiters, like this:

```
<!-- comment (in this case, your STYLE definition) -->
```

When should you use an embedded style sheet? This option is a logical choice only when a single document has a truly unique style.

Importing a Style Sheet

Within a CSS style sheet file or even within a STYLE element, you can tell a browser to apply an imported style sheet to the document it's currently dealing with by using the CSS statement *@import*. Consider the following brief style sheet file.

```
<STYLE TYPE="text/css" MEDIA="screen, projection">
<!-- @import url(http://www.htmlhelp.com/style1.css); @import
url(/stylesheets/newstyle.css);-->
```

All *@import* statements must occur at the beginning of a style sheet. And any rules explicitly defined within the style sheet itself will override any conflicting rules in the imported style sheets.

The order in which style sheets are imported has a definite impact on the results they produce. In the brief style sheet we just laid out, if the first imported style sheet, style.css, specified that STRONG (that is, boldface) elements be shown in red, and the second imported sheet, newstyle.css, specified that STRONG elements be shown in yellow, the resulting display would present all STRONG elements in yellow.

When should you import style sheets? Imported style sheets can be a handy way to introduce modularity into your HTML documents. For instance, you can create categories of style sheets, and then design each category to handle a particular selector. Each member of a category will accomplish different effects for that selector. Table 1-1 illustrates one such scheme.

The category	applies to	and contains the style sheets	which in turn contain rules for
simplst	rules for common HTML elements such as HEAD, BODY, and P	head.css boddy.css p.css	positioning positioning positioning
moredetl	rules for more detailed features such as visibility	morehead.css morebody.css morepara.css	visibility visibility visibility
nittgrit	the level of greatest detail in all elements dealt with	nitthead.css nittbody.cxx nittpara.css	stacking stacking stacking

Table 1-1.   *Modularity Through Style Sheets*

Inlining Style

Style can be inlined—that is, included as part of the definition of an HTML element—by associating the STYLE attribute and appropriate values for it with that element. You can apply the STYLE attribute to any BODY element (including BODY itself). STYLE can have quite a variety of CSS declarations as its value, and any number of them as well. But as with selector syntax (see the "A Quick CSS Tutorial" section earlier in this chapter), when you use multiple characteristics with STYLE, each such declaration must be separated by a semicolon.

For example, the inlining:

```
<P STYLE="color: red; font-family: 'New Century Schoolbook', serif">
```

can be translated as

```
Display this paragraph in red, in the New Century Schoolbook font, if available.
```

When should you inline style? This technique throws away most of the advantages of style sheets (since it mixes content with presentation), so you should only use it when you have to apply a style to a single occurrence of an element.

CLASS as an Alternative to Inlining

You can use the CLASS attribute to specify a category of style to which an element may be assigned. For example, you might create a style sheet that contains the classes *copasetic* and *dangerous*:

```
copasetic { color: lime; background: #ff80c0 }
dangerous { font-weight: bolder; color: red }
```

You can then reference these classes in HTML with the CLASS attribute.

In HTML styles as in programming, mnemonics are valuable; it's a good idea to name classes according to their function. It's obvious that a class named *dangerous* should be used for warning and error messages. Calling it *red* or, even worse, *style2*, wouldn't have made this as apparent.

When should you use classes? They can be a very effective method of applying different styles to structurally identical sections of an HTML document.

Thumbnail Review

1. World Wide Web Consortium sets standards for HTML, DHTML, SGML, and XML, among others.

2. HTML, DHTML, and XML can each be considered subsets of SGML.

3. The dynamism of DHTML consists largely of positioning and visibility controls, as well as the ability to include multimedia material.

4. The meaning of the term DHTML can vary depending upon who's using it.

5. Style sheets, and in particular cascading style sheets, are perhaps the most important DHTML tool.

Looking Ahead

Now that you've gained a grasp of the concepts most basic to DHTML, we'll turn, in Chapter 2, to designing a Web page in which to apply these concepts.

Chapter Two

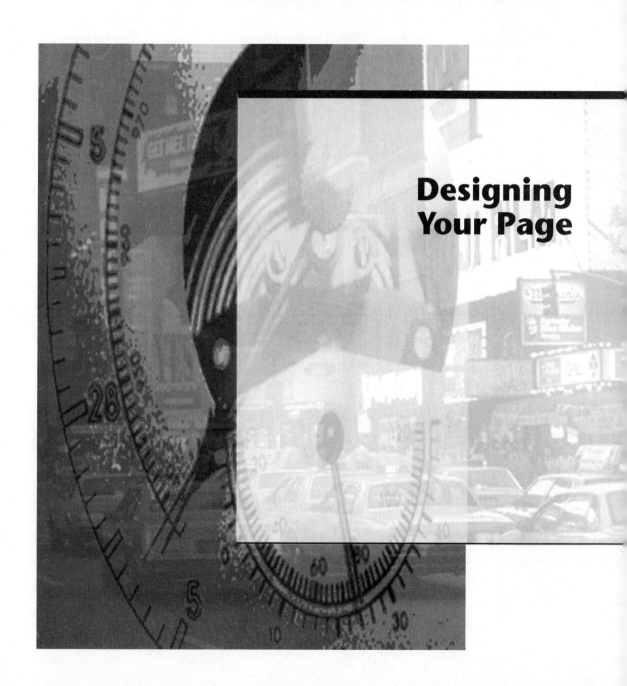

Designing
Your Page

A s we're so often reminded but so seldom have the chance to do, it's a good idea to plan ahead. That holds true in Web page design as in all things.

In this chapter, we'll take the time to plan properly. First, we'll present all the design principles you'll need to lay out an effective DHTML-based page. Then we'll apply those principles to a real-world project: the design of a Web page as a contribution to the members of the National Writers' Union (NWU).

Building the Design

The last thing you want to do in designing anything is to dive straight in. This is especially true of something like your Web page, which is intended to convey interrelated information without obscuring either its differences or its relationships. First, you need to give some thought to abstracts—the *characteristics*, rather than the actual components, you want your creation to contain. This process is particularly important in designing for the Web, where the medium, while it may not be the entire message, is certainly more than just a vehicle for it.

Seek Synergy

Perhaps the most important quality an effective Web page can have is synergy. When designing DHTML-based pages, with all the activity and variety they're capable of, it's all the more critical to keep this ideal of harmonious interaction well in the front of your mind.

A basic principle of teaching is that, the more of a student's senses you can involve in absorbing the information you're trying to impart, the more likely he or she is to retain that information. Substitute *Web surfer* for *student*, garnish with animation, dynamic elements, and multimedia, and you've got the perfect recipe for a Web page, like that sketched in Figure 2-1, that will reach out and grab anyone who taps into your site

But if you fail to consider the impact of the interaction of a page's elements, what you may end up with instead, as Figure 2-2 shows, is the Internet publishing equivalent of a sticky mess that's burned right into the bottom of a pot. The features that make up this page do not constitute a harmonious whole.

In designing your page, seek balance. Avoid a preponderance of text; that might result in any dynamic behavior you later introduce creating confusion

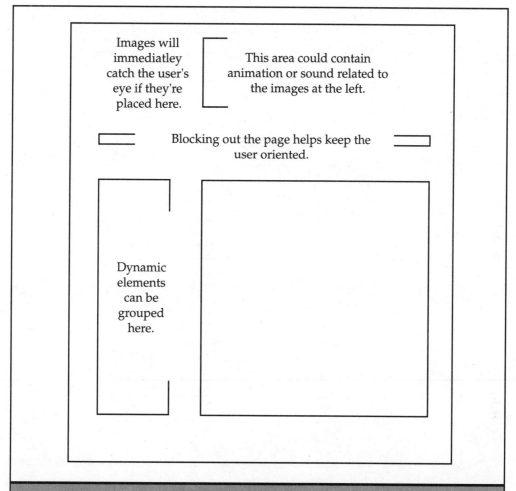

Figure 2-1. *A design like this can be the basis for an effective DHTML page*

rather than clarity. Think, for instance, how annoying it would be to attempt to read text that's constantly changing color, size, or style. And while one picture may be worth a thousand words, a lot of those words come from inside the viewer's head, reflecting attitudes as much as conveying facts. Choose images carefully, so that they create the impression you want. If you do, any dynamic behavior these images exhibit will highlight, rather than obscure, your message.

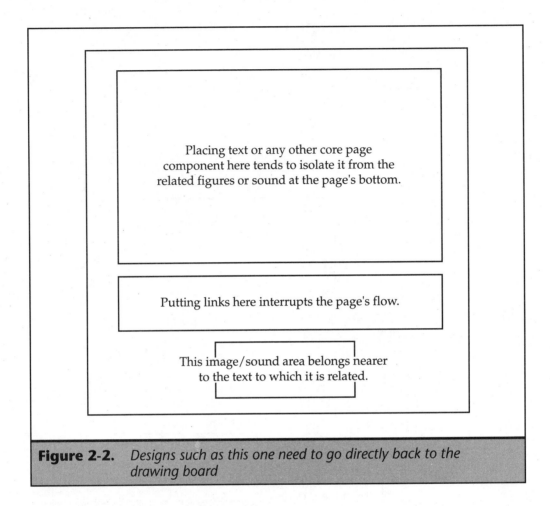

Placing text or any other core page component here tends to isolate it from the related figures or sound at the page's bottom.

Putting links here interrupts the page's flow.

This image/sound area belongs nearer to the text to which it is related.

Figure 2-2.   *Designs such as this one need to go directly back to the drawing board*

Design for Dynamism

Absolutely everything you do in laying out your page must reflect the fact that the page will be active. You must take into account the dynamic nature of the final product at every stage of the design. So the next thing we'll do is walk through each of those stages, with that caveat in mind.

Defining Information Content

Defining the information your Web page will present involves more than mulling over its general subject matter. You'll have to select

■ specific amounts of information to be supplied, for your page as a whole and for each of the items of information you want it to contain

■ how this information will be subdivided physically—that is, where to break paragraphs and how to link within the page

■ how much and what parts of this content will be present in your page's first draft

■ how much and what parts of this content you can feed in as time goes on, *without detracting from the clarity and completeness of the initial presentation*

Let's say, for instance, that you're setting up a home page for the Navajo Community College in Window Rock, Arizona. To make that page an effective entry point into all webbed information about the College, you'll want it to be made up of:

■ a banner or header that tells surfers what the page is

■ an overview of the College, preferably no more than two paragraphs

■ a set of links, to other pages on your site and to pages on remote sites, to related information

If you choose wisely, form will indeed follow function. In the case of our Community College example, as Figure 2-3 depicts, it's evident that:

■ The banner, or welcoming/explanatory text, announcing the page's role should be at the head of the page, and must be present from day 1.

■ The text giving the overview of the College should appear in the center of the page, and should also be part of even the roughest draft.

■ The set of links to related information on your site can be contained in a single small section, and can either be incorporated in the first draft or shortly thereafter.

■ The set of links to related information on remote sites can be contained in a second small section, and need not be included until the page has been fine-tuned.

Defining Style

To some extent, the style—by which we mean the overall feel or tone of your page—will be self-defining. Depending upon the nature of the information the

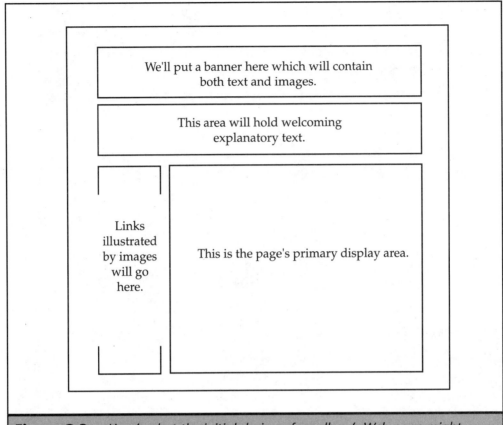

Figure 2-3. *Here's what the initial design of a college's Web page might look like*

page will present, you're going to design a businesslike, chatty, light-hearted, or other appropriate feel into the page from the very beginning. But there are other factors you should consider.

Your audience will have a significant impact upon the style or tone your page should adopt. If, for instance, your page will be viewed within an intranet, and largely by clients of the firm that implemented that intranet, too light or informal a tone might be out of place. Which is to say that you wouldn't want to open such a page with:

"Hi, there, Klingons! Are you ready to do battle with Desktop Data?"

Remember to take into account the degree of computer and Internet literacy of your audience. A Web page that will be viewed primarily by software engineers need not take the pains to anticipate or reassure that would be valuable in a page directed at patrons of a public library in a small rural community.

Remember too that, whatever the demographics of your anticipated audience, there are some features that your page will most likely have to contain, regardless of its style. But you can extend that style to such features. Table 2-1 outlines some of the possible relationships between style and typical Web page components.

The greatest effect of style or tone on Web page components will be in certain categories of sites or content, such as entertainment, education, and the visually oriented—that is, those that lend themselves to a lighter approach.

Defining Visual Elements and Relating These to Text and to Overall Style

When deciding upon the visual elements you'll place on your Web page, you'll find yourself dealing with two categories of images:

- figures that will act as illustration or elaboration of text-based content
- figures that will serve as the sole or primary vehicle for conveying information

Pop Quiz If you plan to use three figures on your page, and intend each of these to illustrate one of the page's most significant points, how should these figures be placed in relationship to the related text? (Answer at the end of this chapter, but you shouldn't have to stretch more than one or two brain cells to get this one.)

Choosing Static Elements

Having thrown you a curve by springing a test on you in the last section, we'll ease off here and give you a crib sheet instead. Web page elements that should remain static include:

- text that is neither input to nor output by a database
- text that need not catch and retain the viewer's attention

- images that act as the sole or primary means of conveying information
- illustrative images that will not benefit from or whose content does not lend itself to being presented in three dimensions
- text, images, or sound that forms part of a logo or signature
- any information for which security is a concern

This style	might affect these features	by requiring that they be
businesslike	navigation buttons or bars	plain but prominent; no unusual colors or textures
	links within your site or to other sites	all rendered with the same font and font characteristics
	email for feedback (on the site itself, or on its content)	not only plain but also unobtrusive
	client browsers	be able to handle such relatively recent HTML features as frames or interaction with databases
friendly but still informative	navigation buttons or bars	prominent, and employing a variety of colors to indicate differences in function
	links within your site or to other sites	all rendered with the same font and font characteristics
	email for feedback (on the site itself, or on its content)	prominent and colorful
	client browsers	be able to handle such relatively recent HTML features as frames or interaction with databases

Table 2-1.   *Style and Its Effect on Components*

Choosing Dynamic Elements

Any Web page components can be made dynamic. Whether you're dealing with text, images, or sound, DHTML lets you tinker big-time with how such components will be presented.

Don't let this power go to your head. Introducing activity for the sake of introducing activity is probably one of the worst design decisions you could make. Any dynamic behavior an element exhibits must have some concrete purpose, such as:

- ensuring that the element won't escape a surfer's attention
- establishing or enhancing the physical structure of a page by means of the element's activity
- establishing or enhancing either physical or conceptual continuity within a page by means of the element's activity
- establishing or enhancing the tone of a page by means of the element's activity

Table 2-2 makes some suggestions for choosing elements that will become dynamic.

Elements in this category	can be made dynamic if they exist as part of	which you wish to
text	a phrase in the body of your content	
	a link	Emphasize for whatever reason.
	instructions to the viewer	
images	any area of your page	Use to establish or illustrate continuity within a concept. For instance, if you need to show the evolution of Russian religious art, stacking a series of images that represent, respectively, icons from the 14th, 16th, and 18th centuries might be an effective technique.

Table 2-2. *Rules of Thumb for Choosing Dynamic Elements*

Elements in this category	can be made dynamic if they exist as part of	which you wish to
	any area of your page	Establish or enhance a tone. As an example, if you're building a page for Net neophytes, you might morph or otherwise alter the appearance of images that act as markers between sections of the page. This will not only enhance the user's grasp of the page's flow, but will also increase their confidence in their ability to effectively navigate, by providing them with unmistakable signposts.
sound	any area of your page	Use as a form of status information. For example, one program we use at home sounds like: a freight train, when we successfully connect to a remote site a ray-gun or other space-opera weapon when we complete an upload or download a siren when we goof up in some way, such as attempting to access a directory for which we're not authorized
	any area of your page	Employ as a breakpoint. For example, if, in the body of your content, you move from less to more significant information in going from paragraph one to paragraph two, you might want to attach a brief musical or other sound bite to that second paragraph. But make sure the attached bite is appropriate. You wouldn't, for instance, want to use the sound of an explosion or an auto accident in such cases.

Table 2-2. *Rules of Thumb for Choosing Dynamic Elements* (continued)

Defining the Activity of Dynamic Elements

Before we discuss how to decide just what it is you want dynamic elements to do, let's quickly review the types of activity each category of elements can exhibit.

Any text on a DHTML-based page can be made to:

- blink
- swim or undulate
- grow or shrink
- change color, texture, or other font characteristics

Images on DHTML Web pages can

- be stacked
- blink
- swim or undulate
- grow or shrink
- change either background or foreground color
- change texture
- change orientation by rotating, moving to the background or to the foreground, or skewing
- morph, that is, transform into an image of something related but different

Sound used in dynamic pages can vary in:

- loudness
- speed
- the refrains it offers, for instance, by repeating a particular musical phrase
- the musical styles it presents, for example, by moving from rock to jazz to rap and back again

Okay, so how do you know which type of activity to associate with which element? The answer lies in the purpose the element is to serve. Let's attach some dynamic behavior to Table 2-2, morph it to become Table 2-3, and zoom in on some animating suggestions.

Elements of this type	if they exist as part of	can make effective use of
text	a phrase in the body of your content	Blinking, growing or shrinking, or changing font characteristics.
	a link	Changing color. Any other dynamic activity on the part of such text might confuse rather than clarify.
	instructions to the viewer	Changing color, or growing to a predefined size.
images	establishing continuity within a concept	Stacking, or skewing, if it's done unidirectionally, as a sort of arrow.
	establishing or enhancing a tone	Morphing. One example of morphing to provide a light tone might be gradually changing an image of the Mona Lisa to cause that venerable woman to grin.
sound	providing status information	A sort of aural morphing, by, for example, changing a soft, gentle background theme, such as the sound of running water, to something related but more emphatic, like the sound of a thunderstorm.

Table 2-3. *Guidelines for Defining the Behavior of Dynamic Elements*

Applying the Design

As mentioned, we'll use a real-world project to illustrate the design concepts we've presented to this point. That project, the creation of a Web page for the National Writers' Union, must produce a page that:

- will act as a source of information on technical writing and editing for anyone seeking to break into those fields, but lacking a technical background

- will therefore have to supply information not only on writing and editing for technical, and in particular for computer-related, topics, but also on the topics themselves

Sidebar

We'll continue to use the page we're designing as a gift to the members of the NWU as our learning tool throughout the rest of this book.

Seek Synergy

It's clear that a page like the one we're beginning to design will consist largely of text, but must also provide images that will illustrate and clarify arcane or abstract technical information. A measure of synergy—that is, of harmonious balance between the page's elements—will go a long way towards preventing readers' eyes from glazing over and their fingers from forming the CTRL+ALT+DEL fork. Figure 2-4 shows one example of an initial layout for such a synergistic page.

Defining Information Content

As Figure 2-5 depicts, the choices we made regarding information content for the page we're designing for the members of the NWU encompass the principles we introduced earlier in this chapter, and which we'll reiterate here:

- deciding upon specific amounts of information for your page as a whole and for each of its sections

- deciding how this information will be subdivided

- deciding how much of this content to present in your page's first draft

- deciding which parts of this content you can forego for the time being

Defining Style

Because of what it seeks to accomplish, the overriding feel of the project page must be friendly and at the same time knowledgeable. We've fleshed out the page's design in Figure 2-6 to reflect these tones.

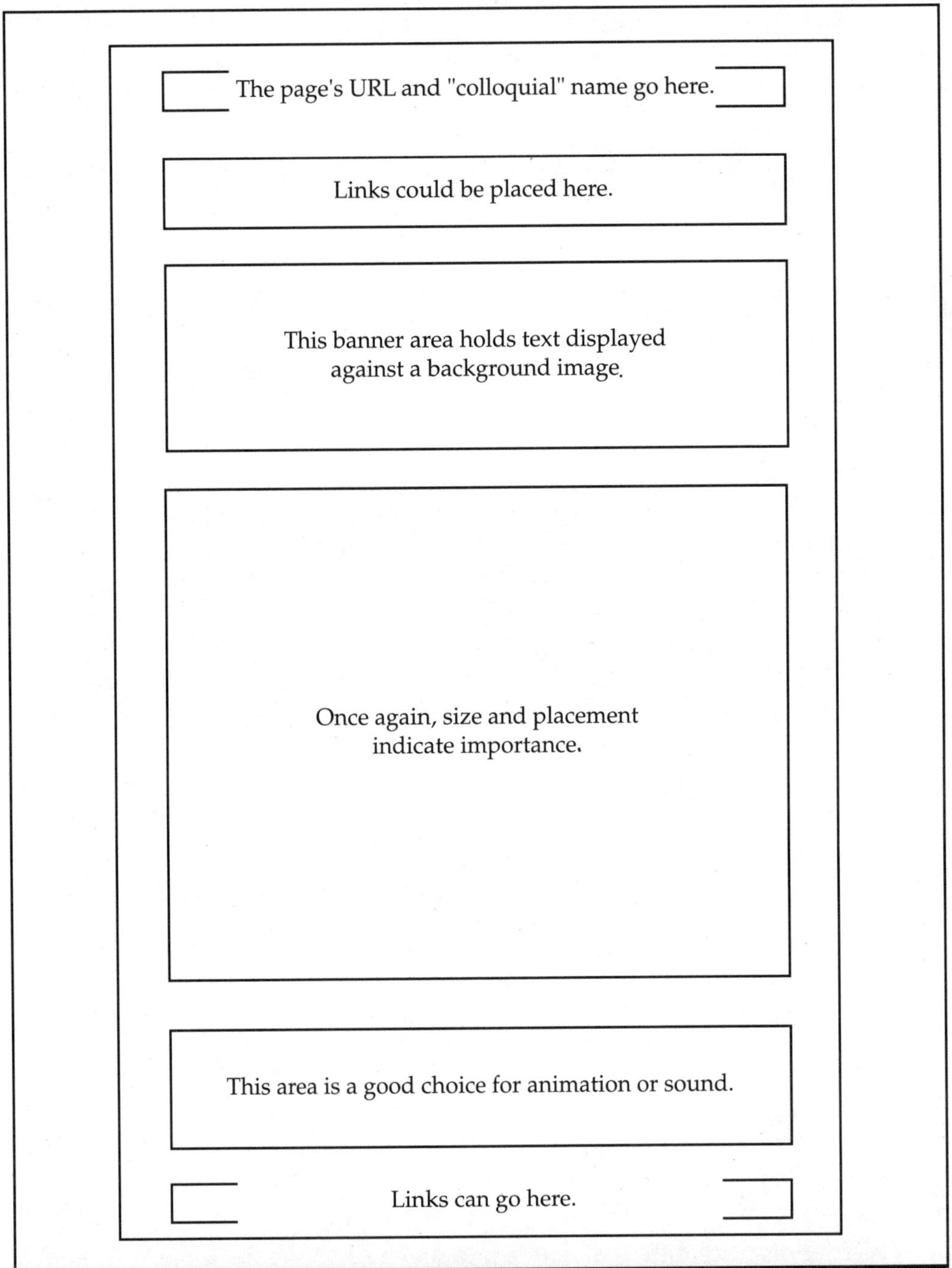

The page's URL and "colloquial" name go here.

Links could be placed here.

This banner area holds text displayed
against a background image.

Once again, size and placement
indicate importance.

This area is a good choice for animation or sound.

Links can go here.

Figure 2-4. *Balance within a page doesn't just happen; it must be designed in*

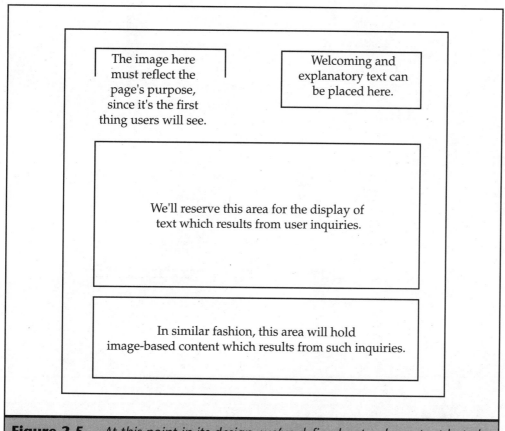

Figure 2-5. *At this point in its design, we've defined not only content but also the distribution of content for the project page*

Defining Visual Elements and Relating These to Text and to Overall Style

Figures 2-4, 2-5, and 2-6 represent the evolution of the initial design of the page we're developing as a contribution to the members of the NWU. At the end of this process, we find a need for only two visual elements, one of which will act as illustration of text-based information, and the other which will act as an important means of conveying the friendly feel we want the page to have.

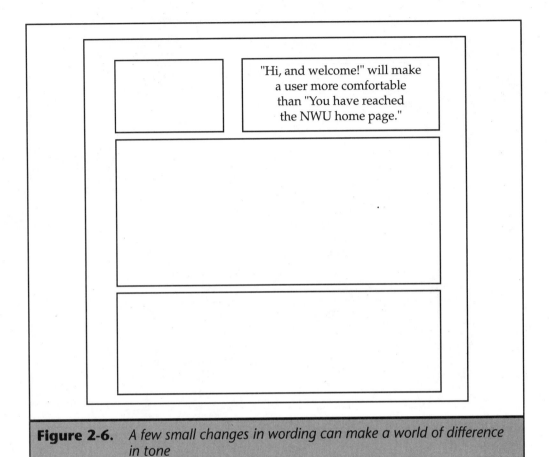

"Hi, and welcome!" will make a user more comfortable than "You have reached the NWU home page."

Figure 2-6. *A few small changes in wording can make a world of difference in tone*

Choosing Static Elements

The elements of the project page illustrated in the preceding three figures that will never exhibit dynamic behavior are

- the page's banner—its content, font characteristics, and placement
- the first paragraph of body text, which explains the page's purpose
- the placement and composition of links, navigation buttons, and feedback/email prompts

---

Sidebar

The forever-static (if anything in data processing can even pretend to approach forever) nature of these elements satisfies the criteria we established in the first major section of this chapter.

Choosing Dynamic Elements

Although the candidates are few, the nature of what the page we're building for the members of the NWU attempts to do, not to mention our own sense of craftsmanship, caused us to spend quite a bit of time selecting the page elements that could become dynamic. In the end, we decided upon three; here's a rundown of them, and of the reasoning behind our choices.

- The link to other sources of information on PCs, chosen because its importance to the page's many nontechnical users merits its being emphasized. However, these components will exhibit only limited activity, perhaps shading within a single vivid color.

- The image, in the page's banner, of a quill pen superimposed upon a PC, chosen because it reinforces both the purpose and the tone of the page.

- The WAV file linked to the page's navigation buttons, chosen as an easy means of alerting users to poor or impossible choices.

Defining the Activity of Dynamic Elements

The page elements that we chose with an eye to possible dynamic behavior fully represent the categories we've introduced. One text, one image, and one sound component will, now or at some time in the future, become dynamic. Table 2-4 summarizes and outlines the reasoning behind the specific activity each of these elements will demonstrate.

To close our discussion of design principles for the project page, we'll let Table 2-5 do the talking.

The element which consists of	will be implemented with	in order to
the link to other sources of information	a series of color changes through a number of shades of red, to be carried out every time the page is displayed	reinforce in users' minds that additional information is available to them
the image in the page's banner	stacking to place the image of a quill pen on top of that of a PC	reinforce in users' minds the purpose of the page, and that it will accomplish that purpose in a friendly way
the WAV file	an aural element, the sound of a cat yowling, which will always be physically present in the page, but will be transparent to users unless they attempt to take unauthorized or nonexistent actions	reinforce in users' minds those actions that are available to them

Table 2-4.   *The What/How/Why of the Project's Dynamic Elements*

For these elements	we chose	because
banner, body	text as the medium, and static as the nature	it's the only sensible choice
links, navigation buttons, and prompts	text as the medium, somewhat dynamic in nature in using color to add emphasis	the anticipated audience may contain many Net neophytes who could benefit from such emphasis
banner image	fully dynamic; we plan to make the superimposed PC transparent to the user upon initially displaying the page, and only gradually make it visible by removing this transparency	a neat trick visually, and reinforces the idea of technology related skills growing out of more basic ones

Table 2-5. *Summarizing Design Decisions for the Project Page*

Answer to the Pop Quiz

Each illustrative figure should be placed as close as possible, perhaps even embedded within, the text it is intended to elaborate upon. (Extra credit will be awarded to those of you who added that the placement of any of these images should not disturb or conflict with that of any other.)

Thumbnail Review

1. Begin your design by deciding not only upon the content but also on the characteristics of your page.

2. Define not only the content but the placement of the information your page will present.

3. Decide which of your page's elements will be static, and which may become dynamic.

4. Define the nature of the behavior each dynamic element will exhibit.

Looking Ahead

With our design kitbag now chock-full of sound principles and salient examples, we can turn, in the next two chapters, to scrutinizing the two applications that are the most significant commercial implementations of dynamic HTML. In Chapter 3, we'll put Internet Explorer 4.0 under the microscope. In Chapter 4, we'll dissect Netscape Communicator 4.0.

Chapter Three

Introducing Internet Explorer 4.0

IE4 contains many more components than the ones that pertain directly to DHTML, and it's worth our time to examine the entire suite. The Explorer's dynamic publishing capabilities are so closely interwoven with its other features that understanding the package as a whole will help us to better understand these capabilities.

The Web PC

Microsoft envisions Internet Explorer 4.0 as a vehicle for completely integrating the Internet into your PC's day-to-day life. The company calls this approach to computing *The Web PC*. While Microsoft considers The Web PC to have four significant functional components, we prefer to boil these down to three:

- the browser and generalized user interface
- extended collaboration and communications capabilities
- administration

Sidebar

We parted company with Microsoft's system of classification regarding Internet Explorer 4.0 because, quite frankly, it didn't make much sense to us. For example, we expected to find that topic near and dear to our hearts, DHTML, in the subcategory called Authoring under Collaboration and Communication. It belongs instead to the Browser category, we assume because the folks in Redmond have made the browser the primary means of integrating Internet and operating system capabilities. For instance, both local and Internet-related tools use the Explorer browser as their user interface.

The Browser

In Internet Explorer 3.0, Microsoft supported Java, ActiveX, and plain-old HTML. Internet Explorer 4.0 continues to support these tools. In addition, it also offers Dynamic HTML authoring. Browser/user interface related features of IE4 include:

- ease-of-use and personalization capabilities

- offline browsing
- performance enhancements
- security enhancements

Let's take a few minutes to peruse each of these.

Ease-of-Use and Personalization

Two things will probably pop out at you quickly regarding the overall look and feel of the IE4 browser.

As Figure 3-1 shows, you can both enter queries and view search results in an area of the screen called the Search Bar, which lets you avoid switching back and forth between a query form and the results.

In a similar fashion, Internet Explorer 4.0 uses a technique, introduced in Office 97 and dubbed IntelliSense, that allows the browser to complete a URL you begin typing if you have entered that URL before. In addition, IE4 makes available, through the right mouse button, a shortcut menu that allows you to edit URLs you've already selected, as shown in Figure 3-2.

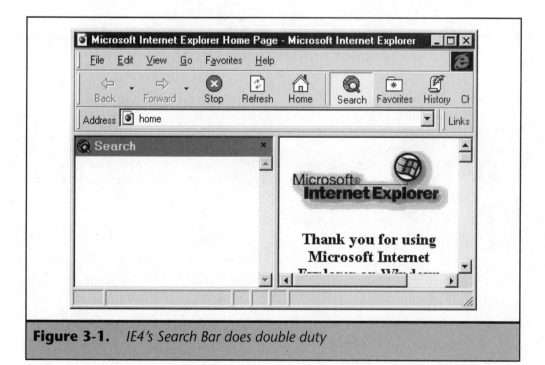

Figure 3-1. *IE4's Search Bar does double duty*

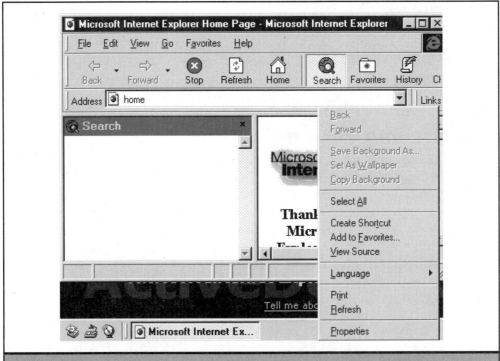

Figure 3-2.   *One click of the right mouse button produces this menu*

Offline Browsing

Internet Explorer 4.0 stores pages you've visited in a cache on the local hard drive so you can browse them offline. Here are some other new features related to offline browsing:

- A red highlight displayed next to a site's icon indicates that the site's content has changed in some way since it was last visited.

- *Thumbnails* give you quick visual summaries of sites.

- When you right-click the Back and Forward buttons, a navigation history appears that lets you quickly reconnect to sites you've previously visited.

- You can print in the background.

- You can choose to print all or only selected frames in a page. (This is called *frameset* printing.)

Performance Enhancements

The most significant performance enhancements in IE4 are those related to download speeds and security. In the case of the speed, let's just say it's lots faster. The suite's security features deserve a little more attention. Table 3-1 summarizes the most important ones.

The feature	functions to
Authenticode	identify the publisher of any software downloaded, confirm that the code in question hasn't been tampered with
Wallet	securely store sensitive data such as: credit cards numbers driver's license number ATM cards numbers
CryptoAPI	provide hooks for programmers into basic security services such as secure channels and code signing, thereby allowing developers to introduce cryptography into the applications they build
NTLM (Windows NT Login manager) challenge/response	provide a further, NT-specific means of authenticating users at login
SOCKS firewall support	allow WinSOCK clients to use various levels of proxies and proxy servers
Platform for Internet Content Selection (PICS)	allow administrators to associate IE4 with such content-filtering applications as Cyber Patrol

Table 3-1.   *Security in Internet Explorer 4.0*

Collaboration and Communication

In the area of collaboration and communication, Microsoft has developed applications to meet the need of two groups of users:

- those who need only basic collaborative tools, such as email, newsgroup reading, chat, Internet telephony, and application sharing
- those who must have fuller, groupware-based tools, such as workflow, group voting, and routing capabilities, in addition to basic applications

Internet Explorer 4.0 is designed for the first of these user categories. Out of the box, it includes:

- Personal Web Server
- application sharing, and video and other conferencing
- basic (as opposed to DHTML-related) authoring
- broadcasting and multicasting
- email
- newsgroup reading

If you find yourself in the second user group, don't think Microsoft has given your needs short shrift. You can pick the groupware-related tools most important to you from the product lines of a number of vendors, and associate them with IE4 as the need arises.

All of Internet Explorer's components, whether intended for basic or more sophisticated environments, rely on a number of protocols, the most important of which we've outlined in Table 3-2. If your environment makes these protocols available, IE4 will fit smoothly into that environment.

Starting with the out-of-the-box group and working through to enhancements that introduce greater sophistication, let's examine the most significant IE4 communication and collaboration tools.

Sidebar

We'll pay particular attention to IE4's broadcasting and multicasting capabilities, because these are closely related to DHTML-based content.

The protocol	serves as
H.323	a standard from the ITU that defines the protocols needed to conduct real-time conferencing across IP networks
IMAP4	Internet Mail Access Protocol, the most recent version of a widely used mail-transfer protocol
LDAP	Lightweight Directory Access Protocol, a standard for storing and retrieving names, email addresses, phone numbers, and other related information. LDAP has quickly become a standard for Internet directories. It has the additional advantage of processing information very quickly.
S/MIME	Secure MIME, an open standard for public- or private-key encryption of email

Table 3-2. *IE4's Protocols*

Personal Web Server

If you're not running Windows 95 as the sole or significant operating system in your environment, you can move immediately to the next section. Personal Web Server (PWS) only runs on Windows 95 machines.

Personal Web Server allows a Windows 95-based PC to act as a Web server, albeit a server for a low-volume site. The relationship of PWS to Windows 95 is similar to that of PWS's big brother, Internet Information Server, and its native operating environment, Windows NT. The installation, configuration, and management of Personal Web Server is closely integrated with the operating system. For instance, PWS uses the Windows 95 taskbar, Control Panel, and security model.

Once again reminiscent of Internet Information Server, Personal Web Server includes an HTML-based administration utility that permits either local or remote administration. (*Remote administration* refers to administering the server from anywhere out on the Internet.) PWS supports standards such as CGI, and, for the down-on-the-metal programmers among you, it includes the Internet Server API (ISAPI) extension to the Win32 API.

Sidebar

ISAPI lets you tweak Internet services by using code written in languages such as C++ or Delphi. As a result, it offers the possibility of executables that run as much as five times faster than standard CGI components developed in languages such as VBScript or Perl.

Application Sharing and Internet Conferencing through NetMeeting 2.0

NetMeeting, shown in Figure 3-3, provides a grab bag of Internet conferencing tools, including:

- a real-time client that not only permits LAN-to-Internet or Intranet-to-Intranet equivalents of chat, but also allows you to share data and applications across multiple points of contact

- standards-based audio and video conferencing

- extensive compatibility with third-party, standards-based conferencing tools

Authoring in FrontPad

FrontPad (see Figure 3-4) is a graphical HTML editor that allows even the most novice user create Web pages. It's based on FrontPage 97 and relies largely on a component tool, the Web Publishing Wizard. FrontPad also lets you include components developed in Java, JScript, Plug-in, and more.

When you save an HTML page you created in FrontPad, the Web Publishing Wizard (shown in Figure 3-5) automatically appears to help you transfer the document to your Web server.

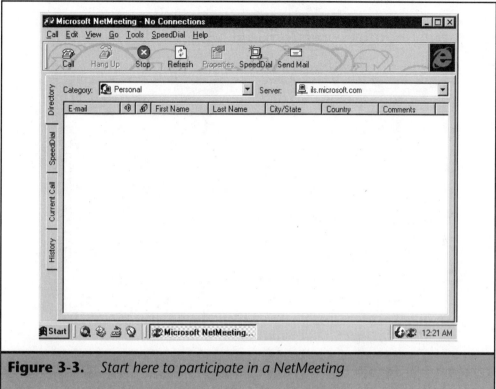

Figure 3-3.   *Start here to participate in a NetMeeting*

The Web Publishing Wizard supports these protocols and services:

- standard protocols such as FTP and UNC
- platform-independent protocols such as as FrontPage and Extended Web
- Internet carriers such as America Online and Sprynet

Broadcasting with NetShow

NetShow is a combination of client and server software that allows Internet Explorer 4.0 to provide audio, illustrated audio, and video on demand, as well

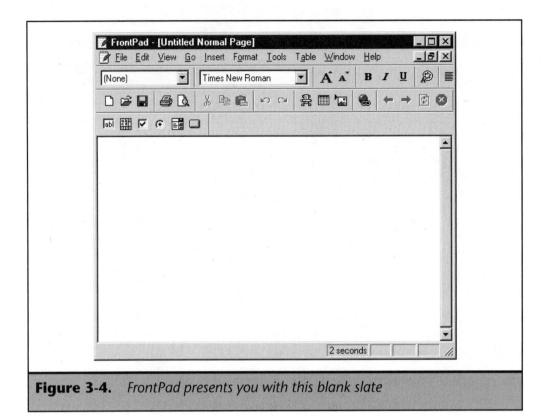

Figure 3-4. *FrontPad presents you with this blank slate*

as live multicast audio, video, and file transfer. This client/server duo supports a variety of transport protocols and media codecs, or compression/decompression utilities, including:

- G723
- H323
- RTP-IP
- TCP
- UDP

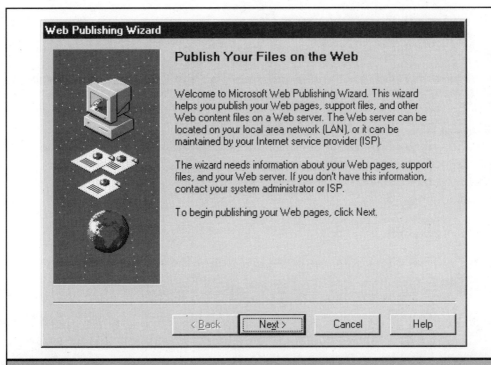

Figure 3-5. *With a wave of its magic wand, this Wizard transfers your HTML documents to the appropriate server*

Sidebar

The NetShow client is an ActiveX control that provides on-demand content streaming. That is, it allows users to access multimedia Web content without having dinner and a cocktail while files download. Therefore, this client also lets content providers offer more varied and sophisticated presentations, such as those incorporating slides or photographs. In fact, NetShow provides basic tools for streaming illustrated audio, and for creating it in the first place, through WAV, AVI, QuickTime, PowerPoint, JPEG, GIF, and URL formats.

Multicasting, or Webcasting

Webcasting, push technology, and *multicasting* are all terms for the Internet equivalent of turning on your radio and tuning in your favorite station. Whatever you call it and whoever provides the implementation, this form of Internet broadcasting comes in two varieties. We'll review them both.

WEBCASTING USING EXISTING TECHNOLOGIES   In order to Webcast using conventional, existing push techniques, IE4, or any other browser, must crawl specified sites at defined intervals, checking for updated content. If you have subscribed to such a site, you can instruct the browser to automatically download any new data on the site to your machine for offline viewing.

How do you subscribe to a Web site? Under Internet Explorer 4.0, at least, you have two options.

- You can set up a subscription to check only for updated content. If IE4 finds such content on a subscribed site, it will notify you, but do no more; it won't download any material.

- You can set up a subscription not only to check for updated content but also to download modified pages, and to let you know that these pages are ready for offline browsing.

Sidebar

One nice touch to IE4's traditional Webcasting is that it uses a single cache for both the browser and the crawler, thus avoiding dual copies of the same HTML file. Another point in favor of this means of Webcasting is that it requires no modification of a site's content.

An inherent limitation of crawl-based Webcasting is that, because of bandwidth limitations, the browser may not be able to successfully carry out more detailed searches of a site. Internet Explorer 4.0 addresses this problem by giving you the option of downloading only HTML material and foregoing any associated images. While this option does, to some extent, throw out the baby with the bath water, it at least consumes less bandwidth and disk storage, and this allows the browser to crawl deeper in search of useful content.

WEBCASTING USING THE CHANNEL DEFINITION FORMAT   Designed by Microsoft as an alternative to the traditional push or crawl-based approach to broadcasting, Webcasting of channels, or logically-related groups of Web content, using the Channel Definition Format (CDF) attempts to succeed in scenarios, such as those described in Table 3-3, that go beyond the capabilities of push.

CDF is a file format, based on the XML standard, through which Microsoft and other vendors seek to accomplish these goals:

- convert an existing Web site into a Channel
- index content independent of format
- streamline scheduling of content delivery
- tailor delivered content to the needs of individual users

Sites where	limit crawling because
The overall layout of the site is not known	a crawler uses a site's page-link tree structure in order to decide what content to push. Many sites provide no further information on how they've organized their content.
The possible relevance of content is not known (this is true for the great majority of sites)	the crawler can't determine whether the crawled content applies to a given request, so it instead substitutes arbitrary values for: the levels of detail to which the crawl will proceed; the amount of disk space retrieved material is allowed to consume
The schedule according to which content is updated is not known (once again, this is the case in the majority of sites)	it can cause the crawler to check for updated material too frequently, or not frequently enough

Table 3-3.   *Even pushing as hard as it can won't help a browser in these situations*

SUBSCRIBING TO A CDF CHANNEL   Caveats aside, any Web site that is indexed by means of a CDF file can be subscribed to as a Channel. This not-at-all-shabby accomplishment requires only that HTML pages, on the site that you wish to offer as part of a Channel themselves, point to the CDF file. The code for one example from the Microsoft Web site of such a CDF-ed HTML file is shown next.

```
<A HREF = "http://www.voicenet.com/~petrovsk/trektriv.cdf"
<IMG SRC = "http://www.voicenet.com/~petrovsk/trektriv.gif"
WIDTH = "100" HEIGHT = "45" ALT="Subscribe to Trek Trivia!>
</A>
```

Internet Explorer 4.0 can even provide for the most recent transport protocols; through its NetShow component, IE4 can receive Channel content that is broadcast via such new protocols.

One protocol already available in IE4 is the one-to-many Multicast File Transfer Protocol, or MFTP

Messaging by Means of Outlook Express

The standard over-the-counter version of the Internet Explorer 4.0 suite includes an email and newsreading client called Outlook Express. This component supports the protocols IMAP4, LDAP, and S/MIME.

Outlook Express has other neat features, including:

- the ability to create multiple, hierarchical email directories
- an Auto-Add utility that builds address books automatically, saving frequently-used email addresses
- support for multiple mailboxes
- enhanced inboxes that make it easier to forward or copy messages

Administration

Internet Explorer 4.0 contains several software configuration and management tools. Most of these are either contained in or interface with the installation wizard for IE4, called Active Setup. Let's take a moment to scrutinize this feature.

Active Setup

Active Setup offers administrators a number of handy tools; we've summarized the most significant of these in Table 3-4.

IE4 INSTALLATION USING ACTIVE SETUP   Before you can use Internet Explorer 4.0 to create all those dazzling DHTML effects you have in mind, you must first install the application, so it behooves us to outline the steps you need to take to do so.

First, as Figure 3-6 illustrates, you must choose an installation option. These are your choices:

- Standard
- Enhanced
- Full

Once you've made this decision, the basic setup engine, weighing in at a skinny 200KB, will download. Next, Active Setup checks to see if you've got

This Active Setup tool	functions to
Modular setup engine	optimize connection time by downloading only the install engine and identifying such potential problems as insufficient free disk space. Only after creating a single installation disk that houses this engine will application components be downloaded.
Scripted installations	permit administrators to both application components and configuration settings for these components, thereby foregoing almost all need for input during the installation process
Migration of existing configurations	automatically import bookmarks, proxy settings, and so on, from previous Internet Explorer or Netscape Navigator installations
Logging	create a transaction-by-transaction log of the installation
Download site switching	allow the machine performing the download to switch to a new download server automatically, in the event of problems with the original server, thereby enabling the installation to proceed uninterrupted

Table 3-4.   *The Active Setup Toolkit*

enough free disk available to handle the installation option you selected. Assuming disk space is no problem, Active Setup will finally download and install IE4. If you've requested any, Active Setup, as its last task, will download and install optional components. (As part of either aspect of installation, Active Setup will also record Dynamic Link Libraries, or DLLs, it places on your machine.)

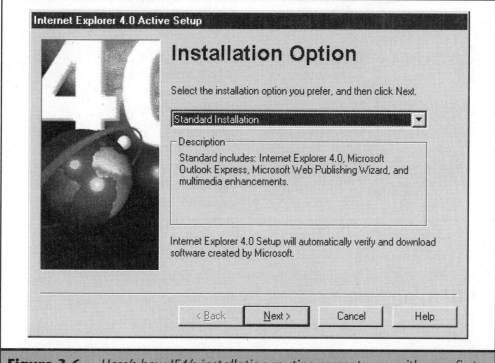

Figure 3-6. *Here's how IE4's installation routine presents you with your first set of choices*

LOGGING OF THE INSTALLATION PROCESS BY ACTIVE SETUP During setup, Active Setup creates several log files; we've outlined the two most important of these in Table 3-5.

DHTML in Internet Explorer 4.0

Now that you understand what DHTML is, you can take a look at how Microsoft has implemented it through IE4. (Do we hear a murmur of "It's about time!" from some of you?)

Styles

IE4 lets Web authors change, on the fly, the element attributes, or style sheet directives, associated with every HTML element in a document.

This log file	tracks
Active Setup Log.txt	all actions that occur during either the Active Setup Wizard or the component install phases of setup
RunOnceEx Log.txt	all actions that occur during the Dynamic Link Library registration phase of the setup process. Keep this log close at hand; it's the only significant tool for debugging improperly installed or registered DLLs.

Table 3-5.   *Active Setup's Logs*

Positioning

Internet Explorer 4.0 provides full-, and fully-W3C-compliant, x-, y-, and z-plane positioning.

Content

Under IE4, you can design the content of any HTML page to change at runtime, based on user-initiated events such as mouse clicks.

New ActiveX Controls

By providing these controls, IE4 allows authors to add animation, or other visual effects, to specific page elements, or to an entire page.

Interactivity with Databases

This one is nifty. Internet Explorer 4.0 offers you several ways to integrate data with HTML elements. For instance, it can automatically generate table rows within an HTML-driven display based on the contents of database records.

ActiveX

Internet Explorer 4.0 supports these two recent enhancements to ActiveX controls:

■ *windowless* controls, which don't require a separate label in memory, thereby using less of this and other precious system resources

■ unusually shaped controls, such as trapezoids

Active Script

Internet Explorer 4.0 supports a number of scripting tools, including Visual Basic Scripting Edition, more commonly known as VBScript, and JScript, Microsoft's 100% Java-compatible scripting language.

Multimedia

Table 3-6 summarizes IE4's multimedia-related DHTML capabilities. You can apply the effects described in this table to individual objects within a Web page, or you can use them to transition between pages.

Internet Explorer 4.0 System Requirements

In this final section of Chapter 3, we'll once again let a table do the talking. Table 3-7 summarizes the hardware and operating system platforms you must provide for Internet Explorer 4.0.

In this area	IE4 offers	through the feature called
Graphics and animation effects	animated images	Sprite
	scalable and rotatable graphics	Structured Graphics
	graphics filters	Effects
	easy migration of objects	Path
Music effects	musical accompaniment	
	software wavetable synthesis	Interactive Music Control
	the ability to mix wave tables together dynamically	Mixer

Table 3-6. *IE4's Multimedia DHTML Capabilities*

In this area	IE4 offers	through the feature called
Page effects	the ability to control the timing of events on pages	Sequencer
	the ability to alter the appearance of a single-page element or of an entire page over a predefined period of time	Transitions
	the ability to apply complex behaviors to controls and page elements	Behaviors
	the ability to set up regions of the screen in which mouse clicks will, and will not, be accepted and processed	HotSpot

Table 3-6. *IE4's Multimedia DHTML Capabilities* (continued)

Thumbnail Review

1. Internet Explorer 4.0 is built around the concept of The Web PC.

2. IE4 enhances many of the security features found in earlier versions of the browser.

3. If you're running Windows 95 as your operating system, Internet Explorer 4.0 even offers a scaled-down Web server.

4. IE4 installation can be automated to a very large degree, and it provides logging as a debugging tool.

5. Dynamic HTML as implemented in Internet Explorer 4.0 offers:

   a) animated images

   b) easy migration of objects

   c) graphics filters

For this feature	Microsoft says to provide	but we recommend
CPU	Intel 486/66 DX or higher	at a minimum, a Pentium 133. If you're installing IE4 primarily as a DHTML creation and distribution tool, and intend to produce and disseminate multimedia content through it, consider a Pentium 200 MHz MMX
Operating System	Windows 95 or Windows NT	NT; 95 just doesn't have the punch needed by any site featuring DHTML
RAM	8MB for Windows 95 16MB for Windows NT	Microsoft must be kidding with this set of recommendations. Or maybe it was a typo on their Web site. In any case, don't even consider using IE4 in conjunction with either OS it supports unless you're giving it at least 32MB of RAM
Available disk space	43MB for a Standard installation, which includes Internet Explorer 4.0, Microsoft Outlook Express, and ActiveMovie 50MB for an Enhanced installation, which includes Internet Explorer 4.0, Microsoft Outlook Express, FrontPad, and ActiveMovie 59MB for a Full installation, which includes Internet Explorer 4.0, Microsoft Outlook Express, NetMeeting, FrontPad, Microsoft Wallet, NetShow, and ActiveMovie	we agree with these recommendations, but do keep in mind that such figures apply only to the application, not to any content it may help you create or distribute

Table 3-7. *IE4 Hardware and OS Requirements*

    d) musical accompaniment

    e) scalable and rotatable graphics

    f) software wavetable synthesis

    g) the ability to alter the appearance of a single-page element or an entire page over a predefined period of time

h) the ability to apply complex behaviors to controls and page elements

i) the ability to control the timing of events on pages

j) the ability to mix wave tables together dynamically

k) the ability to set up regions of the screen in which mouse clicks will, and will not, be accepted and processed

Looking Ahead

In the next chapter, we'll subject Netscape Communicator 4.0, the only significant competitor to Internet Explorer for the DHTML crown, to the same scrutiny we've just put IE4 under.

Chapter Four

Introducing
Netscape
Communicator 4.0

Netscape Communicator 4.0, like its rival in the Battle of the Browsers, Microsoft Internet Explorer 4.0, emphasizes the integration of Web applications. Communicator takes a pared-down approach, unlike Microsoft's implementation, but it doesn't sacrifice functionality. In this chapter, we'll run through Communicator's most important characteristics. We'll follow the same structure we used in Chapter 3 to help you compare the two products. That is, we'll scrutinize these features of Communicator, in this order:

- the browser
- collaboration and communication
- administration
- setup
- DHTML
- system requirements

The Browser

As always, Netscape's browser is more understated than Microsoft's. But don't let appearances fool you. For once, a product lives up to its publicity; Communicator 4.0's user interface is truly seamless and intuitive. Through this single interface, shown in Figure 4-1, you can

- create or edit text for conferencing, email messages, and Web pages
- follow hyperlinks, which are automatically established between all Communicator components and their content
- manage messages from both both Collabra, Communicator's equivalent of a chat room, and Messenger, its mail service
- use a single address book for email and conferencing

Communicator's client application includes both a Standard and a Professional Edition. The Professional Edition offers three applications that are not included in the Standard Edition:

- Calendar
- Auto Admin
- IBM Host-on-Demand

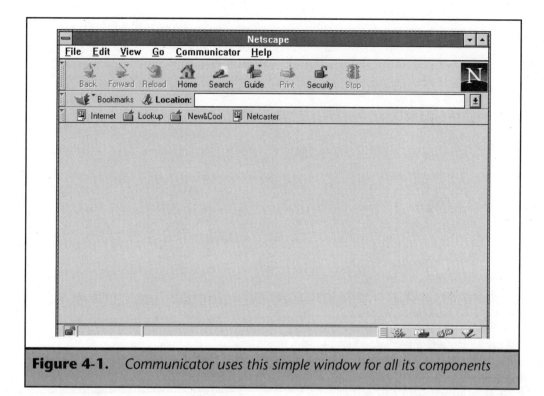

Figure 4-1. *Communicator uses this simple window for all its components*

Before examining these, though, let's take a look at the components that the Standard and the Professional Editions share.

Sidebar

The components of Communicator (both editions) are so tightly integrated that you can't purchase them separately .

Collaborating Through Conference

Netscape's analog to Microsoft's NetMeeting is called Conference. Like NetMeeting, Conference provides you with the ability to share information through standards-based, full-duplex audio conferencing. You can share not only whiteboards but also data and applications across multiple points of contact.

Conference offers full support for the international H.323 standard from the ITU, which defines the behavior of protocols used in real-time conferencing across IP networks.

Discussions Under Collabra

Unlike IE4, Communicator distinguishes between conferencing and the LAN-to-Internet (or Intranet-to-Intranet) equivalent of chat, which it offers in Collabra, shown in Figure 4-2.

Collabra provides both public and private discussion forums, requiring user passwords for the latter. Collabra lets you browse offline, and it supports not only plain text but also rich (HTML-formatted) messages. Collabra postings can contain links to Intranet pages, and those pages can point to Collabra documents.

Collabra uses a variant of the overall Communicator user interface that is nearly indistinguishable from that employed by Netscape Messenger, as Figure 4-3 shows.

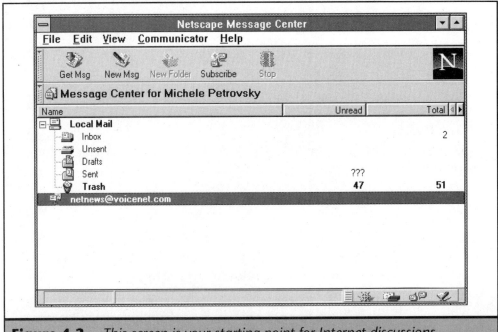

Figure 4-2. *This screen is your starting point for Internet discussions*

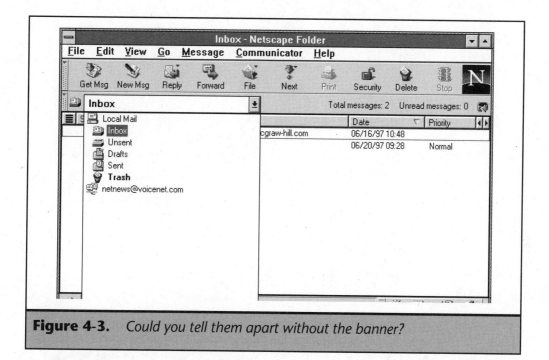

Figure 4-3.　*Could you tell them apart without the banner?*

The two Communicator components have something else in common: Messages from both can be stored in a single file subsystem, and can be viewed offline.

Authoring in Composer

Those of you familiar with the HTML editor in Netscape Navigator Gold 3.0 will feel right at home with Netscape Composer. Communicator's authoring tool, illustrated in Figure 4-4, allows you to create:

- discussion documents
- email messages
- Web pages

Composer's editing environment is shared between Netscape Messenger and Netscape Collabra and includes a feature called *one button publish*, which is Communicator's analog to IE4's Web Publishing Wizard. To upload a document to a Web server, you need only click the Publish toolbar button, shown next.

Unlike Internet Explorer's FrontPad, however, you can use Composer to create email or discussion messages as well as Web pages. Regardless of which Communicator component you are designing a document for, Composer lets you incorporate these elements:

- frame targets
- images
- JavaScript and Java applets
- lists, both bulleted and numbered
- tables

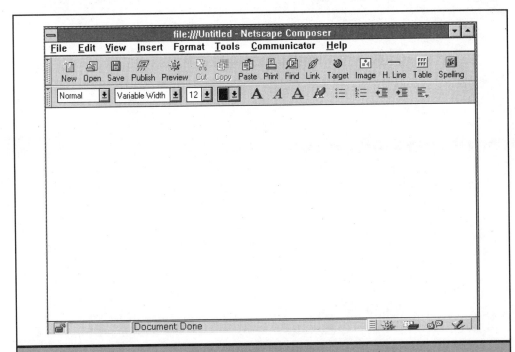

Figure 4-4. *Composer allows you to create a variety of document types*

- varied font and character styles
- varied paragraph formats

Unfortunately, while Composer can create frame targets, it cannot fill them. That is, it cannot directly build frames or image maps into a document.

Webcasting With Netcaster

Netcaster, the Web broadcasting component of Netscape Communicator (shown in Figure 4-5) enables you to provide your users:

- push delivery of information
- dynamically-subscribed and updated Web content
- offline browsing capabilities

Sidebar

As noted in Chapter 3, in the section "Webcasting Using Existing Technologies," Netscape believes that the Channel Definition Format (CDF) approach to Webcasting, which Microsoft has proposed and implemented, is a form of overkill. According to Netscape, Webcasting, that is, dynamically subscribed and crawled channels, can be more reliably and flexibly implemented with existing open standards such as HTML, Java, and JavaScript. In line with this Open Platform approach, Netcaster supports quite a handful of operating environments, among them Windows 3.1, Windows 95, Windows NT, the Macintosh Power PC, and versions of Unix running on several hardware platforms.

Mail via Messenger

The email client component of Communicator, Netscape Messenger, is based on open standards, and provides features such as:

- directory access as a part of message exchange
- mail filtering, searching, and sorting capabilities

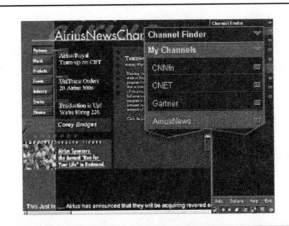

Figure 4-5. *Netscape's approach to Webcasting, unlike Microsoft's, relies on existing rather than developing technologies*

- rich text (HTML-based) mail, such as the message shown in Figure 4-6
- secure exchange of messages
- support for email protocols such as POP3, SMTP, and IMAP4
- support for MIME attachments
- support for mobile users
- tools to allow you to migrate mail messages, directories, and address books from your current email application

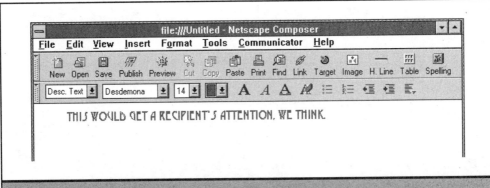

Figure 4-6. *Email doesn't have to be boring anymore*

Why all the fuss about HTML-based mail? Beyond adding visual interest to your messages, an HTML-based mail system gives you the ability to use scripts. This lets you incorporate features such as forms in your messages.

To maintain the address book and file subsystem shared by Messenger and Collabra, Communicator employs the Lightweight Directory Access Protocol (LDAP). Communicator relies on S/MIME (which offers both public and private key-based encryption) and digital signatures to provide security for email. In addition, Messenger uses Internet Mail Access Protocol (IMAP4), which allows you to read your mail but leave it on a mail server.

Additional Components in Communicator Professional Edition

Netscape Communicator's Professional Edition offers three components intended strictly for corporate and Intranet environments. Let's review these now.

Calendar

Netscape Calendar is essentially an enterprise-level group scheduling application. Calendar allows you to handle these three tasks, among others:

- carry out searches of schedules on local or remote servers
- manage meeting schedules and to-do lists
- schedule meetings within an Intranet or even across the Internet, through the standards-based vCalendar meeting format

Sidebar

What is vCalendar? It is a format developed by Versit Corporation as a possible basis for making Web-based scheduling applications more interoperable.

Because most current calendaring and scheduling applications are either host- or LAN-based, Calendar, in its initial release, can work only in conjunction with the Netscape Calendar server. Host-based implementations can handle thousands of users, but they fail to support offline and remote access.

LAN-based applications, on the other hand, offer offline and remote access but often can handle no more than a few hundred users. By using the Calendar server and client combination, Netscape is trying to answer both sets of needs, both providing offline/remote access and supporting large numbers of users.

AutoAdmin

Netscape has included a tool in Communicator called AutoAdmin, which provides centralized setup and management of the suite. When you use AutoAdmin in tandem with the (non-Communicator) Netscape product Mission Control, you can create and manage such parameters as desktop configurations, security policies, and user preferences even from remote locations across the Web.

What's more, the Auto Admin/Mission Control duo even allows you to keep such settings in agreement with those of any proxies you might employ.

IBM Host-on-Demand

Not much mystery about this Professional Edition component—the name really does say it all. IBM Host-on-Demand provides Intranet- or Internet-to-mainframe interconnectivity, as well as emulation of and application access through mainframe terminal types. Host-on-Demand does not itself include Web-server functionality. However, if you use it with Java-enabled Web browsers, it can nonetheless offer access to mainframe- rather than Internet-based information, applications, and services.

In addition to relying on the TN3270 family of protocols rather than on HTML-to-3270 mappers, Host on-Demand offers several options for emulator screen presentation, and it gives users access to PF keys directly from a PC's keyboard.

Because it is written only in Java, Host-on-Demand can run in any environment that also offers a Java Virtual Machine (VM).

The Server Side of Netscape

Unlike Microsoft, Netscape Communications does not provide a Web server application with its most recent, integrated browser. The folks in Redmond provide Personal Web Server with Internet Explorer 4.0 and give you the option of running IE4 in tandem with Windows NT 4.0's Web server application, Internet Information Server. In contrast, the decision-makers at

Netscape have structured their Internet servers into a suite of software called (so help us) SuiteSpot.

SuiteSpot offers servers for applications including:

- Calendar
- Catalog
- Collabra
- Directories (phone and address books, not file systems)
- Media Services
- Messaging
- Proxies

Security

Navigator 4.0 includes a security API. This lets you customize Communicator security to meet specific requirements, such as the need to interact with proprietary or legacy systems that lack adequate security measures.

Platforms

What we find most attractive about Communicator is the number and variety of hardware and operating system environments it supports. Table 4-1 outlines these environments.

On this hardware platform	you can run Communicator 4.0 under the operating system
Intel x86	Windows 95 Windows NT 3.51 and 4.0 Windows 3.1 and 3.11 OS/2 Warp Caldera Linux SCO Unix

Table 4-1.   *Communicator's Operating Environments*

On this hardware platform	you can run Communicator 4.0 under the operating system
Apple	Macintosh OS 7.5 and higher (68K) Macintosh OS 7.5 and higher (PowerPC)
DEC Alpha	Digital Unix 3.2 and higher
Hewlett-Packard	HP-UX 9.05, 10.x, and higher
IBM RS/6000	AIX 4.1 and higher
Silicon Graphics	IRIX 5.3, 6.2, and higher
Sun SPARC	Solaris 2.4 and higher Sun OS 4.1.3

Table 4-1. *Communicator's Operating Environments (continued)*

Sidebar

In addition to the environments outlined in Table 4-1, Communicator can also operate on an Intel platform under five additional operating systems, although Netscape Communications doesn't offer support for Communicator on these systems:

- Caldera Linux 1.2.13
- Digital Alpha (Windows NT 3.51 and 4.0)
- SCO OpenServer Release 5, version 3.2
- SCO Unixware 2.1
- Sun Solaris x86 2.4

Support for Microsoft Platforms

As this book was being written, Netscape Communications, in conjunction with Sun Microsystems, announced its intention to "embrace and integrate" Microsoft platforms and technologies into Netscape platforms and environments. What this means is that in addition to including support for ActiveX, future versions of SuiteSpot and Communicator will also support such Microsoft operating and application systems as:

- BackOffice
- Office
- SQL Server
- Systems Management Server or SMS
- Windows 95
- Windows NT

Furthermore, Netscape has promised to "simplify migration from Microsoft's legacy development environments and databases to the open-system alternatives it supports."

What's particularly interesting about Netscape's decision to take this tack that it has promised to "integrate the SuiteSpot server family with key Windows NT system services." Such integration will include:

- administration tools that allow system and network managers to carry out performance and event monitoring through the Windows NT services called (cleverly enough) Performance Monitor and Event Viewer. While this capability is already present in Netscape's Enterprise Server 2.0, it has yet to appear in other SuiteSpot servers.

- bidirectional synchronization (in English, creating fully two-way communications paths) between the LDAP-based Netscape Directory Server and Windows NT directory services, thereby allowing easier exchange of user information between NT and SuiteSpot

- measures to accomplish secure single logins to both SuiteSpot and NT

- support, in future releases of selected SuiteSpot servers, for Symmetric Multiprocessing (SMP), a paradigm already available in Windows NT that permits the simultaneous use of as many as 32 CPUs in a single machine

Through its Catalog Server 1.0 and Enterprise Server 3.0, Netscape already supports indexing and searching of Excel, PowerPoint, and Word documents. Future versions of SuiteSpot servers are expected to offer integration with Office 97's Web publishing features as well.

Communicator in the Year 2000

Those of you whose job, or whose tendency, it is to fret over details, will be glad to know that Netscape Communications affirms that "Communicator will properly process and use dates before, during, and after the transition from December 31, 1999, to January 1, 2000, provided that the underlying operating system... of the host machine is year 2000 compliant."

DHTML

As you've no doubt guessed, Netscape Communicator 4.0 supports several DHTML-related features. Let's review them now.

 *Like IE4, Communicator 4 implements DHTML through its client side, that is, through its browser component.*

Positioning and Layering

Communicator allows you to position these elements with a great deal of precision:

- HTML directives
- images
- links and other forms of rich text
- plug-ins and applets

It does this by allowing you to define x and y coordinates for them. In a similar fashion, Communicator lets you layer or stack the elements on a page.

Stylesheets

Through a combination of CSS-compliant style sheets and JavaScript, Communicator gives Web designers the ability to control such details of a page's appearance as:

- all element properties as recognized by HTML
- the activity of elements
- the visibility of elements

ActiveX

The folks in Provo weren't born yesterday; they've configured Communicator to provide support for Microsoft Web publishing technologies, including ActiveX- and Visual Basic-reliant applications.

Support for and Controlling Access to Java Applets

True to its role as a major developer and proponent of Java-based programming, Netscape Communications has designed Communicator 4.0 to support several Java Developers' Kit (JDK) components, including:

- data types such as Bignum, Byte, Short, and Void
- enhanced I/O services
- inner classes, that is, the ability to nest classes of elements
- internationalization
- JAR files
- JDBC
- object serialization, or the ability to deal with a number of HTML objects in a single way

Communicator's ability to tailor levels of user access to Java applets is equally significant. The access levels you set can range from restricted forms, such as simple read/write permission, to unlimited access to some applets for specific stations.

Communicator 4.0 System Requirements

We'll conclude our examination of Netscape Communicator 4.0 with Table 4-2, which summarizes the demands the suite will make of a system's resources.

Under these operating systems	Communicator needs this hardware platform	and at least this much memory
Windows 3.1 Windows 3.11 Windows 95 Windows NT 3.51	Intel 486 or later	if you enjoy living on the edge, 8MB RAM; otherwise, 16MB
Windows NT 4.0	Intel 486 or later; we recommend a Pentium 133 at a minimum	16MB
Macintosh Apple System 7.1 or later PowerPC	68020 or later	16MB
Digital UNIX	Alpha	16MB
HP-UX 9.03, 9.05, and 10.x	700 series	16MB
AIX 3.25 and 4.x	RS/6000	16 MB
Silicon Graphics UNIX (IRIX 5.3, 6.2, and 6.3)	MIPS	16MB
Solaris 2.4 and 2.5 SunOS 4.1.3	SPARC	16MB

Table 4-2.   *Communicator 4.0's System Requirements*

Thumbnail Review

1. Through a single user interface, Netscape Communicator 4.0 allows you to create or edit text for discussions, email messages, and Web pages; follow hyperlinks that are automatically established between all Communicator components and their content; and use one address book for email and conferencing.

2. Communicator 4.0, unlike its rival Internet Explorer, does use the Channel Definition Format for its Webcasting services.

3. Communicator 4.0 supports a much greater variety of operating environments than does Internet Explorer 4.0.

Looking Ahead

Now that we've previewed

- the basics of Web publishing
- the concepts underlying DHTML
- document design
- the Big Two of integrated Internet application suites

we can begin, in Chapter 5, to investigate the nuts and bolts of using DHTML.

PART TWO

The Project

Chapter Five

Adding Intelligence to the Client Display

In data processing parlance, saying that a piece of software *has intelligence* means that it knows what it should do in certain predefined circumstances. Until recently, Web browsers were not the brightest software bulbs to be found. For example, Internet Explorer prior to 3.0, Netscape prior to 2.0, and W3C HTML up to and including 3.0 couldn't even handle frames. In other words, they couldn't create or manage multiple windows within a document. And as Figure 5-1 shows, HTML documents that don't have frames can be hard to understand.

Dynamic HTML has broken through this Web-publishing limitation, as well as many others. With DHTML, you can't make the client browser into a mind reader, but you can make it sensitive to quite a few user-initiated actions. What's more, you can fine-tune what the browser will do in response to such actions. In this chapter, we'll learn about adding intelligence to a client

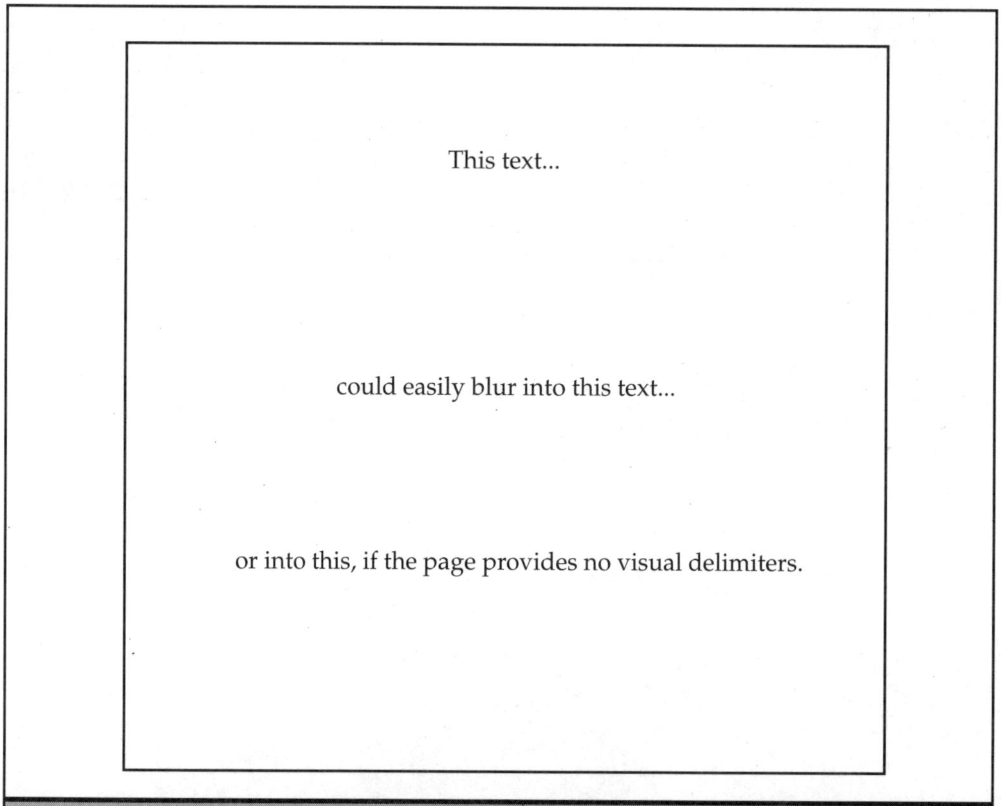

This text...

could easily blur into this text...

or into this, if the page provides no visual delimiters.

Figure 5-1. *HTML documents without frames lack interest, and can even be difficult to structure*

browser display by presenting means of making the browser sensitive to certain steps a user might take, and by giving the browser alternatives it can take in such cases. We'll do this by acquainting you with those HTML elements, and overall document features, that lend themselves to making a browser behave more intelligently.

Elements

In the beginning, there were HTML elements. Or should we call them *document features?* As we've noted so far in this book and will continue to find to be true, the jargon related to Web publishing, like all computer jargon, isn't applied consistently.

In the most informal sense, *elements* are anything you can put on a Web page, including headings, subheadings, images, and text. In HTML-specific terms, however, *element* is synonymous with *tag.* A tag is a directive regarding document composition and display that you enclose in angle brackets (< >) .

Which definition of *element* does DHTML adopt? Both. In the literature on the subject, you'll see the term *element* used to describe everything from the simplest tags to the most complex forms. So, we'll proceed now to distinguishing between elements and features.

Features

First of all, let's summarize the members of the element category we're calling *features*—those elements that represent major areas or components of a page. Table 5-1 outlines this category.

As Table 5-1 illustrates, the term *feature* applies only to the most general definition of HTML document components. The next section goes to the other end of the specificity spectrum and examines the most narrow definition of HTML components.

Sidebar

We made the distinction *depending on where they occur in a document* in Table 5-1 because you have to use HTML tags, reflecting levels of specificity of information or formatting, at certain levels of specificity of document structure. For example, you can only use the tag <TITLE> within a portion of a document marked off by the tag pair <HEAD> </HEAD>. On the other hand, you can use the tag <IMG>, which requires no closing tag, within a number of tagged document sections, many of which can also occur within the <BODY> </BODY> pair.

In the features group	we can place	which, depending on where they occur in a document, can be associated with tags such as
Headings	all levels of document headings	■ <HTML> </HTML>, which must appear in every HTML document, and which indicate the beginning and end of the full document ■ <HEAD> </HEAD>, which mark off the major header of an HTML document ■ <TITLE> </TITLE>, which define the overall page title ■ <A> </A>, which is part of what you need to set up a link to another HTML document
Body	all forms of body text, images, and formatting	■ <BODY> </BODY>, which mark off the body of an HTML document. This body can consist of text, tags, and other forms of information, such as images ■ <P> </P>, which indicate the end of a paragraph ■ <MENU> </MENU>, which define a menu list ■ <H2> </H2>, which create a second-level heading within the body, rather than relating and positioning that second heading in terms of the major document header
Bars, boxes, and buttons	things like: check boxes radio buttons reset buttons submit buttons	■ <HR> </HR>, which is used to create a horizontal line or rule, whose width, thickness, and alignment can be further specified ■ <ADDRESS> </ADDRESS>, which indicate general info on a document's source site or author ■ <IMG> </IMB>, which is used to insert an image into a document at the position where tag is placed. Such images can be specified to be clickable image maps, among other things

Table 5-1. *Document Features as Elements*

HTML Tags

This chapter doesn't have enough pages to list and explain every HTML tag available. Instead, we'll satisfy ourselves with a look, in Table 5-2, at tags that are basic, frequently used, and likely to be needed in top-quality pages. (Appendix A in this book offers a much more extensive listing of HTML tags and extensions.)

In the category	we can place tags such as	which can be applied to document features such as
Basic	the venerable, and required, <HTML>, <HEAD>, <BODY>, <TITLE>, and so on	the major logical and visual divisions of an HTML document
Frequently used	<OL> </OL>, which indicate a numbered (ordered) list <UL> </UL>, which denote a bulleted (unordered) list <DIR> </DIR>, which mark off a directory listing <DL> </DL>, creating a glossary (definitions) list <DT> </DT>, indicating a term to be included in a definitions list	the body of a document

Table 5-2. *HTML Tags as Elements*

In the category	we can place tags such as	which can be applied to document features such as
Likely to be needed if you want to avoid creating a drab page	<SAMP> </SAMP>, which mark off a sample of some kind (usually text) <CITE> </CITE>, which indicate a citation <B> </B>, which define text to be rendered as boldface <I> </I>, which specify text to be displayed in italics <FORM> </FORM>, which define a form to be used within the document	the body of a document

Table 5-2. *HTML Tags as Elements* (continued)

HTML Extensions

In HTML as in programming and formatting in general, *extensions* are not so much enhancements to specific items of existing software vocabulary as they are entirely new entries. In version 3.0, the W3C's standard for HTML tags was extended to include a number of new capabilities, some of which we've summarized in Table 5-3.

As Table 5-3 demonstrates, the trend in Web publishing and HTML has been to provide greater visual interest for the user and finer levels of control for the designer.

To the standard tag	we can add attributes such as	which let you
<FONT> </FONT>	COLOR=" ... " FACE=" ... "	display the text bounded by the font tag pair in the indicated color and style; you can supply such values through names or, in the case of shades of basic colors, through hexadecimal values. Some of the names that you can use as values for COLOR are *blue*, *green*, and *navy*. Two examples of hex values are FF FB F0 for cream and C0 DC C0 for clear green
<UL>	TYPE=" ... "	define the shape of the bullet used in the list, with the possible values: ■ CIRCLE, which defines the bullet character as an open circle ■ SQUARE, which defines the bullet character as an open square ■ DISC, which defines the bullet character as a solid circle

Table 5-3.   *HTML 3.0 Extensions as Elements*

Dynamic Displays

Don't confuse dynamically-displayed elements with intelligence. None of the dynamic elements you might use to liven up an HTML document—such as blinking text, rotating images, and so on—can give your document the ability to react appropriately and spontaneously to user cues. However, you can use such displays to emphasize the results of an intelligent action on the part of the browser. We'll deal with that aspect of dynamic displays shortly. For now, let's just review some of the activities that display elements can take part in.

Here's a little more Web publishing jargon for your growing collection. For activities in the sentence above, substitute behaviors.

Dynamic Displays in HTML 3.0

With version 3.0, the W3C introduced a number of tags that allow you to get elements up and boogeying. Table 5-4 summarizes some of these, as well as similar tags from the most recent non-DHTML versions of Netscape Navigator and Internet Explorer. These tags are, in the strictest sense, extensions to

The new tag or attribute	supplied by	produces
ALIGN (an attribute that you must use in conjunction with the tag <IMG>)	for a limited set of values, HTML 3.0 and IE 1.0 and 2.0 for the full range of its possible values, Navigator 1.0 and 2.0	the detailed definition of the placement of an image on a page
<BGSOUND> (a new tag)	only in Internet Explorer 2.0 and later	background sound for a document
DYNSRC (an attribute that you must use in conjunction with the tag <IMG>)	only in IE 2.0 and later	the ability to include a video as a dynamic image
MARQUEE (a new tag)	only in IE 2.0 and later	text that scrolls continuously, from right to left

Table 5-4. *Extensions and Active Elements*

standard HTML. However, they've become so widely adopted that they can be considered as de facto standard.

Figure 5-2 takes a look at one possible result of using an extension to liven up a display.

Figure 5-3 gives an example of one way you could use the marquee extension.

This book distinguishes between Netscape Navigator, whatever the release, and Netscape Communicator. While Communicator includes an enhanced Navigator, it also contains a number of other components. It is an integrated suite of applications, not merely a sophisticated browser. This inclusion of related but separate applications, and the resulting integration of Web software, under a single umbrella, providing concierge, maitre d', menu, waiter, and busboy all rolled into one, is another of the clear trends in Web publishing's evolution. In later chapters, you'll see how this trend is extending even to providing mood music and a floor show.

The attribute/value
pair ALIGN=LEFT
placed an image here...

...and caused
text to flow, in
accordance with
the image's
placement, into
this area.

Figure 5-2.   *The attribute ALIGN might be considered a precursor to animation*

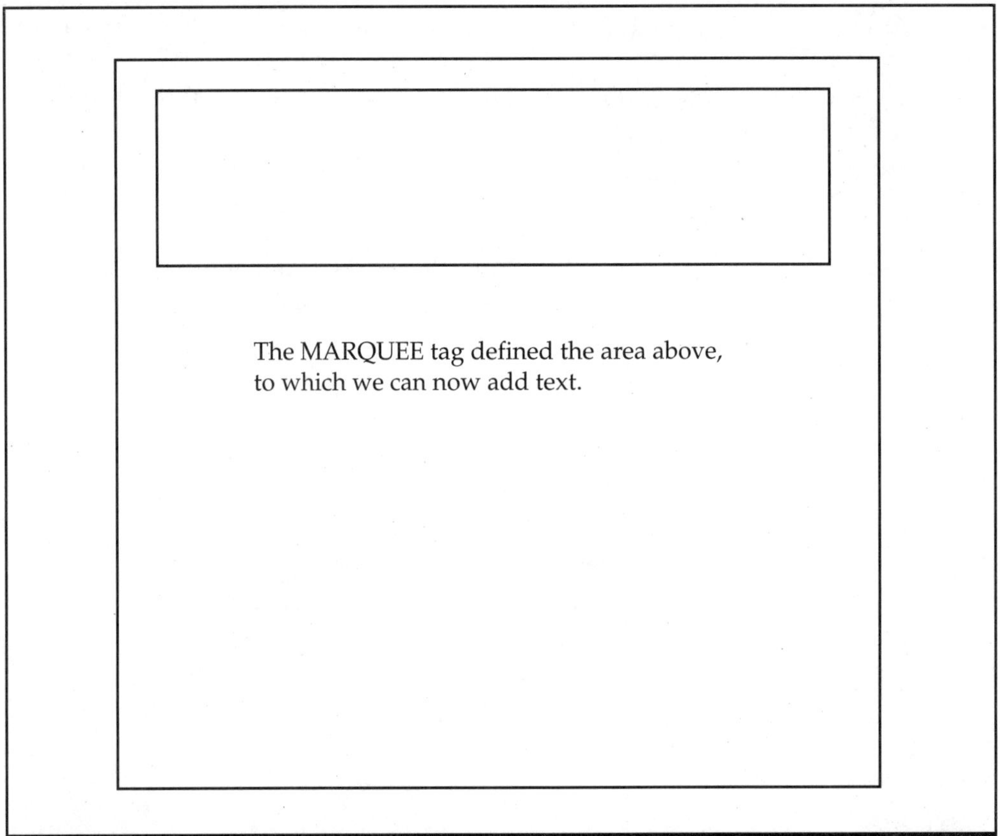

The MARQUEE tag defined the area above,
to which we can now add text.

Figure 5-3. *The tag MARQUEE provides a rudimentary animation capability*

Actions

Once again, understanding actions in an HTML context requires a bit of translation from computer-ese. Programmers and developers refer to actions as *events*. Furthermore, these folks recognize two types of events:

- user-initiated
- system-generated

System-generated events are operating system- or application-generated actions such as regular status messages, warnings, and error messages. User-initiated events, on the other hand, fall within the territory that we, as DHTML gurus-in-the-making, would like to cover. Such events include changes to text, clicks, mouse-overs, and selections of single items from a group of alternatives.

Figure 5-4 shows how system-generated and user-initiated events might intertwine, while Table 5-5 gives you a closer look at user-initiated events and their relationship to displays in HTML documents.

Table 5-5 makes it clear that a browser is basically a client-based user interface to Web sites and Web servers. Figure 5-5 gives a different perspective on this definition of browsers, demonstrating than even the earliest browsers could nonetheless offer a means of extending the scope of that interface.

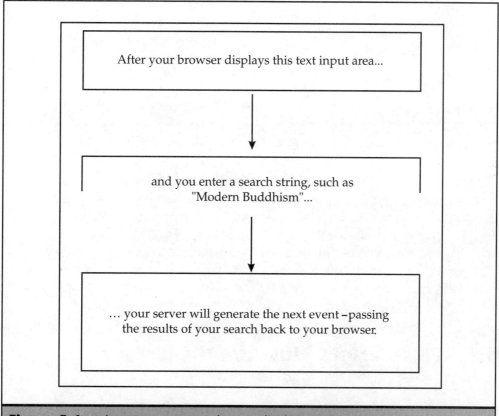

After your browser displays this text input area...

and you enter a search string, such as "Modern Buddhism"...

... your server will generate the next event –passing the results of your search back to your browser.

Figure 5-4. *A system-generated event displays an input area. This event results in a user-initiated action (the entry of text), which in turn brings about another system-generated event*

The user action	might cause HTML to	when the action is carried out on an element defined by
mouse-click	display the URL of an image	the tag <IMG> and the associated attribute ISMAP
mouse-click	display a form	the tag <FORM>
mouse-click	accept text input of up to and including 50 characters from a form	the tag <INPUT> the associated attribute TYPE and attribute value SUBMIT the associated attribute TEXT the associated attribute MAXLENGTH (applied to a text input area) and attribute value 50

Table 5-5.   *User Actions from an HTML Perspective*

Actions That the Client Can Accommodate

Just keep repeating to yourself, "It's only a client; it's only a client." Because that's all a browser is. Beyond carrying out the instructions conveyed to it by an HTML file, a browser, on its own, can do little if anything to give rise to activity or interactivity on the part of a Web page. And not all browsers can carry out all the activity-related instructions we've reviewed so far, let alone the intelligence-related ones we're about to discuss. To provide intelligence to Web browsers and Web page displays, you're going to have to supply scripts.

Actions That Scripts Must Handle

While a browser may appear to be performing these actions:

- accept input from a user
- process that input
- display the results of the processing to the user

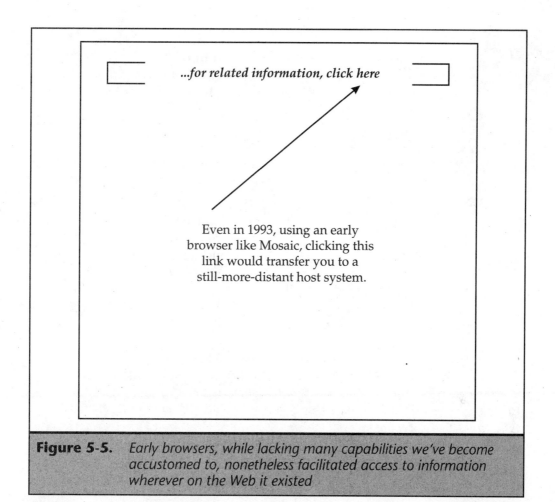

...for related information, click here

Even in 1993, using an early
browser like Mosaic, clicking this
link would transfer you to a
still-more-distant host system.

Figure 5-5. *Early browsers, while lacking many capabilities we've become accustomed to, nonetheless facilitated access to information wherever on the Web it existed*

it is actually only:

- accepting the input
- handing that input off to a server script
- displaying the results of the script's processing

The browser even has to rely on HTML vocabulary and syntax to display script-generated results. Any intelligence shown by a browser usually originates in the scripts stored and executed in its server.

There are more Web scripting languages available than you can shake a shellaighleah at. Some of the best known and most widely used ones are: C and C++; Java; JavaScript (from Netscape) and JScript (from Microsoft); Perl; Visual Basic and VBScript (both Microsoft products).

Deciding on a Scripting Language

How do you decide which scripting language best suits your Web site? It must, of course, be compatible with the underlying operating system and Web server. It must also excel at processing text, because much of your user input will be in this form. It should also be able to quickly process all other forms of user input, such as mouse-clicks and mouse-overs. Finally, it should be easy to learn.

Given these criteria, we recommend that you use Perl, JavaScript, or VBScript. Table 5-6 outlines the reasoning behind this recommendation.

If we had to make a recommendation for a single scripting language irrespective of operating environment, it would be JavaScript. This language is most likely to dominate Web scripting in the near future. Perl, while powerful and flexible, is used most frequently in UNIX environments. VBScript lacks some of the capabilities of Perl or JavaScript. (Interestingly enough, Microsoft is tacitly acknowledging this by offering JScript, which is JavaScript-compliant, and by supporting JavaScript in Internet Explorer 3.0 and higher.)

Here is a rudimentary example of the type of HTML coding that would activate such a script. This Perl code processes a user request for a file.

```
#I /usr/bin/perl
# The first line of a Perl script is always the location on the
server of the Perl implementation.
$file='QUERY_STRING'
# The HTTP protocol automatically passes to the Perl script the
contents of the CGI environment variable QUERY_STRING. This
variable contains the name of the desired file, which is entered
by the user.
```

The language	has these characteristics
JavaScript	although interpreted rather than compiled, it processes input quickly because code is embedded within an HTML document
	it can be associated with fully-Java applications on the server to provide additional processing
	it is easy to learn because it lacks some of the complexities of full-blown Java
Perl	it is associated with many flavors of UNIX, the operating system that most frequently serves as the basis for Web sites
	it excels at text processing
	it processes user input quickly
VBScript	like JavaScript, it is interpreted rather than compiled, so it processes input quickly
	it lets you create and manage scripts as ActiveX objects, in effect letting you choose which scripts to execute on the fly, based upon user input

Table 5-6. *Choosing a Web Scripting Language*

Intelligent Actions

You have to script intelligent actions. Period. There is no other way to make browsers generate action-specific, intelligent responses to user-initiated actions. This being the case, it behooves us to introduce you to some of the vocabulary, grammar, and syntax you'll need to create scripts that evoke intelligent browser behavior.

Using JavaScript to Define Intelligent Actions

As you might expect from a language designed by Sun Microsystems and further developed by Netscape Communications specifically for Web-related programming, JavaScript is chock-full of tools for raising browser IQs. In this section, you'll learn about two tools that apply to DHTML.

Handling Mouse-Clicks

If a user clicks on a form element, let's say a radio button, to choose a particular item, you could use the following JavaScript code fragment to notify the user that the choice is not available.

```
<FORM>
<INPUT TYPE="RADIO" onClick='alert("Sorry; that's no longer a valid choice.")'>

</FORM>
```

This code lets the browser focus on a form's radio button and tells the browser to display a specific popup warning message when the radio button is clicked.

Handling Mouse-Overs

Another hypothetical situation: Your user passes the mouse over a link you've embedded in a page. The user doesn't click, mind you, he or she just runs the mouse over the link. In such a case, you could use this code to display a description of the associated URL in the status bar:

```
<A HREF="http://www.nwu.org" onMouseOver="window.status='National
Writers' Union'"; return true">"Connect to the National Writers'
Union"</A>
```

Using Dynamic Displays to Present Intelligent Actions

As we pointed out in the "Dynamic Displays" section earlier in this chapter, both Internet Explorer and Netscape, even prior to their respective DHTML incarnations, offered a number of extensions that you could use to create dynamic display effects. Of course, you can use these same extensions to present or emphasize intelligent browser responses to user actions.

Let's use the dynamic Web page we're developing for the National Writers' Union as an example. Say that the user has requested a search of the Union's database of computer-related terms for a definition of the word *parse*, and we want to draw the reader's attention to the page's response. Let's assume that the search was conducted by JavaScript code, and it has found a definition and returned it to the browser.

To focus the reader on these results, we might use

- an announcement to tell the user that the search was successful

- a noticeable font and color to display the definition

Let's examine each of these techniques further.

Messages or Announcements

To announce a successful search, we might add the following code to the HTML file that constitutes our basic page.

```
<FRAMESET COLS="90" ROWS="35">
<FRAME NAME="Huzzah" SCROLLING="no">
<A HREF="../usr/bin/apache/cand_txt/hurrah.txt" TARGET="Huzzah">
</FRAMESET>
```

These lines of HTML code will produce these results:

- establish a subwindow (or frame) that is 90 pixels wide and 35 pixels high

- assign the name Huzzah to the frame, and display the frame without scroll bars

- display a canned announcement, stored on the server in a file called hurrah.txt, within the frame

Font Type and Color for the Results of a Search

To reinforce the definition of *parse* in the user's mind, we could add this code to our basic page:

```
<FRAMESET COLS="120" ROWS="55">
<FRAME NAME="Def" SCROLLING="no">
<A TARGET="Def" >
<FONT FACE="ARIAL" COLOR="RED" SIZE="+2">
</A>
</FRAMESET>
```

These lines of HTML code will produce these results:

- establish a subwindow (or frame) that is 120 pixels wide and 55 pixels high

- assign the name Def to the frame, and display the frame without scroll bars

- specify that the results returned by the server-side script will be displayed in this new frame

- specify that the results will be displayed in a red Arial font that's three times as large as the base font for the page

Sidebar

This example assumes that the client browser is probably Internet Explorer, because HTML 3.0 and Netscape Navigator 1.0 or 2.0 don't support the attribute COLOR for the tag <FONT>. We don't mean to imply, however, that IE is the best or even the most widely-used browser. The example simply illustrates the fact that neither HTML itself nor DHTML are truly standardized.

Thumbnail Review

1. You can create dynamic displays solely through HTML.

2. Intelligent responses to users by a browser *must* originate in a script.

3. Scripts can be stored and executed on a Web server, or they can be embedded within an HTML document.

4. Your best choices for a scripting language are JavaScript, Perl, or VBScript.

5. Both JavaScript and VBScript programs can be embedded within an HTML file, but they may need to interact with server-side code.

6. Perl scripts must be located on and run from a server.

Looking Ahead

Investigating activity and intelligence in individual HTML elements has prepared you to move on to fully DHTML-related tools and techniques. We'll begin our scrutiny of these in Chapter 6, where you'll learn how DHTML can use cascading style sheets to position or layer elements on a page.

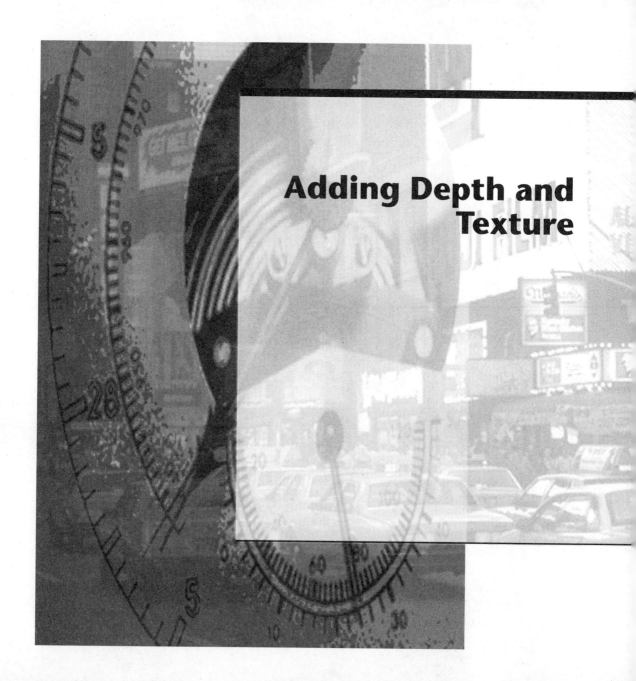

CHAPTER SIX

Adding Depth and Texture

Paintings produced before about the 12th century AD seem flat to us, not only visually, but emotionally as well. Can you imagine, for example, the subject of an Egyptian scroll or a Greek icon in any but a passive context? While such works may evoke a contemplative mood, they convey little or no sense of any action being possible, let alone imminent.

This principle applies to Web page visuals as well. As Figure 6-1 shows, incorporating depth—or visual layers—and texture—or a variety of shapes and sizes—in an HTML document will make the document more interesting for your viewers. It will not only more fully engage their attention, but may also suggest, however subliminally, that something might be about to happen.

In this chapter, you learn how to add depth and texture to an HTML document. That is, you learn how to work with layering.

Cascading Style Sheets

Cascading style sheets, as proposed by the World Wide Web Consortium, let you deal comprehensively with logical or physical groupings within a Web page by allowing you to define styles for such features as color and font.

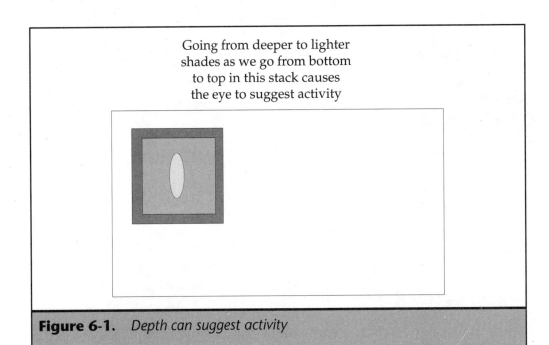

Figure 6-1.   *Depth can suggest activity*

Further, given these abilities, such style sheets offer a way of creating a layered look in a Web document.

The main mechanism through which the W3C standard for cascading style sheets—referred to as CSS1—accomplishes this is something called a selector, *which allows you to choose those features to which a style will be applied.*

CSS1 (or any other) style sheets can manipulate properties such as these:

- font style, for example, italic
- font weight, that is, bold or light
- line height
- text alignment, whether horizontal or vertical
- text color
- text decoration, such as underlining
- text indentation

For instance, a CSS1 style sheet might contain this code:

```
<STYLE>
{H4:color green;
H5:color red;
BLOCKQUOTE:font-style italic;
BLOCKQUOTE:line-height 1.5;
P:text-indent 20;
P:text-align center;
</STYLE>
```

Parents and Children

Style sheets let you embed elements within other elements. An element that contains an embedded element is called a *parent*, and the embedded element is called the *child*. Often, and especially when you don't specify otherwise, child elements take on, or *inherit*, styles assigned to their parent elements. The code we'll discuss in more detail in a moment illustrates one example of a parent/child relationship.

As part of understanding inheritance, you need to understand the difference between style properties and style specifications. A style *property* is a parameter, stored by a browser, that helps it make layout decisions. A style *specification*, on the other hand, is an attribute of a style sheet element that modifies the normal behavior of a property in some way. For example, in the code fragment below, fontfam is a property, while alternate is a specification.

This code fragment illustrates why this distinction is important.

```
<stylesheet>
<style id=look1
    fontfam=alternate
    lmargin="+3em">
</style>
<style id=look2 gis="blockquote"
    inherit=look1
    lmargin="+5em"
></style>
<style id=look3 gis="p" fontshape=plain>
</style>
</stylesheet>
```

Let's say your default left margin has been specified as 1em, and a BLOCKQUOTE element is encountered. In this scenario, *look2* is the style element that will be used. *Look2* itself inherits specifications from *look1*. But the explicit definition of a setting for the left margin in *look2* overrides the specification inherited from *look1*, so the left margin is indented by 5em, not 3em.

Now, suppose that the BLOCKQUOTE element in question encases a <P>. In this case, style element *look3* will take over. But *look3* has no spec for the left margin, so the paragraph inherits its left margin characteristics from its parent BLOCKQUOTE element, which in turn inherited it from its parent. So inheritance here, like that shown in Figure 6-2, will not proceed as we planned; our <P> element will not have a left margin set to 5em, but rather to 6em, the sum of the default margin and the +5 inherited from *look2*.

Note ▶   *A few properties, such as background, can never be inherited.*

Selectors and Classes

Any HTML element can function as a CSS1 selector, which is simply an element that is linked to a particular style. For a given selector, you can then

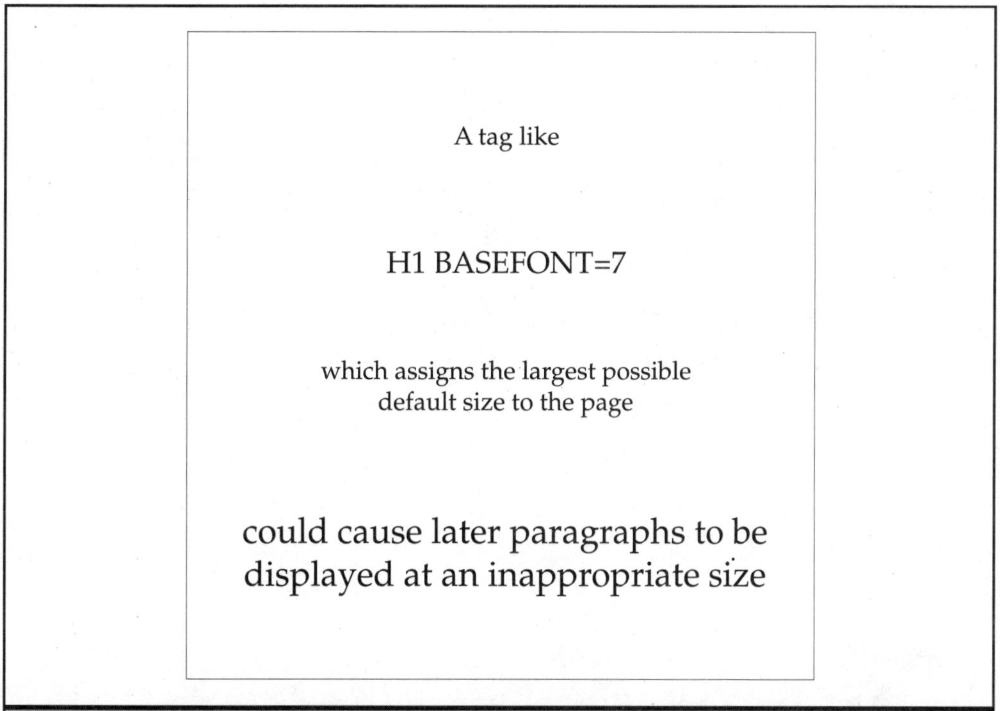

A tag like

H1 BASEFONT=7

which assigns the largest possible
default size to the page

could cause later paragraphs to be
displayed at an inappropriate size

Figure 6-2.   *Be careful that a child doesn't inherit unwanted characteristics*

create *classes* to assign different styles to the same element, to be used in
different circumstances. For example, if you want to echo text input from the
user in different colors, depending upon whether the text was the first or a
subsequent entry, you might want to identify these classes and related
properties for the element/selector TEXTAREA:

```
textarea.first { color: blue }
textarea.again { color: red }
```

You can even create classes without associating them with an element,
which allows you to apply them to any element, as this code sample and
Figure 6-3, point out:

```
code.newshade { color: green )
```

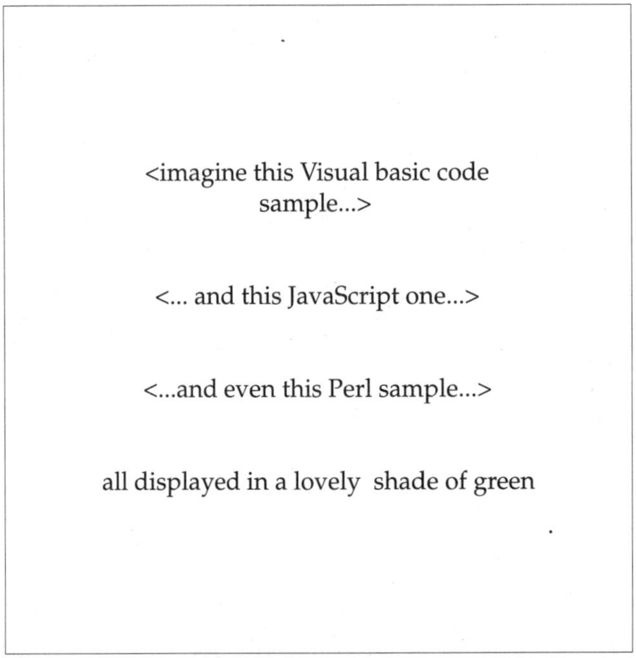

<... and this JavaScript one...>

<...and even this Perl sample...>

all displayed in a lovely shade of green

Figure 6-3. *The same stylesheet class can be applied to a number of situations*

Sidebar

One type of selector is known as an *ID selector*. You can only use ID selectors on a per-element basis, and they are clumsy to work with. Here's an example of an ID selector:

```
#special1 { text-indent: 3strong )
```

You'd apply this ID selector as follows:

```
<P ID=special1>Text for this paragraph will not only be
indented but heavily emphasized.</P>
```

We think you'll agree that the ID selector isn't a good choice because it's too clunky. For this reason, we won't use them in any further examples.

Contextual Selectors

Separate simple selectors, that is, selectors that consist of only one word, by white space within a string, and presto!—you've just defined *contextual selectors*, to which you can then assign any sensible properties. What's more, the rules of cascading order for CSS1 style sheets mandate that contextual selectors are applied before simple selectors. In other words, contextual selectors have precedence over simple selectors. One example of a contextual selector might be

```
A EM { background: red }
```

Pseudo-classes and Pseudo-elements

Pop Quiz

To what element and property does this contextual selector apply? To what element(s) and property or properties does it not apply? The answers are at the end of the chapter.

What's that you just asked? Might there not be situations in which you need different classes for a single element, depending on different circumstances? Indeed there are. Two that come easily to mind and that may have prompted your question are

- distinguishing between a link's being unselected, selected for the first time, or revisited
- setting off the first sentence or paragraph of a logical grouping of text

CSS1 style sheets deal with such special class requirements through a mechanism called *pseudo-classes* and *pseudo-elements*.

Pseudo-classes and pseudo-elements, which are automatically recognized and correctly interpreted by any CSS-compliant browser, can distinguish either between overall element characteristics (as in our inactive/visited links example) or between subsections of an element (as in our sentence/paragraph example). If you wanted to distinguish between inactive, active, and revisited links in your Web page, you could write these lines into your style sheet:

```
A:no_visits { color: green }
A:active { color: red }
A:been_there { color: navy }
```

Or, if you wanted to set off not only the first line but the first letter of your page's body text, you might use this style sheet section:

```
P:first-line { font-weight: bold }
P:first-letter { font-size: 200% }
```

As Figure 6-4 shows, these lines of code would create more than just a bolded first line.

Pop Quiz 2
What will distinguish the letter whose pseudo-element we just defined?

You can apply first-line pseudo-elements to any block-level element, such as paragraphs or headings.

Grouping and Inheritance

When you are setting up style sheets, it's a good idea to group your selectors and selector declarations. Grouping keeps a sheet lean by avoiding redundant code. So if, for instance, you want all subsidiary headings in a Web page to be

The font size of the first letter of the line below is 24; the rest of the line is sized 12.

Hi, and Welcome!

Figure 6-4. *Look at the difference in this line when it's displayed with, and without, pseudo-elements*

displayed in the same font and color, you could accomplish this with a single line such as

```
H2, H3, H4, H5, H6 {color: navy; font-family: serif }
```

In addition to grouping selectors, you can take advantage of the fact that selectors inherit from one another. An element that you ordinarily place within other elements (such as P within BODY) inherits the property values assigned to the outer element unless you explicitly define it otherwise.

> ## Pop Quiz 3
>
> Can you think of a case in which an inner element would not, by default, inherit a surrounding element's property values? Let your intuition take charge here. Also, you get extra credit for more than one example.

Cascading Hierarchy and Defining Styles as Important

As you learned in Chapter 1, in the section "Style Sheets in More Detail," you can apply multiple style sheets to a single Web document. If you decide to do this, however, you have to make it clear which style sheet's directives apply when more than one sheet references the same element. You can accomplish this by using the *! important* designation:

```
! important
```

You can specify that a style will take precedence over contradictory styles applied to the same element. One example of this designation might be:

```
BODY { background: white ! important }
```

One quality of CSS1 style sheets that is largely intended to support users with special needs is that readers of a Web page you build through style sheets can also define their own versions of the sheets. For instance, a visually handicapped individual might alter a previously defined font size, making it larger. When there is a conflict between the display or behavior specified in the author's and the reader's style sheets, the author's wins. For this reason, you should exercise a bit of caution when you declare styles to be ! important. These styles will override any user-defined ! important ones, and this might create problems for readers such as the visually handicapped.

If you don't use the *! important* syntax, conflicts between style sheets are resolved based on level of specificity in the sheets; the more specific style always takes precedence. As a rule of thumb, the more ID and CLASS attributes and tag names there are associated with a selector, the more specific it is, so the more likely it is that the selector will be executed if there is a conflict. Finally, should two style sheets or rules have the same level of specificity, the last one defined will take precedence.

Comments

Comments in CSS1 style sheets (like so much of the programming syntax for Web publishing) follow C programming conventions. So, for example, you might find this comment in a CSS1 style sheet:

```
/* COMMENTS IN CSS1 LOOK LIKE COMMENTS IN C CODE */
```

CSS1 Syntax and JavaScript Syntax

The most significant difference between CSS1 style sheet syntax, which we've been using up to this point, and the syntax used in JavaScript under Netscape Communicator, is in how property names are managed.

In CSS1 style sheets, you use hyphens to separate the words in property names that contain more than one word, as in:

```
<code>margin-right:none</code>
```

In JavaScript style sheets, you capitalize the first letter of the second (and subsequent) words in a property name, as in:

```
<code>marginRight</code>
```

Single-word properties in CSS1 and JavaScript syntax are indistinguishable. This makes it impossible to determine the origin of a line such as this one:

```
<code>font</code>
```

In addition to how they handle single-word property names, CSS1 and JavaScript share another characteristic: Case counts! This means that both types of style sheets distinguish between

```
P:First-line { font-weight: bold }
```

and

```
P:first-line { font-weight: bold }
```

CSS1 and JavaScript style sheets also share these three conventions:

- They list the property names and values of an HTML element inside curly braces immediately after naming the element.
- They use a colon to separate a property name from its value.
- They complete every property name/value pair, including the last one in a list, with a semi-colon.

JavaScript can recognize and correctly interpret CSS1 style sheet syntax. For a complete rundown of the CSS1 and JavaScript syntax used to define and manipulate properties in style sheets, see Appendixes B and C.

CSS1 Layering

In this section, we will present at least a few of the CSS1 properties that you can use to add depth and texture to a Web page. Bear in mind that there are literally dozens more. For a complete review, refer to Appendix B.

Background Color

- uses the syntax: background-color: <value>
- the values allowed are <color>, transparent
- the default value is transparent
- the property can be applied to: all elements
- the property cannot be inherited

■ Example: BODY { background-color: blue }

■ Explanation: sets the background color of all BODY elements to blue

Background Image

■ uses the syntax: background-image: <value>

■ the values allowed are URL, none

■ the default value is none

■ the property can be applied to: all elements

■ the property cannot be inherited

■ Example: P { background-image: url(http://www.d.com)}

■ Explanation: defines the URL at which the image is found

Background Attachment

■ uses the syntax: background-attachment: <value>

■ the values allowed are scroll, fixed

■ the default value is scroll

■ the property can be applied to: all elements

■ the property cannot be inherited

■ Example: BODY { background: blue;
background-image:url(candybar.gif); background-attachment: fixed }

■ Explanation: specifies that the background image will not scroll with text

Background

■ uses the syntax: background <value>

■ the values allowed are background attachment, background color, background image, background position, background repeat

■ the default value is undefined

■ the property can be applied to: all elements

- the property cannot be inherited
- Example: TABLE { background: blue url(leaves.jpg) no-repeat bottom right }
- Explanation: acts as a shorthand for more specific background definitions

Word Spacing

- uses the syntax: word spacing <value>
- the values allowed are normal, <length>
- the default value is normal
- the property can be applied to: all elements
- the property can be inherited
- Example: P.code { word-spacing: -0.2 em }
- Explanation: reduces spacing for words to which this class is applied by 20 percent

Letter Spacing

- uses the syntax: letter spacing <value>
- the values allowed are normal, <length>
- the default value is normal
- the property can be applied to: all elements
- the property can be inherited
- Example: H2{ letter-spacing: 0.1em }
- Explanation: spaces letters within all level-2 headings at one-tenth their normal distribution

Vertical Alignment

- uses the syntax: vertical-align: <value>
- the values allowed are baseline, sub, super, top, text-top, text-bottom, middle, <percentage>

- the default value is baseline
- the property can be applied to: inline elements, that is, those that have no line break before and after, such as EM, A, and IMG
- the property cannot be inherited
- Examples:
  - IMG.middle { vertical-align: middle } will align the image at its vertical midpoint, with the baseline plus half the x-height (the height of the letter x) of the parent
  - IMG { vertical-align: 30% } will align the image by placing its baseline 30 percent above its parent's baseline
  - IMG { vertical-align: text-top } will align the image by placing its baseline according to the tops of its and its parent's font

Text Transforming

- uses the syntax: text-transform: <value>
- the values allowed are none, capitalize, uppercase, lowercase
- the default value is undefined
- the property can be applied to all elements
- the property can be inherited
- Examples:
  - H2 { text-transform: uppercase } will capitalize the first letter of every word in every level-2 heading
  - H2 { text-transform: capitalize } will capitalize all letters in all words in every level-2 heading

Text Alignment

- uses the syntax: text-align <value>
- the values allowed are left, right, center, justify
- the default value is defined by browser capability
- the property can be applied to: block-level elements such as P, all H

- the property can be inherited
- Example: P:newspaper { text-align: justify } would create a class called newspaper;

- Explanation: all text to which this class is then applied would be justified

Line Height

- uses the syntax: line-height <value>
- the values allowed are normal, <number>, <length>, <percentage>
- the default value is normal
- the property can be applied to: all elements
- the property can be inherited
- Example: P { line-height: 200% }

- Explanation: would set the height of all lines in the paragraph to twice their normal height relative to the font size in use. When specified as a number, line height is calculated by multiplying the element's font size by the number.

Margin

- uses the syntax: margin <value>
- the values allowed are <length>, <percentage>, auto, <4 values that specify, respectively, top, right, bottom, and left margins>
- the default value is undefined
- the property can be applied to: all elements
- the property cannot be inherited
- Example: FORM { margin: 1em 2em 3em 4em }

- Explanation: shorthand for the margin-top, -right, -bottom, and -left properties respectively

JavaScript Layering

Using JavaScript to create and control layers is ... well, it's just easier than using CSS1 syntax. That's because JavaScript has a number of built-in, layer-specific properties and methods. We'll review them all in this section.

Translate the term method *as* subroutine *or* procedure; *it's close enough.*

Sidebar

In general—that is, outside the context of working with layers—we recommend CSS1 syntax as readily as JavaScript syntax. Why? For the same reason that we suggest using SGML syntax for comments in HTML documents and script files. It will help ensure that your sheets are recognized by the widest range of browsers possible.

The LAYER Tag

We'll begin our discussion of layering in JavaScript with one of the newest extensions to standard HTML, the LAYER tag, offered by Netscape Communicator 4.0. With this tag, you can indicate any element or group of elements that will form a visual layer on your page. You can then treat everything you place between the opening and closing LAYER tag (between <LAYER> and </LAYER>) as a single item.

Sidebar

Such conglomerations are called, in JavaScript and in many object-oriented programming (OOP) languages—did we just give it away?—*objects*.

What's most important about layers in the context of our exploration of Dynamic HTML is that layers can be stacked. You can specify the order of the layers, the *Z order*, in two ways:

- as ordinal or relative indicators, along the lines of

```
place Layer 2 immediately above Layer 1
```

- by means of explicit integer values for a layer's Z order, saying, in effect

```
the Z value of Layer Cat is 1, and of Layer Dog is 2.
```

Layers can demonstrate any standard or advanced HTML properties. So, they can, for example:

- be opaque
- be transparent
- have unique background patterns or colors

Layer Objects

For every layer defined in a JavaScript-generated HTML page, there exists a *layer object*. This object has properties that you can modify through

- assignment statements, such as

```
mylayer.visibility = hide
```

- JavaScript methods or procedures, which follow the general syntax

```
layerName.methodName(parameters)
```

Layer Object Properties

If you're to use layers effectively, you must thoroughly understand their characteristics, which span many categories, including positioning, background effects, and clipping region, among others. This diverse and extensive set of layer properties might at first seem intimidating, which is why we've once again chosen to present them to you by means of a table.

Table 6-1 acquaints you with JavaScript layer object properties.

The JavaScript layer property	refers to
above	the layer object above the active or current one, among: all layers in the document all layers in the enclosing window, if the current layer is topmost

Table 6-1. *JavaScript Layer Object Properties*

The JavaScript layer property	refers to
background	background for the layer's canvas, that is, for that part of the layer within the clip area; must have a value that: represents an image object whose *src* attribute is a URL is set to null if the layer is to have no backdrop
below	layer object below the current one
bgColor	solid background color for the layer's canvas; value can be specified as: a hex-encoded RGB value a pre-defined color null to create a transparent layer
clip.top/left/right/bottom/width/height	define the clipping rectangle, that part of the layer that is visible. (Any part of a layer outside the clipping rectangle will not be displayed.)
left	horizontal position of the layer's left edge in pixels, relative to the origin of its parent layer
name	name assigned to the layer through the ID attribute in the <LAYER> tag
pageX	horizontal position of the layer, in pixels, relative to the page
pageY	vertical position of the layer, in pixels, relative to the page
parentLayer	either: the name of the layer object that contains, in other words, is parent to, the current layer the name of the enclosing window object, if the current layer is not nested in another
siblingAbove	among all layers that share the same parent layer, the layer object above the current one; null if the layer has no sibling above

Table 6-1. *JavaScript Layer Object Properties* (continued)

The JavaScript layer property	refers to
siblingBelow	among all layers that share the same parent layer, the layer object below the current one; null if the layer has no sibling below
src	source, specified as a URL, of a layer's content
top	vertical position, in pixels and relative to the origin of a parent layer, of a layer's top edge
visibility	whether a layer is visible; values: show: layer is visible hide: layer is invisible inherit: layer inherits the visibility of the parent layer
zIndex	relative Z order of the current layer with respect to all siblings, and to parent; the higher its Z order, given as an integer, the nearer a layer is to the top of a stack of siblings

Table 6-1. *JavaScript Layer Object Properties* (continued)

Layer Object Methods

Now that you know what properties JavaScript layers can take on, you can refer to Table 6-2 to learn how to manipulate those properties.

Relating Layers to Documents

Every document created by a JavaScript style sheet that uses layers has a property that consists of an array of all the top-level layers in the document. And every layer in such a document has a property that consists of an array of all the top-level layers inside the current layer. To see how this works, scan through this code snippet and then take a look at Table 6-3 for further explanation.

The JavaScript layer object method called	allows you to
layer.moveBelow(layer)	place the current layer below that specified as an argument, without changing the current layer's horizontal or vertical position
load(sourcestring, width)	simultaneously make the contents of the file named in the *sourcestring* argument the source of content for the current layer and change the width at which the layer's contents will wrap first argument: string second argument: an integer pixel value
moveAbove(layer)	place the current layer above the layer specified in the argument, without changing either layer's horizontal or vertical position
moveBy(x, y)	change the current layer's position by the number of pixels specified in the two integer arguments; negative values would move left/down as appropriate
moveTo(x, y)	change the position of the current layer to the specified integer pixel coordinates, which must be within the containing layer
moveToAbsolute(x, y)	change the position of the current layer to the specified integer pixel coordinates, which must be within the current page
resizeBy(width, height)	change the current layer to reflect the specified integer height and width pixel values; has the same effect as setting clip.width and clip.height
resizeTo(width, height)	change the current layer to have the specified integer height and width pixel values; layer contents may be clipped by these new boundaries

Table 6-2. *JavaScript Layer Object Methods*

The line	has a property of the type	with the value	and an index within its array of
<HTML>	document		
<BODY>	document		
<LAYER ID = "LAYER1">	layer	layer1	1
<P>put the content for Layer 1 here. </P>			
</LAYER>			
<LAYER ID = "LAYER2">			
<P>Put Layer 2's content here. </P>	These lines will generate an error, because this second layer is not nested within another.		
</LAYER>			
</BODY>			
</HTML>			

Table 6-3.   *Relating Document and Layer Properties*

```
<HTML>
<BODY>
<LAYER ID = "LAYER1">
<P>Layer 1 content. </P>
</LAYER>
<LAYER ID = "LAYER2">
<P>Layer 2 content. </P>
<LAYER ID = "LAYER2.1">
<P>Layer 2.1 content. </P>
</LAYER>
</LAYER>
</BODY>
</HTML>
```

What Table 6-3 illustrates is that—assuming you place your layers correctly—JavaScript lets you access any object in one of the layers by means of

- the layer's array index, which must of course be a non-negative integer
- the name specified by the ID attribute in the <LAYER> tag

When you use array indices to access layer elements, the elements appear from back to front. An index value of zero represents the bottommost layer, an index of one represents the next highest layer, and so on. In this way, a stack of five layers might be represented by the array

```
layr_stak[4]
```

whose individual cells would then be numbered

```
layr_stak[0], layr_stak[1], layr_stak[2], layr_stak[3],
layr_stak[4]
```

Adjacent layers, that is, those displayed at the same depth but controlled by different arrays, can have the same zIndex values. But within an array, only one layer can be pointed to by each index of the array.

To conclude this discussion of JavaScript layering arrays, here is a list of all the (generalized-syntax) valid ways that you can access layer objects:

- `document.layers[index]`
  This accesses the layer indicated by *index*.
- `document.layers["layerName"]`
  This accesses the layer indicated by *layerName*.
- `document.layers["layer2"].document.layers["layer2.1"]`
  This accesses the layer indicated by *layer2.1*, which is nested within *layer2*.

Creating Layers

JavaScript allows you to make new layers on the fly by using the operator *new* on an existing layer object, as shown here:

```
smalllayer = document.layers["smalllayer"]
/* This first line references an existing layer by its name,
rather than its index, within its array. */
newsmalllayer = new Layer(300, smalllayer)
/* This line has, as its first argument, the width in pixels of
the new layer, and as its second, the name of the parent layer.
Note that this second argument is optional. */
```

When you dynamically create layers or modify their contents, you need to follow these rules:

- You can only have one layer open for writing at a time.
- You can only use the *new* operator after a page has completely loaded.
- You cannot open a layer's document and write to it until the page containing the layer has completely loaded.

Writing to Layers

While, and only while, defining a layer, you can write to its document, that is, to its content, with an appropriate write method. Here is an example:

```
<LAYER ID="layer1">
<H1>Level-1 header stuff</H1>
<SCRIPT>
document.write("<P>Here is some content</P>")
</SCRIPT>
<SCRIPT>
function changeLayerContent() {
document.layers["layer1"].document.write("<HR><P>More stuff for
content.</P><HR>");
document.layers["layer1"].document.close();}
</SCRIPT>
</LAYER>
```

Given this code, the layer whose ID is *layer1* will have, as its initial content, the paragraph

```
Here is some content.
```

and as its final content, the paragraph

 `More stuff for content.`

Note that if you write a layer document dynamically, you have to explicitly close it.

Layers and Events

Because every JavaScript layer functions as a separate document, each layer can also carry out event handling as if it were a top-level window. <LAYER> can use the built-in JavaScript event handlers

- onBlur (invoked when the layer loses keyboard focus, that is, when the layer becomes stippled out)
- onFocus (invoked when the layer gains keyboard focus)
- onLoad (invoked when a layer is loaded, whether or not the layer is visible)
- onMouseOut (invoked when the mouse moves out of a layer)
- onMouseOver (invoked when the mouse moves into a layer)

These handlers let you define how the layer will behave in each of these scenarios. You can even define what will take place if an event occurs at a point on the screen where layers overlap. In such cases, the event belongs, so to speak, to the top most layer. Therefore, you must specify actions to be taken with this in mind. One last point, though—hidden layers cannot own events.

 *You can also use the <SCRIPT>/ </SCRIPT> tag pair even within layers. The functions defined in the script will then apply only to the layer that contains them.*

Answers to Pop Quizzes

1. The contextual selector *A EM* applies only to a link, and within that, to the background color and font emphasis.
2. The letter to which the pseudo-element font-size: 200 percent is applied will be rendered twice its normal size, relative to its base font.

3. One example of a property that would not be inherited, simply because doing so would be illogical, is the property *margin-top*. Think about it; you wouldn't want a paragraph to share a top margin with the document as a whole.

Thumbnail Review

1. Both CSS1 and JavaScript syntax can create layers.

2. CSS1 and JavaScript style sheets share many points of syntax.

3. JavaScript style sheets offer many built-in features that CSS1 scripts do not, such as:

   a. the <LAYER>/</LAYER> tag pair

   b. properties such as *visibility* and *zIndex*

   c. methods or procedures such as *moveToAbsolute(x, y)*

   d. the ability to access layer elements through array indices

Looking Ahead

Whew! This chapter was a bit of a stretch. But we now have everything we need to begin, in our review of animation in Dynamic HTML.

Chapter Seven

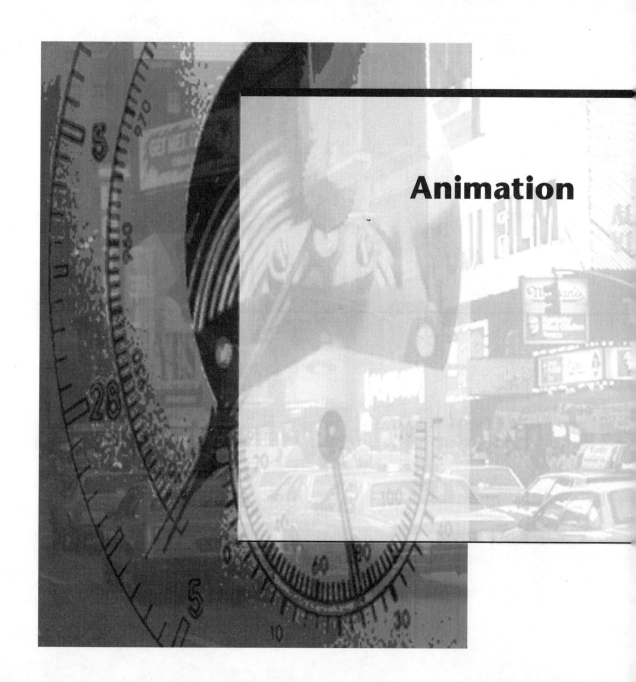

Animation

Y ou might say that the entire motion picture industry is built on a house of cards. Literally. Films rely on the same quirk of physics that many of us discovered as children when we drew a series of images, each on its own blank card, riffled the deck, and watched the images flow into a single, if stutterstepping (picture *Seinfeld*'s Kramer entering a room), sequence.

With this metaphor in mind, you can understand why we discussed layering in Chapter 6 before moving on to animation in this chapter. Now, we'll look at the Web publishing equivalent of riffling the deck.

Animating Layers with JavaScript

JavaScript includes a function called *setTimeout()* that is ideal for animating layers. *setTimeout()* is handy because it can call another function, even itself, after a particular interval of time. *setTimeout()* has two forms:

```
setTimeout("code to be executed", delay)
setTimeout(fn, delay, args...)
```

Suppose you want to execute the function *TrekTrivia*, with the arguments *Neelix* and *alien*, 15 milliseconds from the current system time. Either of the following lines of JavaScript code would do the job.

```
setTimeout("TrekTrivia('Neelix', 'alien')", 15)
setTimeout("TrekTrivia", 15, "Neelix", "alien");
```

Here's an even flashier example of using *setTimeout()*. The following code will expand the layer to which it is applied by 10 pixels in both length and width until the layer is 500 pixels wide, as illustrated in Figure 7-1.

```
function expand(layer) {if (layer.clip.right < 500)
{layer.resizeBy(10, 10);
<!--What this line says is: if the right side of the layer's clip
region is at a position less than 500 pixels, bump up both the
height and the width of the layer by 10 pixels.-->
setTimeout("expand", 10, layer); }return false;}
<!--Wait ten milliseconds, and bump them again, as long as they
still satisfy the < 500 criterion.-->
```

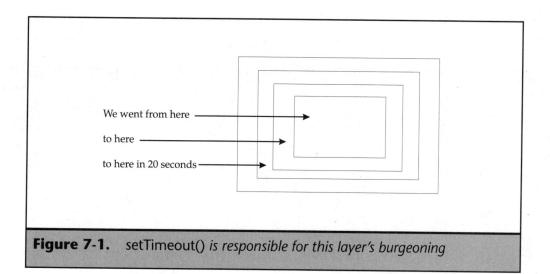

Figure 7-1. setTimeout() *is responsible for this layer's burgeoning*

Animating Images

Easy and interesting animations can result if you:

- change the source of an image
- simultaneously move the image

But don't get ahead of yourself, or more correctly, of your user's browser. As Figure 7-2 shows, if you change an image source too quickly or too often, the image may not download quickly enough to keep the animation coherent.

One way around this hurdle is to do what's called pre-fetching. Pre-fetching relies on the fact that, when a layer loads, all its content, including images, are loaded, whether or not the layer is visible. So, you can include a hidden layer in a page that contains all the images needed to animate the page. When the page loads, all source files for images will go straight into the client browser's cache; they just won't be immediately visible.

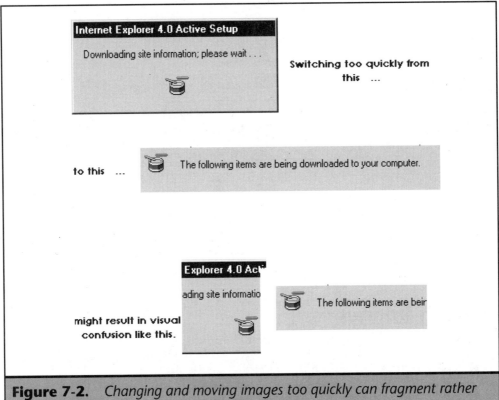

Figure 7-2.   *Changing and moving images too quickly can fragment rather than animate*

Animating for the Project Page

We've come up with a great recurring motif for the page we're designing as a contribution to the members of the National Writers' Union. The motif involves an old-fashioned quill pen and three PCs. Let's create those elements now, as illustrated in Figures 7-3, 7-4, and 7-5.

```
<HTML>
<HEAD>
<TITLE>Dear Tech Writer</TITLE>
</HEAD>
<BODY>
<LAYER ID="redpc"LEFT=120 TOP=150>
<IMG SRC=http://www.ispnet.com/~petrovsk/content/images/redpc.gif>
```

```
<!--We've just defined our first PC layer.-->
<!--Note that, like all our code samples, this one carries a
fictitious URL.-->
</LAYER>
<LAYER ID="bluepc" LEFT=300 TOP=150>
<IMG SRC=http://www.ispnet.com/~petrovsk/content/images/bluepc.gif>
<!PC layer number 2 >
</LAYER>
<LAYER ID="whitepc" LEFT=200 TOP=150>
<IMG SRC=http://www.ispnet.com/~petrovsk/content/images/whitepc.gif>
<!PC layer number 3 >
</LAYER>
<LAYER ID="quillpen" LEFT=60 TOP=170 above="whitepc">
<!our quill pen layer >
</LAYER>
```

By default, a JavaScript layer is stacked on top of the one *defined immediately before it*. So this code places our four images in this order:

- the red PC on the bottom
- the blue PC next in the stack
- the white PC next
- the quill pen above the white PC

Figure 7-3.   *Here's a look at the source image for our red PC layer*

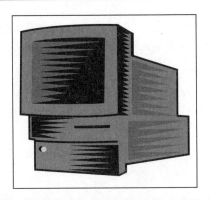

Figure 7-4. *Now we'll show you our blue PC*

Moving the Pen

To suggest something along the lines of *The pen is mightier than the PC*, we want to move the quill pen image across the screen repeatedly. Here's some JavaScript code to do that:

```
<SCRIPT>
function movePen() {
<!--First we define the function.-->
var pen = document.layers["quillpen"];
<!--Then we define the variable upon which it will rely.-->
if (pen.left < 300) {pen.moveBy(10, 0);}
<!--If the left side of the text contained by the variable, that
is, by the quillpen layer, is at a position less than 300 pixels,
move that text 10 pixels along the x axis, or 10 pixels to the
right.-->
else {pen.left = 20;}
<!--Otherwise, place the left corner of the quillpen text at 20
pixels.-->
setTimeout(movePen, 15);}
<!--Wait 15 milliseconds, and then do it all again.-->
</SCRIPT>
```

Presto! When *movePen()* executes, the quill pen:

Figure 7-5. *You can't beat a good quill pen*

- marches across the screen to the 300th pixel
- reappears at the far left side of the screen, at 20 pixels
- marches across the screen again

What's more, because of the way we stacked our original four layers, the pen will seem to march in front of all the PCs.

Starting the Pen Moving

But how do we kickstart the pen? Perhaps the easiest way to make it march might be to set up a button that you can click to invoke *movePen()*. Here's the code we'll need:

```
<FORM>
<!--To have an input button available, we must first have a form.-->
<INPUT type=button value="Move the quill pen"
OnClick="movePen();return false;">
<!--Then we define our input button to execute movePen when the
button is clicked.-->
</FORM>
```

In this code, the text to be displayed:

- is not associated with any layer
- is therefore the only text in the page
- as a result, is presented at the top of the page

 *To state explicitly where the button should appear on the screen, we would have had to put it in its own layer and define the position of the layer.*

More Advanced Animation Techniques: Stacking Pen and PCs, and Moving the Pen

At this point in the design, we're really beginning to feel our oats. When the quill pen gets to the far right side of the screen, we've decided to turn it around and make it march back, that is, to its origin at the left. What's more, on this return trip, we'd like to have the pen march behind, rather than in front of, the three PCs.

To do all this, we must:

- change the stacking order of the layers each time the pen changes the direction of its march
- use two image files, each of which represents a direction of movement for the pen
- make these image files animated GIFs
- retain the static nature of the three image files that represent the PCs

Stacking the Pen and the PCs

We'll need two functions to change the stacking order of our four layers; let's call them *changePcs()* and *restorePcs()*. Both could use any of the ways JavaScript offers to change layers' stacking order:

- explicitly setting a layer's *index* property
- using the function *moveAbove()*
- using the function *moveBelow()*

 *Don't mix and match these methods for reordering stacking. Doing so can cause you to lose track of a layer's position in the stack relative to the other layers there.*

Because we want to take our own good advice, both *changePcs()* and *restorePcs()* will use only *moveAbove()* to set stacking order for our four layers.

```
function changePcs ()
{ var redpc = document.layers["redpc"];
var bluepc = document.layers["bluepc"];
var whitepc = document.layers["whitepc"];
var pen = document.layers["quillpen"];
pen.moveAbove(redpc);
bluepc.moveAbove(pen);
whitepc.moveAbove(bluepc);}
function restorePcs ()
{var redpc = document.layers["redpc"];
var bluepc = document.layers["bluepc"];
var whitepc = document.layers["whitepc"];
var pen = document.layers["quillpen"];
bluepc.moveAbove(redpc);
whitepc.moveAbove(bluepc);
pen.moveAbove(whitepc);
```

Adding a Layer to Reverse the Pen's Direction of Movement

In a way, we're about to do some sleight of hand. To make the quill pen's image appear to reverse direction when it reaches the screen's far right side, we're going to change it to an image of a pen marching to the left. For this card trick to be effective, we must do it so quickly users don't notice it. But there's a problem with this: Such speed may be too much to allow for the new pen image file to download completely. Should this problem arise, we could end up with bits of the pen moving in both directions. To avoid this very unaesthetic and unprofessional display, we'll take advantage of JavaScript's ability to pre-fetch.

That means that we must write code that will:

■ create a hidden layer

■ place the image of the quill pen, marching right to left, in that hidden layer

Here's our code:

```
<LAYER ID="quillpenR" VISIBILITY="hide">
<IMG SRC= http://www.ispnet.com/~petrovsk/content/images/penR.gif>
</LAYER>
```

GIVING THE PEN A DIRECTION VARIABLE   Next, we need to construct a means of tracking the direction of our quill pen. We'll do this by creating two variables that we'll incorporate into the *quillpen* layer. These variables will

- allow us to initialize the pen's direction of movement to one going from left to right
- provide the means for changing that direction

```
function initializePen() {
var pen = document.layers["quillpen"]; var penR =
document.layers["quillpenR"];pen.direction = "forward";
pen.forwardimg = pen.document.images["pen"].src; pen.reverseimg =
penR.document.images["penR"].src;}
```

MAKING THE PEN MOVE   Now we can move our quill pen with panache. Here's the code we'll use:

```
function movePenP()
{var pen = document.layers["quillpen"];
if (pen.direction == "forward")
     {if (pen.left < 300) {pen.moveBy(10, 0);}
     else {restorePcs();changeDir();}}
     else {if (pen.left > 20) {pen.moveBy(-10, 0);}
else {restorePcs();changeDir();}}
setTimeout("movePenP()", 15); return;}
```

CHANGING THE DIRECTION OF THE PEN'S MOVEMENT   The function *changeDir()*, which we called twice in the last section, doesn't, of course, actually make our quill pen march from right to left. Rather, *changeDir()*:

- displays a new pen image file, in which the pen is marching in the direction we prefer
- sets the direction variable to reflect this new direction of movement

```
function changeDir ()
{var pen = document.layers["quillpen"];
if (pen.direction == "forward")
        {pen.direction = "backward";
        pen.document.images["pen"].src = pen.reverseimg;}
else
            {pen.direction = "forward";
            pen.document.images["pen"].src =
pen.forwardimg;}return;}
```

THE PEN BEGINS MOVING   Wanting to deserve fully our budding
reputations as JavaScript gurus, we're going to add one more touch to the pge
we're building for the members of the NWU. We'll position the button that
starts the quill pen moving, by placing the button in its own layer. The code
we'll need will look like this:

```
<H1>Dear Tech Writer</H1>
<LAYER ID="penButton" LEFT=30 TOP=100 >
<FORM>
<INPUT type=button value="Move the quill pen"
OnClick="initializePen(); movePenP(); return false;">
</FORM>
</LAYER>
```

Thumbnail Review

1. The function *setTimeout()* is a handy JavaScript animation tool.

2. One simple means of animating an image is to simultaneously change
   its source file, and move it.

3. You can also produce animation by creating a number of layers, and
   moving them relative to one another.

Looking Ahead

In Chapter 8, we'll consider some animation questions in more detail, when
we examine positioning elements to provide optimal animation functionality.

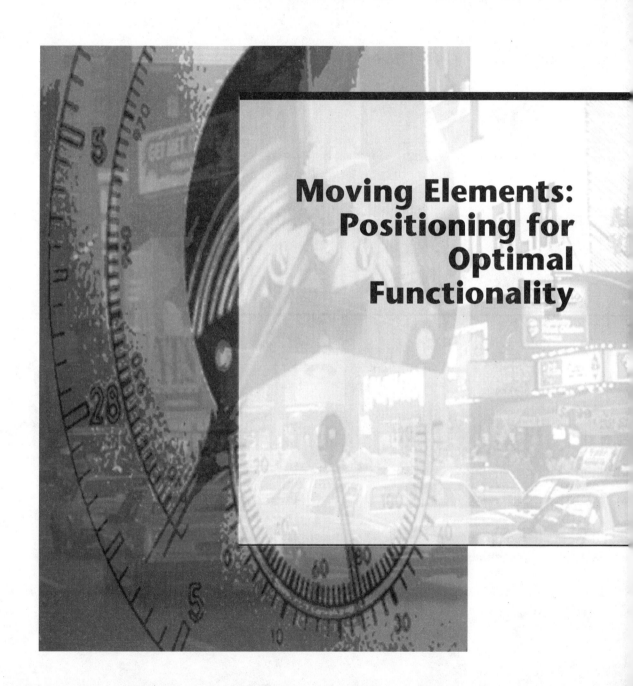

Chapter Eight

Moving Elements: Positioning for Optimal Functionality

W̶e know that effective DHTML-based pages don't just happen. So this chapter, as well as Chapters 9 and 10, revisits some of the design concepts introduced in Chapter 2, but in more detail and in the context of Dynamic HTML. We'll investigate how to design with the special requirements of an active page in mind. This chapter's special requirement? Designing, from the ground up, a page that will easily, effectively, and efficiently lend itself to dynamic positioning and manipulation of elements.

Visual Integrity

Any Web page, and especially an active one, benefits from a unique and consistent visual identity. Such a signature makes it easier for users to recognize the page's purpose, as well as any relationships it may have to other pages.

Whether or not it includes graphics, the header of your page must serve as the page's banner. It should include a prominent title at or very near the top of the page. As Figure 8-1 demonstrates, any graphics in the header should either

- be below the title
- if above it, be small enough to ensure that the title and introductory text do not scroll out of the user's immediate line of sight

Even today, most monitors present a desktop of only 640x480 pixels. Keep this in mind when selecting and positioning header graphics. 640x480 doesn't give you much to work with.

Any page elements such as subtitles, section titles, or footers, which help establish the relationship of a document to others in a series or category, should be standardized across your site, like those in Figure 8-2. In addition, footers should always contain historical information about the page, and may need to supply a redundant set of links, since, in a long document, any links at the top of the page may be lost to the user who's reading its latter sections.

You should even, as much as possible, decide upon such characteristics as the font family, size, and style to be applied to categories of elements, or the spacing to be applied to those categories, before jumping into your HTML generator-of-choice. Such advance planning is particularly important in large sites, if the pages offered by those sites are to form a coherent body of displayed content.

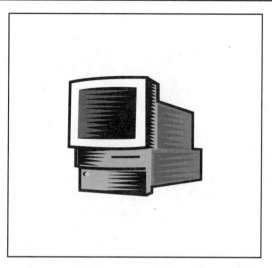

Neither the size of the image above, nor that of this
text, indicate that both are part of the same page
header area

Figure 8-1. *This is how **not** to position graphics in headers*

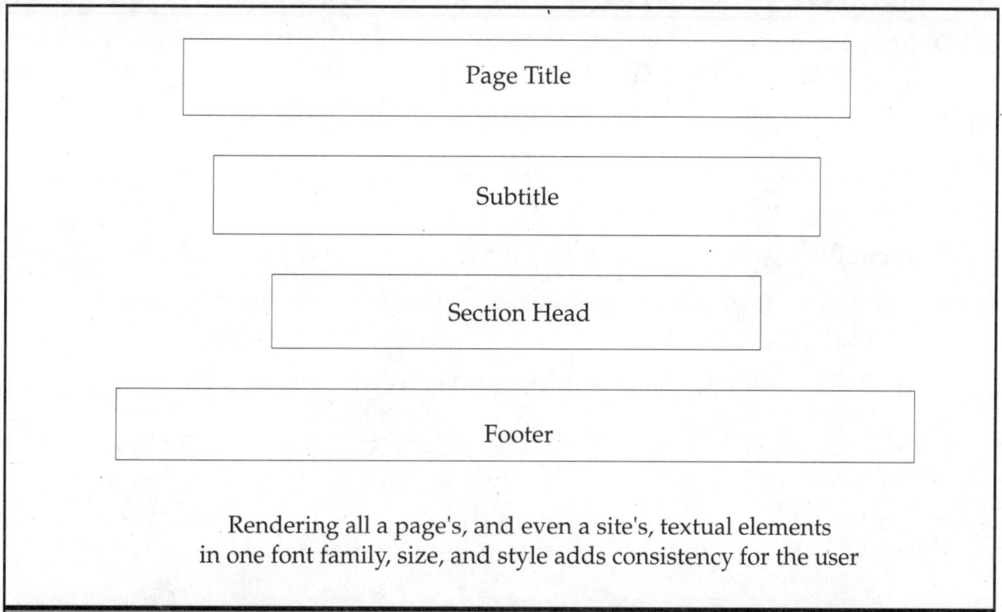

Page Title

Subtitle

Section Head

Footer

Rendering all a page's, and even a site's, textual elements
in one font family, size, and style adds consistency for the user

Figure 8-2. *Standardization in element design supplies continuity
among content*

Efficient Design

Most Web browsers, and as noted most PC screens, cannot display more than about half of a typical Web page at any one time. What's more, studies have found that only about 10 to 15 percent of Web surfers *ever* scroll *any* page they access. For example, one very common, and very annoying, flaw in the design of the Web pages of even some topflight corporations is that document width spreads well beyond the area most monitors can display.

So, one measure of efficient page design would be the number or percentage of elements you consider vital that you've placed in the top four inches of your page. This part of any page is critical; it's the only area you can be sure most users will see. Another such yardstick would be the number or percentage of critical elements you've positioned within a typical monitor's default display width. Finally, no well-designed Web page will contain graphics wider than about 535 pixels or higher than about 320 pixels, since, even if a user has a monitor to die for, the typical Netscape or Internet Explorer window still defaults to a width appropriate to smaller screens.

Suitability of Size

Given the almost infinitely linkable nature of Web publishing, content need not and in many cases should not be the primary criterion used in establishing the length of Web pages. That length should instead derive from four factors:

- bandwidth or modem speed *available through client browsers* to your target audience

- the nature of browsing (for example, online or offline)

- the nature of content (for example, whether or not it lends itself to being highly segmented)

- the relationship between content and screen size

Ideally, to avoid any visual loss of context through scrolling, Web pages, in particular home and menu pages, should consist of no more than two 640x480 screens of information. Such pages should also prominently display local navigational links at both the beginning and the end of the page.

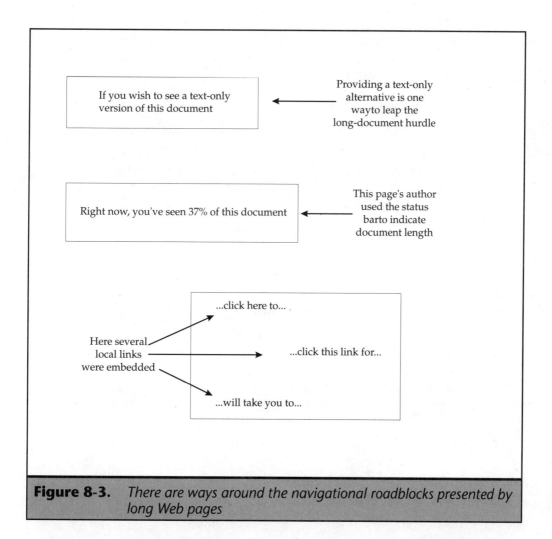

Figure 8-3.   *There are ways around the navigational roadblocks presented by long Web pages*

However, in some cases, such as those involving database searches and displays, or graphics, long Web pages may be unavoidable. If you have to deal with such documents, some solutions, as illustrated in Figure 8-3, might be to

- customize either the vertical scroll bar's slider, the screen's status bar, or both, to include some indication of total document length as a relationship to screen contents

- embed local navigational links at regular intervals throughout the document

- provide a link to a separate file that contains the full text of your document, without graphics or other niceties, but formatted to make it readily readable and printable

---

Sidebar

Long Web pages do have advantages. They're easier to organize and maintain, and often, in spite of their size, quicker to load than a series of smaller linked pages.

In a nutshell, think *short* for

- home pages
- menu pages
- navigation pages such as lists of download sites
- pages intended to be accessed solely online
- pages that contain very large graphics

But go *long* when you're dealing with

- pages that must be especially easy to maintain
- pages whose content would suffer from being highly divided

Gridded Pages

Design grids can be a valuable Web page development tool. We'll discuss them in some detail in this section.

The Advantages of Design Grids

Most well-designed paper publications rely upon design grids. Such grids can be even more useful in electronic publishing, where

- spatial relationships must be even more carefully specified
- such relationships change constantly in response to user input and system output

Obviously, no one grid will work for every Web page. But you should always create some such blueprint to establish the basic layout of a page. An effective grid should define

- the placement of major blocks of text and figures
- the placement and style of headings, links, and buttons

Even before roughing out a page grid, it's a good idea to gather representative samples of the text and figures that the grid will outline.

Why are grids so important a page design tool? They allow you to establish page layouts that are

- consistent across your site
- easy to maintain
- reinforcing of content

An effective page grid might include

- An image map with paging buttons at the top and bottom of every page. Image maps have become a standard feature on many Web sites; they offer a combination of visual appeal and the efficient use of limited display space. In addition, image maps are probably your best tool for overcoming the rather inflexible nature of pages built with standard HTML tags.
- A links column at page left, to present links and to add visual interest.
- An invisible table underlying the column structure of the page.

Coding a Gridded Page

If one picture is worth a thousand words, one code sample must then be worth at least 17,892. That being the case, we'll stop discoursing for the time being, and instead offer sample HTML code that creates a template for a gridded Web page.

```
<HTML>
<HEAD>
```

```
<TITLE>Page Grid for Dear Tech Editor</TITLE>
</HEAD>
<BODY BGCOLOR="#FFFFFF" BACKGROUND="~/whatevr.gif">
<!--Header Graphic-->
<IMG SRC="~petrovsk/WHATEVR2.GIF" WIDTH="535" HEIGHT="27"
BORDER="0">
<P> <TABLE WIDTH="535" BORDER="1" CELLSPACING="2" CELLPADDING="0">
<TR>
<FONT FACE="Palatino" SIZE="3">
<!--Links Column-->
<TD WIDTH="150" HEIGHT="300" VALIGN="top">
<IMG SRC="~petrovsk/WHATEVR3.GIF" WIDTH="170" HEIGHT="1"
VSPACE="3">
<!--You can use similar code for other areas of the grid, such as
the text column or footer graphic area.-->
<!--Next we'll code some of the page's image map.-->
<MAP NAME="~petrovsk/navgate.map">
<!--PREV> <AREA SHAPE="RECT" COORDS="488,0 509,26">
<!--NEXT> <AREA SHAPE="RECT" COORDS="514,0 534,26">
```

Working with Frames

It's a small step from gridded pages to frames. Frames allow you to display, simultaneously, multiple HTML documents on a single screen. But frames-based pages are *not themselves HTML documents*. They are what are called *meta-documents*, because they contain no body HTML tags, but rather only the parameters that define their frames, and the URLs of material that will fill those frames. Because of their makeup, frames not only offer functionality that is particularly well suited to certain types of content, but also can streamline site maintenance.

Sites whose content information changes frequently can make effective use of frames, because you can design an entire frame-based site around a single navigation file. Even in less volatile sites, frames can provide structural coherence to contextually varied content.

One interesting, and well-implemented, example of the latter use of frames can be found at the URL

```
http://www.dartmouth.edu/~eng128/reading_room/pl/book_1/index.htm
```

Here you'll find a virtual reading room for lovers of the works of John Milton. As Figure 8-4 illustrates, the leftmost frame presents internal navigation links, while the major frame displays both poetry and criticism.

The following code sample is drawn from the source HTML for the Reading Room:

```
<HTML>
<HEAD>
<TITLE> MILTON READING ROOM: PARADISE LOST, BOOK 1 </TITLE>
</HEAD>
<FRAMESET COLS="110,*" FRAMEBORDER="yes" BORDER="1"
BORDERCOLOR="999999">
<FRAME SRC="~petrovsk/NOWWHAT.HTM" MARGINHEIGHT="10"
MARGINWIDTH="10" NAME="navigation" SCROLLING="auto" RESIZE="false">

<FRAMESET ROWS="*,70" BORDER="1" >
<FRAME SRC="~petrovsk/NOWWHAT2.HTM" MARGINHEIGHT="10"
MARGINWIDTH="10" NAME="Navigation" SCROLLING="auto" RESIZE="true">
</FRAMESET>
</FRAMESET>
</HTML>
```

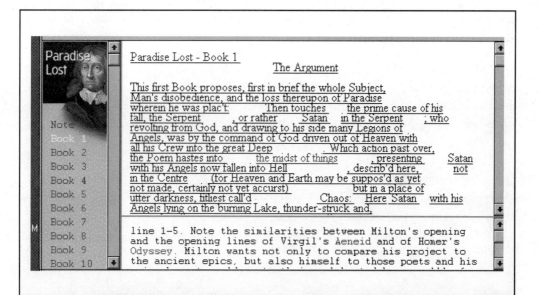

Figure 8-4. *Paradise may have been lost, but not because of this page's layout*

Frames and Interactivity

Because frames let you change portions of a page's contents without rewriting the entire screen, and because frames can interact, changing the contents of, or clicking a link in, one frame can change the contents of that frame or of another.

Sidebar

The Milton Reading Room makes good use of this characteristic of frames. If you stop by the site, note how annotations in the major frame are linked to commentary that originates at remote sites.

You can also set up frames to help users choose content. For instance, any site that offers very large downloadable files might benefit from

- a home page set up as a frameset
- an area within that page that provides a nearly empty frame, containing only a link to be followed if a user wants to download significant content into that frame

Once upon a time, page designers shied away from frames because of their prescribed borders and relative inflexibility. But today's browsers and scripting languages allow you to tailor not only many frame parameters but also frame interaction.

Such interaction rests on two attributes of framed documents, target and name, and on the concept of the window. For example, in Netscape Communicator, a window is anything that can display an HTML file. It is this definition, which Communicator shares with all HTML 3.2-compliant browsers, that allows you to implement interactivity within and between frames.

JavaScript, Frames, and Interactivity

You must build frames using both the FRAMESET and FRAME tags. Here's a simple, noninteractive JavaScript example.

```
<FRAMESET COLS="*,3*">
<FRAME SRC= ~whoever/somecontent.html>
<FRAME SRC= ~whoever/someheader.html>
</FRAMESET>
```

If your frames are to interact, you must be able to reference them explicitly. Naming frames lets you do so. Let's rewrite the preceding code sample, adding the attribute NAME.

```
<FRAMESET COLS="*,3*">
<FRAME SRC= ~whoever/somecontent.html NAME="frame1">
<FRAME SRC= ~whoever/someheader.html NAME="frame2">
</FRAMESET>
```

Now that they're named, your frames, with the addition of the attribute TARGET, can be the destination for and source of links.

Sidebar

By default, an activated link will load the linked-to file into its own window. With the TARGET attribute, you can change this.

In the context of our code samples, an anchor such as

```
<A HREF="~somepath/someinfo.html" TARGET="frame2"> More
information</A>
```

might be embedded in the file ~/somecontent.html so that a user who clicks *More information* will cause the file ~/someinfo.html to replace ~/someheader.html in frame2.

What will HTML 3.2-based browsers do if you specify as a TARGET a frame that has no NAME attribute? Communicator, for one, will open an empty new browser window.

To frame Web documents that contain multiple links, there's no need to target each such link individually. Instead, you can use a related tag-and-attribute pair, <BASE TARGET>. Placing this construct at the top of an HTML file is functionally equivalent, as Figure 8-5 shows, to using the TARGET attribute in every one of the file's anchors.

We can substitute the single tag

BASE TARGET= "FRAME1"

for all of...

TARGET=FRAME1"

TARGET=FRAME1"

TARGET=FRAME1"

TARGET=FRAME1"

TARGET=FRAME1"

wherever they might occur in a document.

Figure 8-5. *One BASE can be worth many TARGETs*

So, we might eliminate the line

```
<A HREF="~endofpath/someinfo.html" TARGET="frame2"> More
information</a>
```

from our most recent example, and instead add the line

```
<BASE TARGET="frame2">
```

at the earliest point in the file somecontent.html.

Visual Basic Scripting Edition, Frames, and Interactivity

Microsoft's online documentation suggests three means of altering frame contents with VBScript: Those are to

- change the frame's HREF with the directive LOCATION.HREF
- change the frame's HREF with the directive NAVIGATE
- write directly to the frame's document object

All these methods not only must *reference a frame other than the active one, but also will* completely *replace a frame's contents. VBScript alone can't replace only parts of those contents. To do that, you must also use an ActiveX control within the frame.*

Now let's take a look at VBScript code that manipulates frame contents through all three of the suggested methods. (Keep an eye peeled for the method *OnClick ()*.)

```
<!--the file ~/default.htm-->
<FRAMESET COLS=50%,50%>
<FRAME NAME=LEFT SRC=LEFT.HTM>
<FRAME NAME=RIGHT SRC=RIGHT.HTM>
</FRAMESET>
<!--the file ~/left.htm, which defines the leftmost frame-->
<HTML>
<BODY>
<INPUT TYPE="BUTTON" NAME="CMD1" VALUE="DOCUMENT.WRITE">
<INPUT TYPE="BUTTON" NAME="CMD2" VALUE="LOCATION.HREF">
<INPUT TYPE="BUTTON" NAME="CMD3" VALUE="NAVIGATE">
<SCRIPT LANGUAGE=VBSCRIPT>
<!--SUB CMD1_ONCLICK() WINDOW.PARENT.FRAMES(1).DOCUMENT.WRITE
"<H1>New Text</H1>" WINDOW.PARENT.RIGHT.DOCUMENT.CLOSE  END SUB
SUB CMD2_ONCLICK() WINDOW.PARENT.FRAMES(1).LOCATION.HREF="NEW.HTM"
END SUB
SUB CMD3_ONCLICK() WINDOW.PARENT.RIGHT.NAVIGATE("NEW.HTM") END SUB
-->
</SCRIPT>
</BODY>
</HTML>
<!--the file right.htm, which defines the right-hand frame-->
<HTML>
<BODY>
<!--This is a blank frame.-->
</BODY>
</HTML>
<!--the file new.htm, which defines a new blank frame-->
```

```
<HTML>
<BODY>
<!--This is a new blank frame.-->
</BODY>
</HTML>
```

Creating Frame Content Dynamically with JScript

When the page we've coded below loads, and the client browser finds the page's SCRIPT tags, the browser will execute the code those tags contain, as the page is being parsed. This JScript code:

- writes content to the page by means of a browser-supplied object
- uses the global document object's Write method
- passes what's written to a string

```
<SCRIPT LANGUAGE="JavaScript">
<!--    These next lines of code execute when the script tag is
parsed.-->
var d = new Date()
var h = d.getHours()
if (h < 12)
document.write("Good morning!")
else
if (h < 17)
document.write("Good afternoon!")
else
document.write("Good evening!")
document.write("<br><br>Welcome to the world of JScript.  ")
document.write("<br>Just in case you were wondering, it's " + d +
".")//-->
</SCRIPT>
```

Thumbnail Review

1. Visual integrity, suitable size, and contextual coherence are all important Web page design goals.

2. Most categories of Web content are better served by short pages.

3. Long Web pages should contain numerous navigational links and referents.

4. Grids help you effectively lay out the placement and style of important page components like major text, graphics, headings, links, and buttons.

5. Frames can be a precursor to DHTML-based pages.

6. A number of client-side scripting languages, including JScript, JavaScript, and VBScript allow you to dynamically manipulate the contents of frames.

Looking Ahead

Chapter 9 might be subtitled "Ground-Up Design, Part Two: Getting Set to Scan." In the next chapter, we'll review design principles that help determine element positions at runtime. Then Chapter 9 will present sample code that does just that.

Chapter Nine

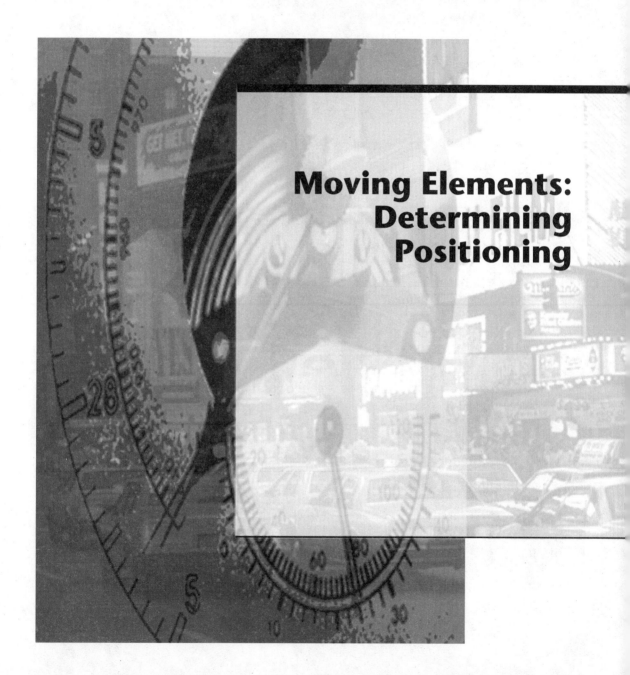

**Moving Elements:
Determining
Positioning**

A t this point in our discussion of Dynamic HTML, we've already established a handful of positioning-related paradigms:

- explicitly coded x/y positioning
- positioning and multiple frames
- positioning through table-based gridded pages
- positioning within image maps

In this chapter, we'll expand upon these technique types. Specifically, we'll put them under a microscope to examine their usefulness in two areas:

- establishing a page's visual focal point
- functioning as a referent for animation

Explicitly Coded X/Y Positioning

We'll begin this section with an overview, as shown in Table 9-1, of selected attributes, in whatever syntax, that you can use to explicitly position elements. Then we'll examine each of these attributes in more detail, discussing their applicability to dynamic positioning.

Background Position

In CSS1 style sheets, *background-position* sets the *initial* position of a background image within a block-level or replaced element. You can assign *background position* in four ways:

- through absolute lengths
- through keywords, either horizontal- or vertical-related
- through percentages

As Figures 9-1 and 9-2 show, you get somewhat different results when you define *background position* in terms of percentages than you do when you set it up in terms of pixel lengths.

Note, though, that working with pixels lengths can sometimes produce unexpected results, as Figure 9-2 illustrates.

The attribute	has the general syntax	the possible values	the initial value	can be applied to	and follows
Background Position	background-position: <value>	percentage length{1,2} bottom center left right top	0%,0%	Block-level and replaced elements	CSS1
Layer Position	position <value/ parameter>	absolute top left pagex pagey relative	relative	inline elements	Java-Script
Vertical Alignment	Valign <value>	baseline sub super top text-top left middle right bottom text-bottom percentage	baseline	inline elements	Java-Script
	vertical-align: <value>	baseline sub super top text-top left middle right bottom text-bottom percentage	baseline	inline elements	CSS1

Table 9-1. *Explicitly Positioning Elements*

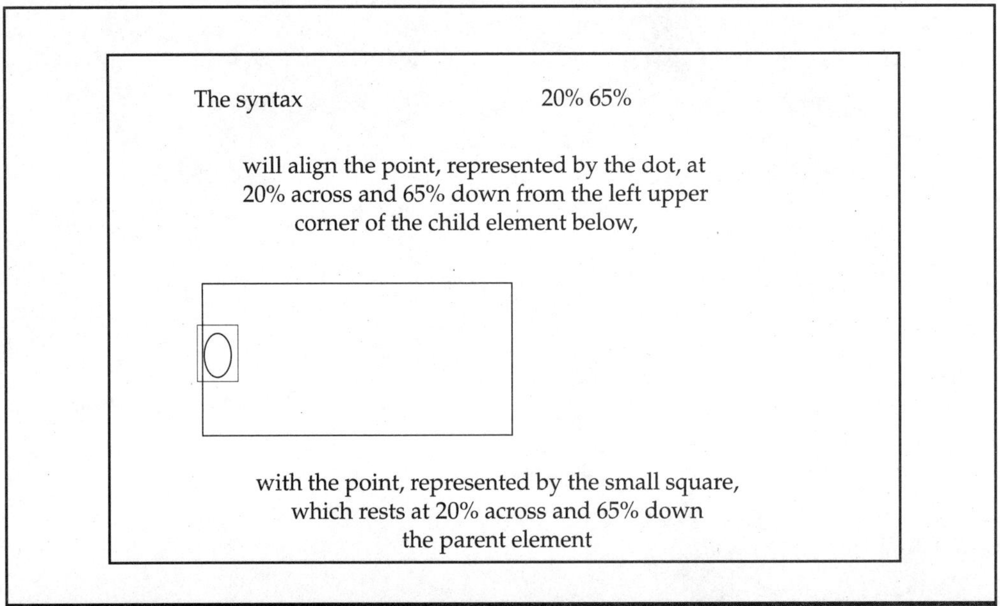

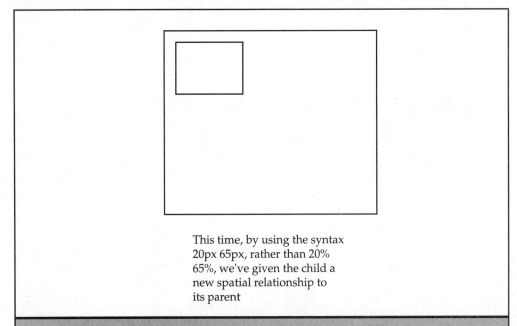

The syntax   20% 65%

will align the point, represented by the dot, at
20% across and 65% down from the left upper
corner of the child element below,

with the point, represented by the small square,
which rests at 20% across and 65% down
the parent element

Figure 9-1. *A background image positioned with percentages might look like this in relation to its parent element*

This time, by using the syntax
20px 65px, rather than 20%
65%, we've given the child a
new spatial relationship to
its parent

Figure 9-2. *Using pixel lengths to position a background might result in this look*

But in either of these two cases, you must include two parameters, the first indicating horizontal position, and the second, vertical position. In either case, if you supply only a horizontal value, vertical position will be set at 50%. In addition, CSS1 syntax lets you combine lengths and percentages, and even use negative positions.

Pop Quiz Where against an element would the values 20% 65% and 5px 10px place a background image?

Table 9-2 summarizes how *background-position*'s keywords and possible keyword combinations are interpreted.

The keyword or keyword combination	will place the origin of the image at this point within the element
top left	0%, 0%
top	50%, 0%
right top	100%, 0%
left	0%, 50%
center	50%, 50%
right	100%, 50%
bottom left	0%, 100%
bottom	50%, 100%
bottom right	100%, 100%

Table 9-2. *Background Positioning in Detail*

Layer Position

When using JavaScript to define layers, you can precisely position those layers by using the keywords *absolute* and *relative* in combination with row/column pixel values and the parameters

- left—to specify horizontal position
- pagex—to specify horizontal position relative to the document window
- pagey—to specify vertical position relative to the document window
- top—to specify vertical position

So, for example, the line

```
<LAYER ID = "LAYER1" POSITION ABSOLUTE PAGEX 200 PAGEY 270>
```

would place the layer in question at an absolute 200/270 x/y position within the document window, while the line:

```
<LAYER ID = "LAYER1" POSITION RELATIVE LEFT 200 TOP 270>
```

would place the layer in question at an x/y position in relation to its parent layer. Figure 9-3 shows you the result of positioning relative to the entire display.

Now, take a look at Figure 9-4 to see what positioning relative to a parent might produce.

Vertical Alignment

If you need to be sure of the position of an inline element relative to its parent, you can use the functionally equivalent CSS1 *vertical-align* or JavaScript *VALIGN* attributes.

Sidebar

Recall that an inline element is one that is not bounded by line breaks, such as IMG. In this context, and given our discussion of the use of "invisible" tables to grid out a page, you can consider *vertical-align* and *VALIGN* in terms of their effect on a display as a whole.

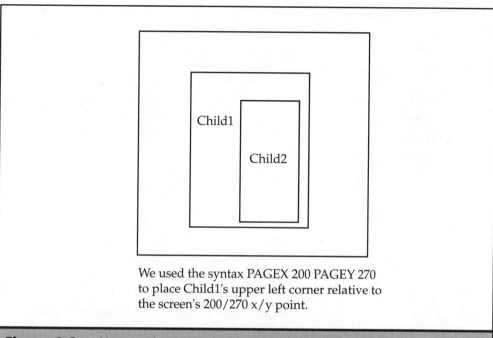

We used the syntax PAGEX 200 PAGEY 270
to place Child1's upper left corner relative to
the screen's 200/270 x/y point.

Figure 9-3. *Here, we've positioned relative to the screen as a whole*

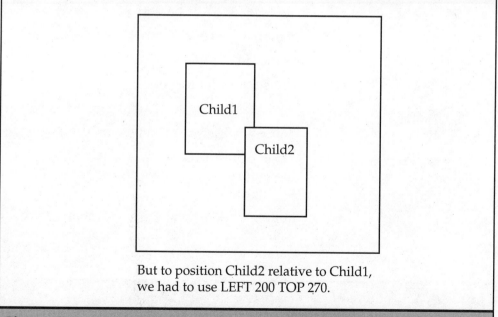

But to position Child2 relative to Child1,
we had to use LEFT 200 TOP 270.

Figure 9-4. *Here, the second layer is positioned relative to the first*

Whichever you use, you may express the required value as:

- a keyword
- a percentage, even a negative one

In either case, the element that you're aligning will be positioned according to the relationship between its line height attribute and the baseline of its parent element. When you use keywords to specify vertical alignment, they will be interpreted as shown in Table 9-3.

The keyword or keyword combination	will place the element in this relationship to its parent
baseline	baselines of element and parent aligned
left	left margins of element and parent aligned
middle	vertical midpoint of element aligned with a position equal to [baseline plus half the x-height (the height of the letter x) of the parent]
right	right margins of element and parent aligned
sub	as a subscript to parent
super	as a superscript to parent
text-top	tops of element's and parent's font aligned
text-bottom	bottoms of element's and parent's font aligned
top	top of element aligned with tallest element on the same line, regardless of parent/child relationships
bottom	bottom of element aligned with shortest element on the same line, regardless of parent/child relationships

Table 9-3. *Vertical Alignment in Detail*

Given its makeup, it should come as no surprise that the *vertical alignment* attribute is most frequently used to:

■ align images, as in

```
IMG.{vertical-align: middle }
```

■ align mathematical and scientific notation, as in

```
exponent { vertical-align: super }
```

Figures 9-5 and 9-6 show you what using *vertical-align* in such situations might produce. You should be able to see that in Figure 9-5, alignment has taken place according to the midpoints of the vertical planes of the two entities involved.

In Figure 9-6, on the other hand, we see only one item, albeit a relatively unusual one.

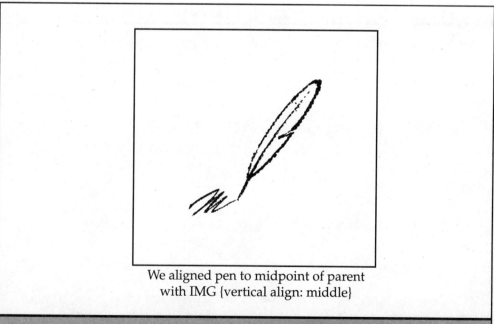

We aligned pen to midpoint of parent
with IMG {vertical align: middle}

Figure 9-5. *Here, the image's vertical midpoint aligns with the approximate vertical midpoint of its accompanying text*

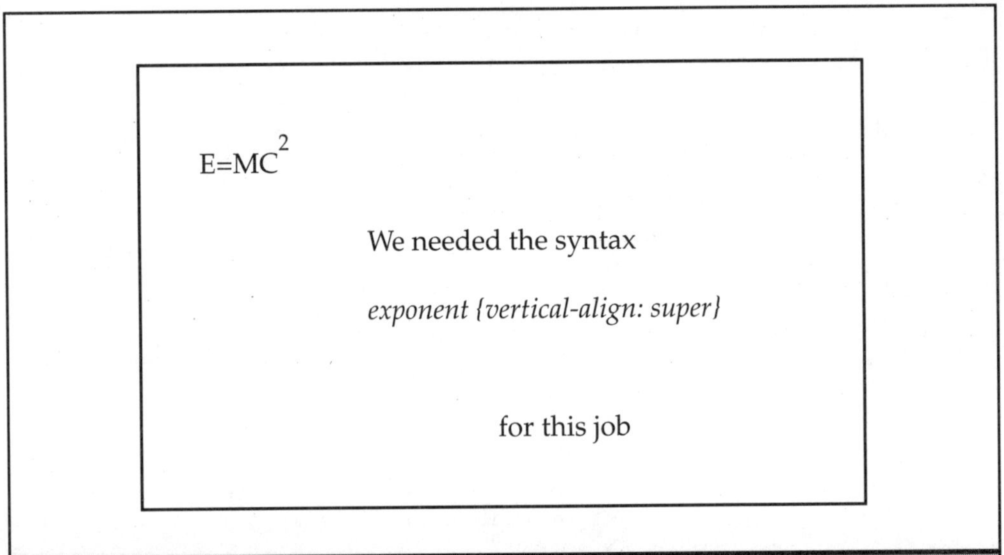

$$E=MC^2$$

We needed the syntax

exponent {vertical-align: super}

for this job

Figure 9-6.   *Anyone who's ever read an engineering manual would feel right at home with this use of **vertical-align***

Explicit Positioning and DHTML

It stands to reason that explicitly-positioned elements are ideally suited to serving as the keystone around which you position active elements. In the remainder of this section, we'll investigate explicit positioning in just this role.

Explicit Positioning as a Visual Focal Point

Image maps offer one opportunity to explicitly position elements as visual anchors. For instance, you'll recall that in Chapter 8, we coded part of an image map as follows:

```
<MAP NAME="..~/navigate.map">
<! PREV> <AREA SHAPE="RECT" COORDS="488,0 509,26">
<! NEXT> <AREA SHAPE="RECT" COORDS="514,0 534,26">
```

Now suppose that we want to add a background image to our map to enhance the map's overall visual coherence. Here's code that would do that. (Figures 9-7 and 9-8 illustrate one possible result in a before-and-after fashion.)

```
<! First we'll fully define the map. >
<P> <IMG SRC="../petrovsk/dhtml/images/snazzy.gif"
USEMAP="../petrovsk/dhtml/images/snazzymap.html">
<! Now we'll define the map's active area. >
<MAP NAME="../navgate.map">
<! PREV> <AREA SHAPE="RECT" COORDS="488,0 509,26">
<! NEXT> <AREA SHAPE="RECT" COORDS="514,0 534,26">
</MAP>
<! Finally, we'll add a background image outside the map's active
area, but within the overall canvas formed by snazzy.gif. >
<IMG SRC="../petrovsk/dhtml/images/snazzybgd.gif" ALIGN="LEFT"
<! Note that we've included an HTML 3.0 attribute, LEFT, in our
JavaScript code, using it to much the same purpose as the CSS1
attribute background-position. >
</P>
```

Figure 9-7 shows what this map might look like without a visual focus.

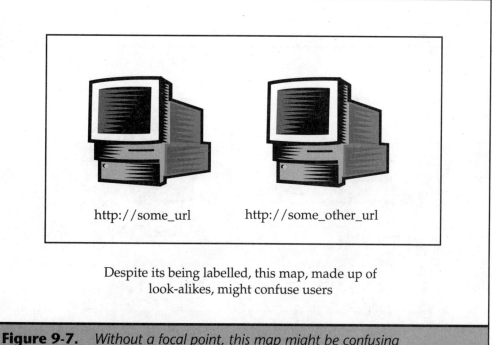

Figure 9-7. *Without a focal point, this map might be confusing*

In Figure 9-8, on the other hand, we see our map through a more directed eye.

Explicit Positioning as a Referent for Animation

You may recall that very early in Chapter 7, we momentarily waxed nostalgic, referring to *"the ... quirk of physics that many of us discovered as children when we drew a series of images, each on its own blank card, riffled the deck, and watched the images flow into a ... sequence."* This simple principle is the basis for much Web animation; let's inspect it a little more.

Most Web animations rely on a sequence of image-format files such as GIFs. The individual GIF files that make up the sequence each contain the same overall image. In each file the image is slightly altered, however, creating a Web analog to a film animation cell or one of the cards in our childhood deck. To suggest movement, these images are displayed in sequence at specific points on the screen.

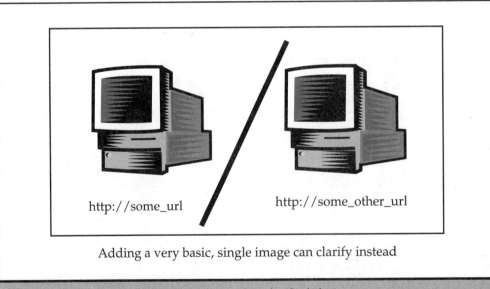

http://some_url

http://some_other_url

Adding a very basic, single image can clarify instead

Figure 9-8. *By adding an image, we've clarified the map*

What if, for instance, you want to display an animated effect consisting of a mouse scurrying away from a cat? You might use such a series of GIF files, and incorporate them into your page with code like this:

```
<P>
<! Our first GIF will display a cat who's, very roughly, .9 inches
wide and 1.1 inches tall, at the left of the screen.  This image
will be the anchor, so to speak, for our animation effect. >
<IMG SRC="felix.gif" ALIGN="LEFT" WIDTH=59 HEIGHT=67>
<! Our next series of images will display a mouse moving steadily
further away from his arch enemy Felix.  Note that each cell in this
animation sequence shows a slightly different image of Misha. >
<IMG SRC="misha1.gif" ALIGN="BASELINE" WIDTH=39 HEIGHT=47>
<IMG SRC="misha2.gif" ALIGN="MIDDLE" WIDTH=39 HEIGHT=47>
<IMG SRC="misha3.gif" ALIGN="RIGHT" WIDTH=39 HEIGHT=47>
```

Multiple Frames and DHTML

Once again, we'll make use of code originally presented in Chapter 8. But this time, we'll modify the VBScript code there.

Multiple Frames as a Visual Anchor

Suppose that, in coding the Reading Room page, the folks at Dartmouth did some things differently. Imagine, first of all, that they chose VBScript rather than JavaScript as their page's coding language. Imagine further that they decided to place, in the leftmost, navigation-oriented frame they'd designed, a new image of John Milton, which they felt would better catch the user's eye. Here is VBScript code that would do the job.

```
<! the file ../default.htm>
<FRAMESET COLS=50%,50%>
<FRAME NAME=LEFT SRC=LEFT.HTM>
<FRAME NAME=RIGHT_TOP SRC=RIGHT_TOP.HTM>
<FRAME NAME=RIGHT_BOTM SRC=RIGHT_BOTM.HTM>
</FRAMESET>
<!--the file ../left.htm, which defines the left, navigation frame-->
<HTML>
<BODY>
<P> <IMG SRC=" ../milton.gif" ALIGN="RIGHT"> </P>
```

Multiple Frames as a Referent for Animation

Having such success with this code fragment might encourage the designers at Dartmouth to add animation to their page. Their first step in doing so could be to add another frame. Their code might then look like this:

```
<!--the file ../default.htm-->
<FRAMESET COLS=50%,50%>
<FRAME NAME=LEFT SRC=LEFT.HTM>
<FRAME NAME=LEFT_BOTM SRC=LEFT_BOTM.HTM>
<FRAME NAME=RIGHT_TOP SRC=RIGHT_TOP.HTM>
<FRAME NAME=RIGHT_BOTM SRC=RIGHT_BOTM.HTM>
</FRAMESET>
<!--the file ~..left.htm, which defines the left, navigation frame-->
<HTML>
<BODY>
<P> <IMG SRC=" ../milton.gif" ALIGN="RIGHT"> </P>
<!--the file ~/left_botm.htm, which defines the animation frame-->
<HTML>
<BODY>
</HTML>
```

Multiple Frames and Dynamically Implementing Animation

As the final step in their incorporating the dynamic display of not only text but also images and animation into their Reading Room, Dartmouth's Web page designers might come up with VBScript-based code such as the following.

```
<! the file ~..default.htm>
<FRAMESET COLS=50%,50%>
<FRAME NAME=LEFT SRC=LEFT.HTM>
<FRAME NAME=LEFT_BOTM SRC=LEFT_BOTM.HTM>
<FRAME NAME=RIGHT_TOP SRC=RIGHT_TOP.HTM>
<FRAME NAME=RIGHT_BOTM SRC=RIGHT_BOTM.HTM>
</FRAMESET>
<!--the file ~..left.htm, which defines the left, navigation frame-->
<HTML>
<BODY>
<P> <IMG SRC=" ../milton.gif" ALIGN="RIGHT"> </P>
<FORM>
```

```
<INPUT TYPE="BUTTON" NAME="BOOK1" VALUE="NAVIGATE">
<INPUT TYPE="BUTTON" NAME="BOOK2" VALUE="NAVIGATE">
<INPUT TYPE="BUTTON" NAME="BOOK3" VALUE="NAVIGATE">
<INPUT TYPE="BUTTON" NAME="BOOK4" VALUE="NAVIGATE">
</FORM>
<SCRIPT LANGUAGE=VBSCRIPT>
<!--SUB BOOK1_ONCLICK()
WINDOW.PARENT.LEFT_BOTM.NAVIGATE("ANIMATION1.HTM") END SUB -->
<!--SUB BOOK1_ONCLICK()
WINDOW.PARENT.RIGHT_TOP.NAVIGATE("BOOK1.HTM") END SUB -->
<!--SUB BOOK1_ONCLICK()
WINDOW.PARENT.RIGHT_BOTM.NAVIGATE("NOTES1.HTM") END SUB -->
<!--SUB BOOK2_ONCLICK()
WINDOW.PARENT.LEFT_BOTM.NAVIGATE("ANIMATION2.HTM") END SUB -->
<!--SUB BOOK2_ONCLICK()
WINDOW.PARENT.RIGHT_TOP.NAVIGATE("BOOK2.HTM") END SUB -->
<!--SUB BOOK2_ONCLICK()
WINDOW.PARENT.RIGHT_BOTM.NAVIGATE("NOTES2.HTM") END SUB -->
<!--SUB BOOK3_ONCLICK()
WINDOW.PARENT.LEFT_BOTM.NAVIGATE("ANIMATION3.HTM") END SUB -->
<!--SUB BOOK3_ONCLICK()
WINDOW.PARENT.RIGHT_TOP.NAVIGATE("BOOK3.HTM") END SUB -->
<!--SUB BOOK3_ONCLICK()
WINDOW.PARENT.RIGHT_BOTM.NAVIGATE("NOTES3.HTM") END SUB -->
<!--SUB BOOK4_ONCLICK()
WINDOW.PARENT.LEFT_BOTM.NAVIGATE("ANIMATION4.HTM") END SUB -->
<!--SUB BOOK4_ONCLICK()
WINDOW.PARENT.RIGHT_TOP.NAVIGATE("BOOK4.HTM") END SUB -->
<!--SUB BOOK4_ONCLICK()
WINDOW.PARENT.RIGHT_BOTM.NAVIGATE("NOTES4.HTM") END SUB -->
</SCRIPT>
</BODY>
</HTML>
```

Answer to Pop Quiz

When using percentages or lengths to specify values for the CSS1 property *background-position*, you have to specify the horizontal position first, followed by the vertical. So, a value such as *20% 65%* says, in effect:

place the point 20% across and 65% down the background image at the point 20% across and 65% down the element.

A value such as *5px 10px* specifies

put the upper-left corner of the image 5 pixels to the right of and 10 pixels below the upper-left corner of the element

Thumbnail Review

1. Explicitly positioning focal or referent elements lets you dynamically position others in relation to them.
2. Explicitly positioned elements can serve as a visual focal point or as a referent for animation, among other uses.
3. Image maps can be enhanced with the addition of a background image as a focal point.
4. You can easily create an animation with a series of images positioned relative to a stable referent.
5. Frames can facilitate the dynamic positioning of both text and graphics.

Looking Ahead

We've done a lot in this chapter, but there's more to come. In Chapter 10, we'll delve deeper into the concepts and techniques for dynamically positioning elements that we introduced here.

Chapter Ten

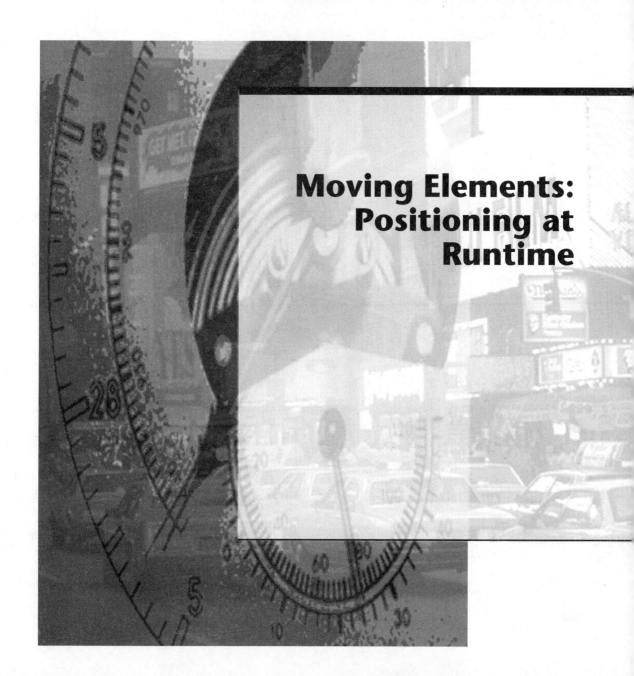

Moving Elements:
Positioning at
Runtime

W e've arrived at what's just about the midpoint of this book. So it seems appropriate that we mark our progress by synthesizing everything we've learned about DHTML. This chapter presents the final design of the page we're building as a gift to the members of the NWU web page. It also discusses the programming logic (as opposed to HTML coding) requirements of the page, and it presents the basic code, both HTML and JScript, for the page.

Completing the Design of the Page

In Chapter 2, we roughed out the general design of our page. As a jumping-off point for our current discussion, let's recap that first draft.

The goal of the page is to provide information for people who want to break into technical writing and editing (about computer-related topics in particular), but who lack a technical background. Therefore, the page must not only present content about technical writing and editing, but also about the technical topics themselves.

- The page will contain only two visual elements; one will illustrate text-based information, and the other will convey the friendly feel we want the page to have.

  - The page will have three groups of static elements:

  - the page's banner—its content, font characteristics, and placement

  - the first paragraph of body text, which explains the page's purpose

  - the placement and composition of links, navigation buttons, and feedback/email prompts

- The page will have three elements that will exhibit at least some degree of dynamic behavior:

  - the links to other sources of information on PCs

  - the image in the page's banner, which shows a quill pen superimposed upon a PC

  - the WAV file linked to the tools by means of which users can navigate within and outside of the page

That's the page's skeleton. Now let's put some flesh on its bones.

The Page's Logical Structure

The page's inherent logic stems from the goal of the page, as outlined in the previous section. This goal requires that we segregate the page's navigational, text, and visual components. Furthermore, the anticipated audience dictates that the page:

- allow users to search one or more databases
- allow users to send email inquiries
- provide links to related sites, organized according to topic areas

The Page's Physical Structure

As always, form will follow function. In this section, we'll describe and illustrate that the page's physical structure is based on the logical one.

Our project's page uses frames to set off navigation, text, and illustrations of text, and to separate static from dynamic areas. Figure 10-1 shows the page's layout at this stage.

Let's summarize the effects of this layout.

1. By reserving two frames for the results of user database searches or email inquiries, one for text and the other for related graphics, we have

   - allowed ourselves, as designers and coders, to associate these frames with a variety of content sources
   - maintained the users' orientation within the page as a whole, even while they're viewing the results of their searches or inquiries

2. By making all frames non-resizeable, we have

   - made it easier to maintain the page
   - made it easier for users to orient themselves within the page

3. By using both scrollable and non-scrollable frames, and by making only selected frames scrollable, we have

   - made it easier to maintain the page
   - optimized our use of the page's space
   - made it easier for users to orient themselves not only within the page as a whole, but also within and between functional areas of the page
   - shortened users' learning curves

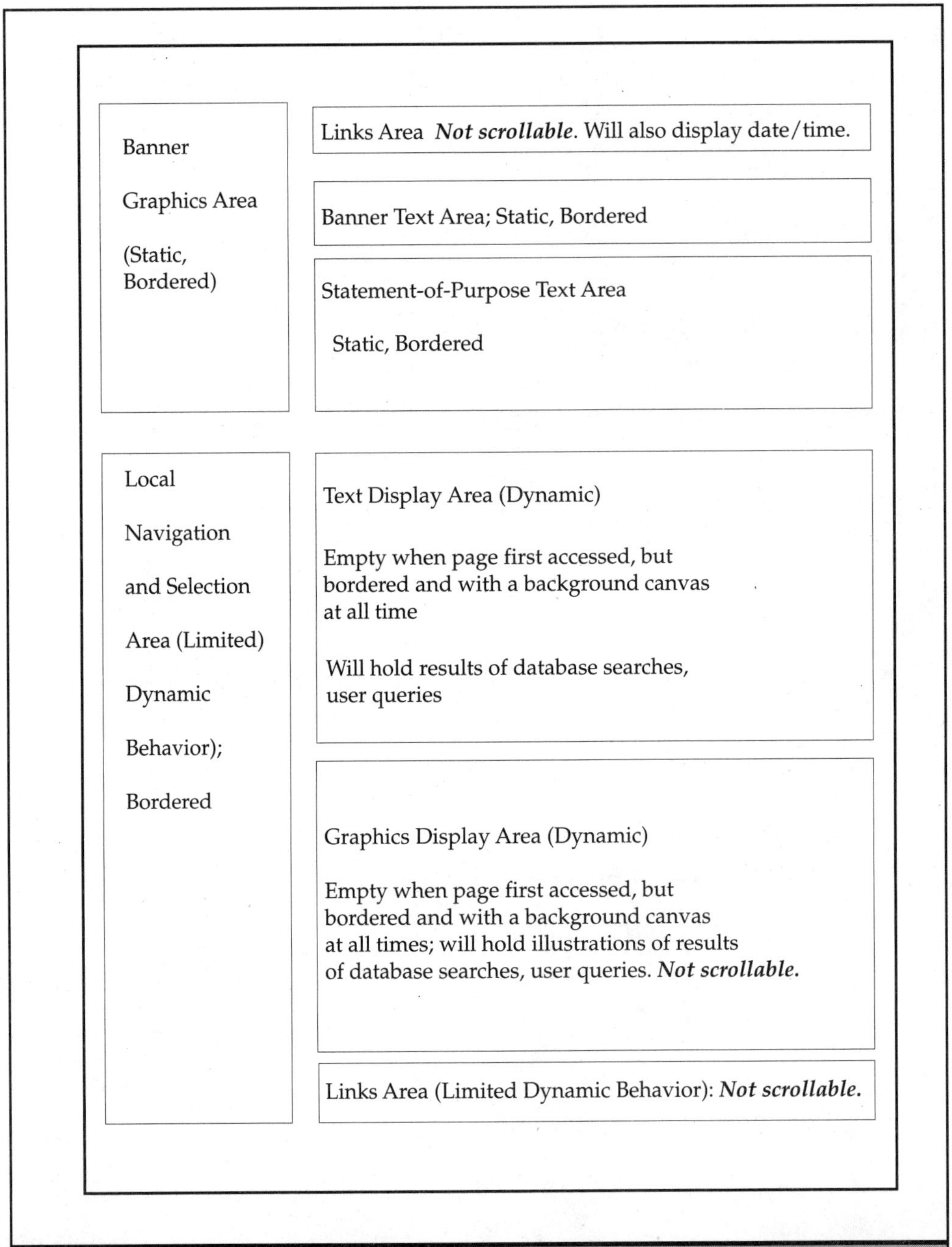

Banner
Graphics Area
(Static,
Bordered)

Links Area *Not scrollable*. Will also display date/time.

Banner Text Area; Static, Bordered

Statement-of-Purpose Text Area

   Static, Bordered

Local
Navigation
and Selection
Area (Limited)
Dynamic
Behavior);
Bordered

Text Display Area (Dynamic)

Empty when page first accessed, but
bordered and with a background canvas
at all time

Will hold results of database searches,
user queries

Graphics Display Area (Dynamic)

Empty when page first accessed, but
bordered and with a background canvas
at all times; will hold illustrations of results
of database searches, user queries. *Not scrollable.*

Links Area (Limited Dynamic Behavior): *Not scrollable.*

Figure 10-1. *All these frames help support the page's logical structure. For this reason, and because of the nature of the material housed in each one, none of these frames will be resizeable, and most areas will not be scrollable.*

A design as ambitious as this will require every DHTML trick you've learned and more. Implementing this design will also mean using rather sophisticated programming logic. You'll investigate this logic, in the context of JScript, in the next section.

(Those of you whose browsers don't handle frames, and those of you who simply consider them cumbersome—as indeed they can be if inefficiently designed and coded—can take heart. The final form of the our project, which we'll present in Chapter 18, makes allowance for no-frames environments.)

Controlling the Display of the Page

The project page, which we designed with activity and interactivity in mind, must be displayed in different ways at different times; in other words, its presentation is subject to a number of conditions. Therefore, our next step in implementing the page should be to review the mechanisms JScript offers for conditional execution.

Controlling the Flow of Execution in JScript

To begin with, let's review JScript's execution-control capabilities. All conditional tests in JScript are Boolean; that is, they result in only one of two possible values: true or false. You can apply such tests to data of a number of types, including numeric and string, and you can use several different programming logic structures to run your tests:

- conditional statements such as *if...* and *if... else...*
- implicit conditional statements that offer only a single true/false choice
- a number of types of reiterative structures, that is, loops
- two bailout mechanisms, *break* and *continue*

Conditional Statements

In JScript, as in every programming language we've ever run across, *if* and *if... else...* statements execute one or multiple lines of code depending upon whether the condition that the statement tests for is met.

Here are some examples of the various flavors of *if* that JScript offers.

Example 1:

```
if (annoyed) response = ("We're running a little slowly today;
please be patient.<br>");
/* This line of code tests for the truth or lack thereof of the
condition represented by the variable annoyed. If the test passes,
that is, if the value stored in the variable equals true, the
action specified in the remainder of the line will be taken. If
annoyed turns out to be false, nothing will be done. Note also
that, unlike some programming languages, JScript requires no
corresponding keyword then with its if statements. */
```

Example 2:

```
if (ears.shape == "pointy " && brows.angle == "upswept")
{ response = ("You must be a Vulcan! <br> ");}
/* In this form of JScript if, we're testing for a combination of
conditions. What's more, by using the && operator, we're telling
the system that the action specified in the rest of the line will
be taken only if both conditions are met. */
```

Example 3:

```
if ((nose.texture == "wrinkled") || (forehead.texture ==
"wrinkled"))  {
response = ("You must be either a Bajoran or a Klingon. <br>");}
else
response = ("What planet are you from? <br>");
/* In this most complex example, we're once again testing for a
combination of conditions. However, because we used the ||
operator, we're telling the system that the action specified in
the response = ... part of the line will be taken if either one or
the other of the test conditions is met. What's more, in the
portion of this block of code governed by the keyword else, we're
telling the system what to do if neither of the tests in the
earlier line passes. */
```

Implicit Conditional Statements

JScript also offers an implicit *if*, which uses a question mark (?) after the condition to be tested, rather than the keyword *if* before it. The implicit *if* specifies only two actions, separated by a colon (:). The first action will be carried out if the test passes, and the second will be executed if it fails. Here is an example:

```
response += nextquery (<= 1) ? " Tastes great!" : " Less filling!";
/* This implicit if, when translated, says "response equals
response plus nextquery.  If the result of this operation is less
than or equal to 1, display the phrase specified before the colon
(:). Otherwise, present the phrase after it." */
```

JScript, once again like every programming language, won't even bother with the second or subsequent parts of compound tests connected by \ \ if the first test condition has passed. Keep this in mind when you're structuring compound conditional statements.

Pop Quiz Given how JScript handles compound tests structured as ORs, how do you think it will execute such tests if they're built as ANDs?

Looping

JScript, like C, makes three types of loops available:

- *for* loops
- *for... in* loops
- *while* loops

Let's investigate these reiterative structures more closely.

for LOOPS *for* loops in any language are the control structure of choice in situations that require a predetermined number of execution cycles. Or, to give an example in English, let's suppose you want to write a small piece of code to handle this problem: You're an avid gardener (in addition to being a crackerjack programmer) and you need to track the productivity of the three varieties of cucumbers you've planted this season.. You plan to inventory plant production once each week for the eight full weeks in July and August. The following is an excerpt from your code.

```
var weeks = 8;
// We've created a variable to store the length of our survey.
var burpless97 = new Array(weeks);
var bushking97 = new Array(weeks);
var lemon97 = new Array(weeks);
/* In this section, we've set up three arrays, to track each of
our cucumber varieties. We've dimensioned these arrays to be just
big enough to hold the results of our weeks' survey. */
for(var iteration = 1; iteration = weeks; iteration++  {
// Everything to be done within our for loop must be encased in
curly braces.
...    burpless97[iteration];
...    bushking97[iteration];
...    lemon97[iteration]; }
/* For every value of iteration from one through eight inclusive,
we'll look at the corresponding ordinal member of each of the
three arrays. */
```

Tip ▶ *Be careful with for loops; they're deceptively simple looking. For instance, none of the loops below will behave very nicely.*

```
for(var iteration = 2; iteration = weeks; iteration++)    ...
/* A simple typographical error will cause this loop to execute
one too few times, and to ignore the first element of each array.
*/
for(var iteration = 1; iteration > weeks; iteration++)    ...
/* This simple typographical error causes  an infinite loop and
the crash of the script, since the value of iteration will
eventually exceed the array's index range. */
for(var iteration = 1; iteration <= weeks; itereation--)    ...
/* This second typo, a misspelling, causes  an infinite loop and
the crash of the script in a different way--the value of  iteration
will always be less than the value of weeks, since iteration and
itereation are not the same variable. */
```

for... in LOOPS JScript uses another common structure, the *for... in* loop, to examine all the properties of an object by scrutinizing all the elements of the array corresponding to that object. The loop control variable in a *for... in* loop need not, indeed cannot, be incremented or decremented, since it is not a number, but a string that acts as a generic representation of the components of the object. Here's an example:

```
for (1 in gardenGrid)
{ // Your code }
```

Pop Quiz 2 Why have we used two different styles for commenting our code samples?

while LOOPS *while* loops don't rely on a predetermined number of iterations. Instead, they depend for entry and exit on a condition reflected in the contents of a variable. For instance, you may want to carry out the same set of actions as long as a visitor to your site requests a per-page display of hits that is between 10 and 20 inclusive. So you write code like this:

```
var hitsrequest = 10;
while (hitsrequest >= 10 && hitsrequest <= 20)  {
// do what you need to do
// then update the loop control variable by taking in the next
per-page hits request  }
```

Pop Quiz 3 As was the case with *for* loops, you must set up the control conditions for *while* loops very carefully. Neither of the following would be of any use. Can you say why?

```
var hitsrequest = 9;
while (hitsrequest >= 10 && hitsrequest <= 20)

var hitsrequest = 10;
while (hitsrequest >= 10 )
```

break AND continue   In JScript, you can use the *break* statement to stop execution of a loop or other block of code under specified conditions. The JScript *continue* statement is mirror-image to *break*. You don't use it to exit a code block prematurely, but to jump immediately to the beginning of the next iteration of the block, updating the loop control variable appropriately if needed.

Let's use *break* and *continue* to interrupt the execution of a *for* loop in two ways:

```
for (count = 1; count <= 10; count++) {
// a bunch of code here
if (noresponse) break; }
/* If there's no response to, for example, an earlier prompt to
the user, don't bother with the rest of the loop. */

for (count = 1; count <= 10; count++) {
// a bunch of code here
if (count = 7) continue; }
/* If you want to do whatever for every element of an array except
the seventh, this code is what you need. */
```

Coding the Project Page in JScript

While we won't end up with a completely coded and scripted page in this chapter (this is only Chapter 10, after all), we will define the page's frames and use some of the JScript execution-flow mechanisms we learned earlier to expedite the page's loading.

Defining the Page's Frames

No beating around the bush; here's the code.

```
<!--the file ~/draft.htm>-->
<HTML>
<HEAD>
<FRAMESET COLS = 23%, 77% >
<FRAMESET ROWS = 40%, 60%>
<FRAME NAME="BANNERIMG" MARGINHEIGHT = 1 MARGINWIDTH = 1 SCROLLING
= "NO" NORESIZE >
<FRAME NAME="NAVIGATE" MARGINHEIGHT = 1 MARGINWIDTH = 1 SCROLLING
= "YES" NORESIZE >
```

```
</FRAMESET >
<FRAMESET ROWS = 8%, 14%, 18%, 32%, 20%, 8%>
<FRAME NAME="TOPLINKS" MARGINHEIGHT = 1 MARGINWIDTH = 1 SCROLLING
= "NO" NORESIZE >
<FRAME NAME="BANNERTEXT" MARGINHEIGHT = 1 MARGINWIDTH = 1
SCROLLING = "NO" NORESIZE >
<FRAME NAME="PURPOSETEXT" MARGINHEIGHT = 1 MARGINWIDTH = 1
SCROLLING= "NO" NORESIZE >
<FRAME NAME="DISPLAYTEXT" MARGINHEIGHT = 1 MARGINWIDTH = 1
SCROLLING="YES" NORESIZE >
<FRAME NAME="DISPLAYFIGS" MARGINHEIGHT = 1 MARGINWIDTH = 1
SCROLLING="YES" NORESIZE >
<FRAME NAME= "BOTMLINKS" MARGINHEIGHT = 1 MARGINWIDTH = 1
SSCROLLING ="NO" NORESIZE >
</FRAMESET>
</HEAD>
```

Loading the Page's Frames

We won't go into the internals of individual .htm files at this point. Instead, we'll build the JScript code that will expedite the page's loading. But before we can do that, there are a few things you need to know.

JScript, like its parent language JavaScript, deals with frames as if they were autonomous windows. In fact, you can consider a browser window itself to be a frame, which functions as the parent object to any frames you create. The identities of parent window and all child frames are stored in an internal, read-only array, which is indexed beginning at zero (0). In this array, the identity of the overall or parent window is stored in the first cell of the array; the identities of all frames created within the parent window are stored in succession after the parent, in the order in which the frames were defined. Table 10-1 outlines the array that contains the identities of all frames on the project page.

Got that straight? Good. We still have code to write—the code that controls the order in which the project page's frames will load.

```
<SCRIPT LANGUAGE="JavaScript">
<!--You read that correctly, despite this being JScript.-->
var numframes = 1;
for (i=1; i<9; i++) {
<!--By beginning our loop at 1, we avoid messing with the overall
```

```
window.-->
if (( i = 1) || (i = 4) || (i = 5)) {
if (i=1) {BANNERIMG = parent.frame[i].open ("BANNERIMG.HTM" };
if (i=4) {BANNERTEXT = parent.frame[i].open ("BANNERTEXT.HTM" };
if (i=5) {PURPOSETEXT = parent.frame[i].open ("PURPOSETEXT.HTM" };
}
break; }
for (i=1; i<9; i++) {
if (( i = 2) || (i = 3) || (i = 6) || (i = 7) || (i = 8) {
if (i=2) {NAVIGATE = parent.frame[i].open ("BANNERIMG.HTM" };
if (i=3) {TOPLINKS = parent.frame[i].open ("BANNERTEXT.HTM" };
if (i=6) {DISPLAYTEXT = parent.frame[i].open ("PURPOSETEXT.HTM" };
if (i=7) {DISPLAYFIGS = parent.frame[i].open ("PURPOSETEXT.HTM" };
if (i=8) {BOTMLINKS = parent.frame[i].open ("PURPOSETEXT.HTM" };}
break;}
</SCRIPT>
</BODY>
</HTML>
```

The frame called	will be stored in this array element numbered as	which is positioned
window (the overall window)	0	first in the array
BANNERIMG	1	second in the array
NAVIGATE	2	third in the array
TOPLINKS	3	fourth in the array
BANNERTEXT	4	fifth in the array
PURPOSETEXT	5	sixth in the array
DISPLAYTEXT	6	seventh in the array
DISPLAYFIGS	7	eighth in the array
BOTMLINKS	8	ninth in the array

Table 10-1. *The Project Page Frames Array*

Answers to Pop Quizzes

1. JScript, following standard Boolean logic, requires that both or all of a set of conditions joined by the && operator be true if the code associated with the set of conditions is to be executed.

2. In JScript, one-line comments are preceded by a double forward slash (//). Multiline comments, on the other hand, must be encased in the traditional in C and C++ delimiters, /* and */.

3. In the first example, the code within the loop would never execute, because the initial value of the loop control variable is outside the range that has been set for the loop. In the second code fragment, we've created an infinite loop because we incorrectly specified the test to be applied to the loop control variable.

Thumbnail Review

1. The physical structure of a Web page must always support its internal logical.

2. Frames provide an excellent means of implementing the internal logic of a page in the most physically efficient way possible.

3. You can use client-side scripting languages such as JScript to control both the behavior of individual page elements and the page's overall activity.

4. Scripting languages offer a number of mechanisms that let you control the flow of execution of the script, thereby controlling the behavior of the page as a whole.

Looking Ahead

The project page is now well on its way to being implemented. In the next chapter, we'll return to a more concepts-oriented discussion of the various ways you can use Dynamic HTML to let users interact with databases.

Chapter Eleven

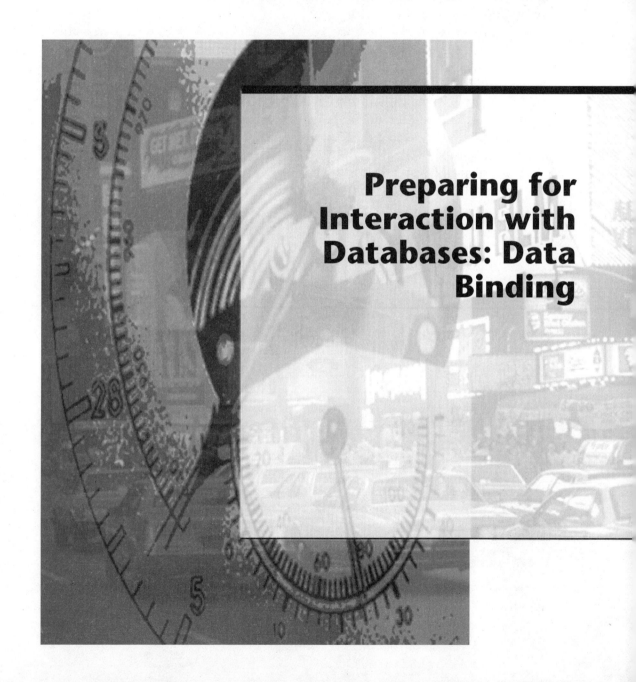

Preparing for Interaction with Databases: Data Binding

The term *data binding* sounds rather intimidating, doesn't it? In some of the data processing contexts in which this phrase is used, its meaning lives up to that impression. Among those who program the complex interactions of operating system and applications—down-on-the-metal programmers—data binding can refer to the practice of locking in a value to a symbolic name or area of memory. However, in the context covered here—the interaction of a client Web browser with a server-stored database—data binding refers to something much less arcane: the ability of a browser to access, inquire of, or modify fields and records in such a database.

That's the good news. The less encouraging fact is that client-side scripting, of whatever flavor and however well written, cannot of itself implement browser-related database interaction. To do that, you must code in the classic sense.

So, in the rest of this chapter, we'll investigate such coding, in the two browser environments most of you are likely to be using:

- Internet Explorer 4.0
- Netscape Communicator 4.0

Sidebar

Remember that many browsers and many users will simply not be able to handle pages created with the techniques this chapter describes. In designing leading-edge documents, don't forget to allow for more mundane presentations of those documents.

Interacting with Databases Under Internet Explorer 4.0

If you're dealing with Explorer 4.0, you'll most likely write your database manipulation code in Visual Basic. So this section begins by examining the three means VB offers to client browsers to manipulate server databases:

- through programming to carry out specific database manipulation
- through programming to employ data controls
- through a combination of these two

Programming to Manipulate Databases

Visual Basic's database-related programming commands manipulate the set of objects that the language recognizes as having to do with data access in any form. Although programs built upon this combination of features may be a bit more complex than those using VB's data controls directly or solely, data-access object-based coding provides a greater range of data manipulation capabilities.

 *It's unlikely that applications you'll be developing will be simple or straightforward enough to permit you to use only data-access controls to implement database manipulation.*

Before we go any further, let's clarify what we mean by *data-access object-based programming* and *data controls*.

Objects, and therefore, of course, the data-access objects, in Visual Basic, adhere to the generalized definition of objects we presented in Chapter 1. You can view them as an analog to or a simple way of referring to a compound variable. The significant difference between objects, as all forms of object-oriented programming structure them, and compound variables in more traditional programming languages such as FORTRAN, is that although those earlier compounds could include only data, albeit sometimes data of a variety of types, objects can encompass data *and* programming instructions, the latter known in "OOP-ese" as *methods*.

VB's data controls, on the other hand, are the language's analogs to the database creation, maintenance, modification, and querying commands that are part of every *database management system* (*DBMS*). That is, data controls deal directly with a database and its contents. (For this reason, such controls are sometimes called *database engine rules*.) Data-access object-based programming, in contrast, must be passed off to the database engine before it can be carried out. This interprocess communication doesn't, however, make object-based manipulation of a database clumsy. Quite the opposite, in fact. With object-based code, you can do more than simply add, modify, or delete fields and records. You can, for instance, run precise and sophisticated data entry validation checks on information keyed in by users, before that information ever gets to the database engine.

To wrap up this brief comparison of object-based and control-based database manipulation in Visual Basic, Table 11-1 outlines the language's most important keywords and syntax related to data-access objects and data controls.

The entity	is a	and works like this
DBEngine .Workspaces	data-access object tool, VB's internal means of tracking and manipulating items defined as being workspace objects	`Set MySpace =` `DBEngine.Workspaces(0)`

OpenDatabase	data-access object method that is part of the workspace object	`Set MyDb =`
		`MySpace.OpenDatabase`
		`("C:\SCI-FI\EARLY\`
		`JULESVERNE.MDB")`

OpenRecordset	data-access object method	`Set PCFacts =`
		`PCFactsDb.OpenRecordset`
		(more stuff here, including the name of the database that will serve as the source for the recordset, as well as the specification of the type of recordset being created).

dbOpenDynaset	data-access object method	`Set PCFacts =`
		`PCFactsDb.OpenRecordset`
		`("SELECT * FROM INTELFAQ", _`
		`dbOpenDynaset)`

dbOpenSnapshot	data-access object method	`Set PCFacts =`
		`PCFactsDb.OpenRecordset`
		`("SELECT * FROM INTELFAQ",`
		`_ dbOpenSnapshot)`

dbOpenTable	data-access object method	`Set PCFacts =`
		`PCFactsDb.OpenRecordset("C:\`
		`PC\INTRO\BASICSTF.MDB",`
		`dbOpenTable)`

3-D check box	bound-defining, or bound, control	allows the user to input yes/no, true/false type values.

Table 11-1. *Data-Access Objects and Data Controls in Visual Basic*

The entity	is a	and works like this
3-D panel	bound-defining, or bound, control	allows the user to input data of a variety of types.
Check box	bound-defining, or bound, control	allows the user to input yes/no, true/false type values.
Combo box	bound-defining, or bound, control	allows the user to input data of a variety of types.
Data	data control (the one and only)	allows the designer to link forms to databases without any programming.
Data-bound combo box	bound-defining, or bound, control	allows the user to input data of a variety of types; can be linked to a specific input data type.
Data-bound grid	bound-defining, or bound, control	allows the user to input data of a variety of types; can be linked to a specific input data type.
Data-bound list box	bound-defining, or bound, control	allows the user to input data of a variety of types; can be linked to a specific input data type.
Image	bound-defining, or bound, control	displays less complex graphics.
Label	bound-defining, or bound, control	acts as a caption; can present data of a variety of types.
List box	bound-defining, or bound, control	displays lists from which the user can select; can present data of a variety of types.
Masked edit	bound-defining, or bound, control	
Picture box	bound-defining, or bound, control	displays more complex graphics.
Text box	bound-defining, or bound, control	displays or allows the user to input data of a variety of types.

Table 11-1. *Data-Access Objects and Data Controls in Visual Basic (continued)*

Programming to Employ Data-Access Objects

Before you can do anything at all with it, you must *open* a database. Here's a fragment of code in Visual Basic which accomplishes that.

```
Dim MyDb As Database, MySpace As Workspace
'Here we've set up two arrays: MyDb, which we'll use for records
retrieved, and MySpace, which we've defined as belonging to the
built-in Visual Basic category of objects called workspaces.
Set MySpace = DBEngine.Workspaces(0)
' Next, we assign our newly created MySpace to the head of the
overall workspace array.
Set MyDb = MySpace.OpenDatabase("C:\SCI-FI\EARLY\JULESVERNE.MDB")
' Finally, we call the built-in Visual Basic method OpenDatabase
on the new MySpace workspace.
```

Sidebar

Several points here:

- The *OpenDatabase* method is part of the *Workspace* object in VB, ergo *MySpace*.

- The file extension .MDB refers to a Microsoft Access database.

- The *OpenDatabase* method can do more than just open; it can specify the mode in which that opening will take place, for example, reserving a database to one program or user, or ensuring that it be opened as read-only, thereby precluding accidental but potentially disastrous modifications.

Now that our database is available, we can begin to think about how we want to manipulate it.

Before you can manipulate a database in any way whatsoever, Visual Basic requires you to define what it calls a *recordset* for the data to be massaged. Think of the recordset as a template, not so much for data itself, as for the way in which that data will be retrieved. VB allows you these three types of recordsets:

- dynaset (pointers that lead to fields and records in one or more tables *within a single database*)

- snapshot (read-only data, again from one or more tables *within a single database*)

- tables (the real McCoy, that is, actual physical database structures that hold actual data)

Table 11-2 outlines the differences among Visual Basic's recordsets.

The recordset called a	consists of	but down on the metal, is stored as	can be manipulated by	but cannot	and therefore
dynaset	a logically related group of field values from one or more database tables	a set of pointers to the data representative of the dynaset after its most recent modification (if any)	only one user at a time	be reindexed	isn't a good choice for multiuser/ multiprocess applications; doesn't provide the ability to sort or filter by means of reindexing.
snapshot	a copy of data	a read-only copy in memory	multiple users or applications	be modified in any way	isn't a good choice for database interactivity other than that which produces displays or reports.
table	data structured exactly as it is represented within the database	no buts about it; it's the same as it's presented to you	multiple users, or applications	be referenced across tables or databases	isn't a good choice for multitable databases, or for multidatabase applications.

Table 11-2. *Comparing Visual Basic's Recordsets*

Table 11-3 presents code fragments that define each VB recordset type.

Sidebar

- Visual Basic gives you several keywords that affect what you can do with a dynaset once you create it. These include

- *dbAppendOnly* (you can add new records, but do no more; in other words, reading or modifying not allowed)

- *dbDenyWrite* (explicitly denies use of the dynaset to anyone other than the individual who opened it)

You can set up a   with Visual Basic code like this:

dynaset	```Dim PCFactsDb As Database, PCFacts As Recordset, MySpace As Workspace Set MySpace = DBEngine.Workspaces(0) Set PCFactsDb = MySpace.OpenDatabase("C:\PC\INTRO\BASICSTF.MDB") Set PCFacts = PCFactsDb.OpenRecordset("SELECT * FROM INTELFAQ", _ dbOpenDynaset)```
snapshot	```Dim PCFactsDb As Database, PCFacts As Recordset, MySpace As Workspace Set MySpace = DBEngine.Workspaces(0) Set PCFactsDb = MySpace.OpenDatabase("C:\PC\INTRO\BASICSTF.MDB") Set PCFacts = PCFactsDb.OpenRecordset("SELECT * FROM INTELFAQ", _ dbOpenSnapshot)```
table	```Dim PCFactsDb As Database, PCFacts As Recordset Set PCFacts = PCFactsDb.OpenRecordset("C:\PC\INTRO\BASICSTF.MDB",dbOpenTable)```

Table 11-3. *Defining Recordsets in Visual Basic*

Programming to Employ Data Controls

Although they aren't quite as flexible as VB's data-access objects, the language's data and bound controls have, in version 4.0, been updated to a very close second. Table 11-4 summarizes these new and improved Visual Basic controls.

Combining Data-Access Objects and Controls

Just how do bound controls (the correct Microsoftian term) relate to data? These controls specify, in their property lists:

■ the screen field to which data will be placed or from which it will be taken in

■ the related data source, which must, for all bound controls, be a data control

The control type called	has these new characteristics	which	and can handle the data types
data	can create any of the three recordset types	overcomes earlier versions' being limited to creating dynasets	
	can assign a recordset created with a data-access object to a screen control such as a text input area, or can assign a previously defined screen control to a recordset as it's being created		
	offers two new properties: Beginning of File or BOF, and End of File or EOF	act as triggers for specific program-defined actions	

Table 11-4.   *Data and Bound Controls in Visual Basic 4.0*

The control type called	has these new characteristics	which	and can handle the data types

bound	offers five new types of bound-defining screen controls:
	  Combo box
	  Data-bound, or
	    DBCombo box
	  Data-bound, or
	    DBList box
	  Data-bound, or
	    DBGrid
	  List box
		flesh out VB's earlier list of bounds-defining controls; that list includes
		  3-D check box
		  3-D panel
		  Check box
		  Image
		  Label
		  Masked edit
		  Picture box
		  Text box
			3-D check box: values such as true/false, yes/no, 1/2 (the last as literals, not numerics)
			  3-D Panel: date, numeric, or text
			  Check box: values such as true/false, yes/no, 1/2 (the last as literals, not numerics)
			  Combo box: date, numeric, or text
			  Data-bound combo box: date, numeric, or text
			  Data-bound grid: date, numeric, or text
			  Data-bound list box: date, numeric, or text
			  Image: binary
			  Label: date, numeric, or text
			  List box: date, numeric, or text
			  Masked edit: date, numeric, or text
			  Picture box: long binary (the internal format for storing graphics)
			  Text box: date, numeric, or text.

Table 11-4. *Data and Bound Controls in Visual Basic 4.0 (continued)*

Bound controls directly manipulate data in a recordset, as changes are made in the control, without the need for any additional programming to update a database record.

The data control, on the other hand, is one of those *programming-for-nonprogrammers* tools Microsoft loves. This control lets you set up access to a database without writing so much as a single line of code. Here's what's involved in using the VB data control.

1. From the toolbox, as shown in Figure 11-1, pick the data control.

2. Place the control on your form, with appropriate sizing and positioning.

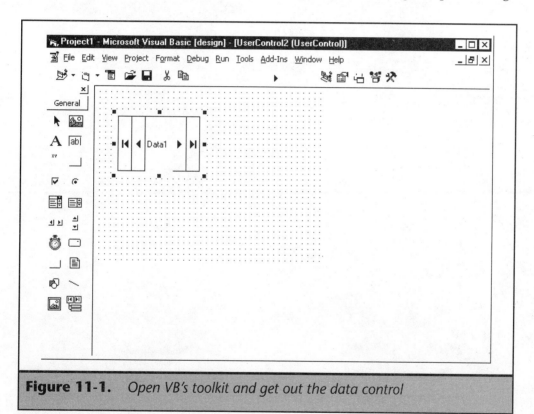

Figure 11-1. *Open VB's toolkit and get out the data control*

3. Define the control's *DatabaseName* property, as Figure 11-2 shows.

4. Define the control's *RecordSource* property; Figure 11-3 shows an example of how we did so.

5. Finally, specify the data control's *RecordsetType* property; take a look at Figure 11-4 for our definition.

Using Current-Record Data Binding

Current-record binding is the name given by Microsoft to their recently developed technique for sorting and filtering retrieved data solely through the

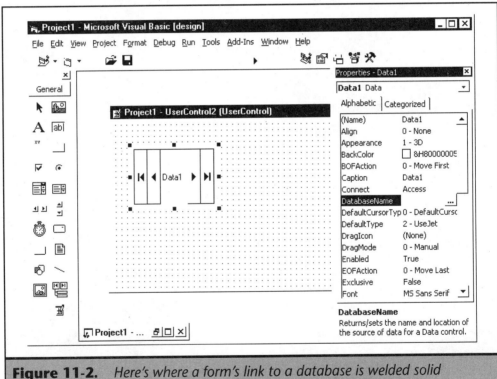

Figure 11-2. *Here's where a form's link to a database is welded solid*

client browser. This technique spares the user the delays that often accompany waiting for the results of server-based sorts and similar operations. Also, current-record binding improves overall throughput and reduces bandwidth demands by reducing the number of calls to the server. Microsoft's description of how current-record binding works can be a little confusing, however, so we offer you Table 11-5 as a means of describing how current-record binding differs from HTML/database interaction in general, and translates some of the terminology that is used to describe it.

One last point about current-record binding. We don't think it will make server-based scripting go the way of the dinosaur anytime soon, since, at least

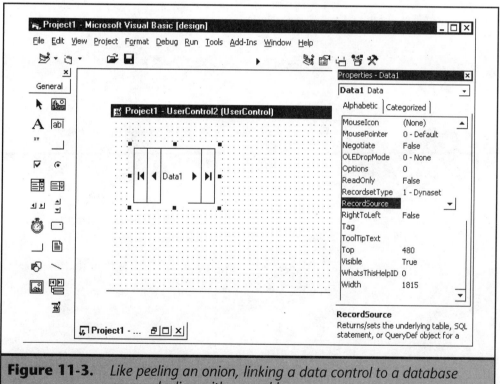

Figure 11-3.   *Like peeling an onion, linking a data control to a database means dealing with several layers*

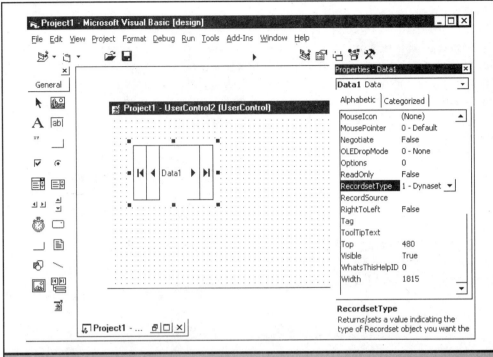

Figure 11-4. *Because it offers the broadest range of access options, we associated our data control with a table*

in early autumn 1997, *only Internet Explorer 4.0 supports such data binding.* This means of linking pages to databases does have several advantages, such as:

- all processing for data display is client-side
- because individual, per-record-requested conversations with the server aren't needed, server resources are freed for other tasks, and client browsing proceeds more quickly
- because you embed data source and even field definitions in your page, you don't need CGI scripting to pass variables defining data to be retrieved to the server

However, it remains to be seen whether these factors alone are enough to carry an entire Web site, or even a collection of dynamic Web pages.

This phrase	means
Merge data with HTML elements on the client	directly associate data contained in a recordset with page elements such as form fields.
Data source object included in the page	the database from which the recordset is derived.
Reference the data source object using the DATASRC and DATAFLD attributes	the HTML attributes through which the association of page element with database is accomplished.
DATASRC, the name of the data source object	do, in Java, what we did earlier in Visual Basic when we wrote `Set MyDb = MySpace.OpenDatabase("C:\SCI-FI\ EARLY\JULESVERNE.MDB")`
DATAFLD, the name of the column that holds the data	give this attribute a value equal to the database field name you want to access.
When the page author changes the position of the current record	when a pointer (there's one in every database, for just this purpose) moves to indicate that a new record is desired.
Data from the new, current record is displayed	whatever page element has been linked to the database automatically updates its (the element's) contents.
Does not require controls; you can bind directly to HTML elements	the DATASRC and DATAFLD attributes eliminate, in theory at least, the need for the VB data control.

Table 11-5. *Making Sense of Current-Record Binding*

Data Binding Under Netscape Communicator 4.0

The first thing we should tell you is this: *You don't have to do it alone*. Really. Netscape Communications has taken a somewhat novel, and certainly sensible, approach to data binding. They've lined up quite a group of third-party vendors whose products work in conjunction with Netscape One to produce dynamic Web pages as easily as possible. Table 11-6 gives you a glimpse of three of these products.

However, not all Web sites will be able to use such products. For instance, if you're operating and publishing through an ISP, and your ISP's Web server doesn't provide them, you're in a bit of a bind. So next we'll examine how to create native Netscape data binding.

Coding NC4 Database Access

Holy Web Server, Batman! Or should we say, Holy LiveWire? Coding for database access under Netscape Communicator 4.0 may, unless you're a Java or JavaScript guru, require another Netscape product, LiveWire, which you'll learn about next.

Looking at LiveWire

Netscape LiveWire and LiveWire Pro are suites of tools that allow you to create and administer Web applications and Web sites. LiveWire includes

- LiveWire Database Connectivity Library
- LiveWire JavaScript Compiler
- LiveWire Site Manager
- Netscape Navigator Gold

Sidebar

In writing this book, we worked with a downloaded, preview release of Communicator, which didn't include any LiveWire tools. The commercial versions do so, however.

The product	can be used to	and comes from
CenterStage	work with JavaScript to present a standard interface for integrating Web-based data with applications	OnDisplay Software (info@ondisplay.com).
HeatShield	build data-bound Web pages that can include secure access even across firewalls connect to any ODBC data source	XDB Systems (PatB@xdb.com).
Web Automation Toolkit	generate Java or JavaScript code to automate extraction of data from Web pages. Includes the ability to bind data objects to variables support for Secure Sockets Layer (SSL) transmission an Object Repository that supports complex queries across multiple resources	Web Methods (info@webMethods.com).

Table 11-6.   *DHTML Products for Netscape One*

LiveWire Pro offers all the features of LiveWire, and adds

- Seagate Software's Crystal Reports, in the Windows NT version only
- Informix-OnLine Workgroup SQL database

Table 11-7 outlines the most significant features of LiveWire's components.

This component	offers features such as
Database Connectivity Library	native SQL connectivity to Informix, Oracle, and Sybase databases.
	connectivity to databases such as Access, DB2, and Paradox.
	passthrough-SQL—that is, the ability to include database-specific SQL statements and commands.
	transaction-based processing such as rollbacks.
JavaScript Compiler	command-line and server-side execution.
	a variety of linking and execution switches.
Site Manager	graphical view of an entire Web site.
	drag-and-drop for site restructuring.
	automatic link reorganization and updating.
	external link checker to track activity and status of outside links.
	wizards and templates for the creation of Web pages and sites.
	site importer to download entire Web sites for local editing and updating.
Crystal Reports	visually-based forms builder and data analysis tools.
	libraries of predefined reports (templates and styles).
	ability to integrate report generation and HTML pages to produce reports automatically.
Informix-OnLine Workgroup SQL Database	single-developer, single-server license allows unlimited users.

Table 11-7. *Getting to Know LiveWire and LiveWire Pro*

Sidebar

You can run LiveWire from a number of hardware and operating system platforms, including various flavors of UNIX, Windows 95, and Windows NT on the OS side, and Intel, Silicon Graphics, and Sun on the hardware side. However, certain basics remain:

- Live Wire will consume at least 10MB of hard disk storage; LiveWire Pro will eat up about 85MB of disk space.

- Be realistic; provide at least 32MB of RAM. (Remember what it is you're trying to do here!)

Coding in Live Wire

Under LiveWire, you must access databases controlled by the Netscape Enterprise and FastTrack servers through a server-side JavaScript object, the *database object*. The database object offers several methods for manipulating a database:

- *connect* connects to a database and establishes user privileges for the connection

- *cursor* defines a *cursor object*, analogous to a recordset, for a database

- *execute* carries out passthrough SQL statements

- *SQLTable* prints an HTML table whose contents result from an SQL query

Investigating the similarities between recordsets and in particular dynasets on the one hand, and LiveWire's cursor object on the other, we find that the cursor object allows you to:

- access database fields—that is, columns—as elements of an array (the *cursorColumn* property, an array that holds a column from the recordset) or through the column name

- insert, update, or delete rows in a recordset directly, through the methods *insertRow*, *updateRow*, and *deleteRow,* respectively

- navigate through the result set by means of the *next* method

The following code sample:

- connects to an Oracle database
- sets up a cursor for the PCFacts table of that database
- calls the next method once, to get the cursor moving through the result set
- displays parts of one record from that set
- updates other fields of the same record
- shuts down the cursor
- disconnects from the database

```
database.connect("ORACLE", "mjp-servr", "oracle", "oracle","PCFacts_db");
// The arguments to database.connect are, respectively:
// database type; must be one of "INFORMIX," "ORACLE," "SYBASE," or "ODBC."
// database server name; for an ODBC database, the name of the ODBC service in
Control Panel
// user name, which allows you to connect to the database; valid values can vary with DBMS
// password to connect to the database; can also vary with DBMS
// database name
pcfactsCursor = database.cursor("select * from PCFacts_db where SERIES='pentium'", true);
// pull out all fields of every record in the current database that have the value
// pentium in the SERIES field
pcfactsCursor.next();
write("Processor: " + pcfactsCursor.cpu + "Speed: " + pcfactsCursor.mhz + "<BR>");
// display some stuff from the extracted record
pcfactsCursor.os1 = "Windows NT Server 4.0";
pcfactsCursor.os2 = "Linux";
// update two fields of the extracted record
pcfactsCursor.close();
// close the cursor
database.disconnect();
// disconnect from the database
```

Thumbnail Review

1. Associating HTML pages with databases, for either input or output, requires server-side programming in most instances.

2. In Internet Explorer 4.0, such programming will probably involve either data-access objects and methods, or data and bound controls, from Visual Basic.

3. IE4 also provides the technique known as current-record binding, which can be completely client-based.

4. Netscape Communicator 4.0, in conjunction with LiveWire, allows you to program database interaction very similar to that provided by Internet Explorer.

Looking Ahead

Pat yourselves on the back once again; you absorbed a great deal of information in this chapter. In Chapter 12, you'll put all that database-interaction expertise to good use, when you learn how to code to filter and sort the information you retrieve, through HTML pages, from a database server.

Chapter Twelve

Data Binding to Sort or Filter Retrieved Information

Oops! Thought we could slip one by you; should have known you'd be more discerning. In closing Chapter 10, we promised a more conceptually oriented discussion during our examination of HTML/database interaction. Then, in Chapter 11, we wimped out, and loaded you down with code syntax, keywords, and fragments. In this chapter, though, as well as in Chapters 13 and 14, we will keep our original promise. And there's a practical reason for returning to a more broadly based investigation.

Database management systems are almost as thick on the ground as leaves in autumn. Table 12-1 lists a few of the most widely used, and relates them to the operating systems and Web servers under which they commonly run.

All of the DBMSs listed in Table 12-1, and many more, use dialects of a programming language, the standard for which was developed by IBM in the 1980s and adopted shortly thereafter by the American National Standards Institute, or ANSI. The parent programming language shared by everything from Access to Sybase, and more, is known as *SQL*, short for *Structured Query Language*. And just as anyone who speaks Russian can pretty well understand Ukrainian, FoxPro could, with little adjustment, understand Informix or SQL Server. The similarities far outnumber the differences.

That's why, in the remainder of this chapter and in Chapters 13 and 14 as well, any code fragments or examples will be in a generalized SQL format, and won't attempt to address the syntax or keywords of specific DBMSs.

Databases for the Project Page

So far, our consideration of design parameters for the page we're developing as a contribution to the members of the NWU has been largely logical and physical. We've not yet blended in anything to do with databases. Let's tackle that aspect of the page now. Because of what it's intended to do, the page will be linked to several small databases; we've illustrated these in Figure 12-1, and outlined them in Table 12-2.

Clearly, the programming that controls all of these databases must provide for sorting and filtering information returned to users.

SQL to Produce Query Results

Before you can sort results, you must, of course, produce them. How do you use SQL to retrieve information from a database?

This database	will run under these operating systems	and in harmony with these Web servers
Access	OS/2 Windows 3.*x* Windows 95 Windows NT Server Windows NT Workstation	Internet Information Server Peer Web Services Personal Web Server
dBASE	OS/2 Windows 3.*x* Windows 95 Windows NT Server Windows NT Workstation	Internet Information Server Peer Web Services Personal Web Server
FoxPro	OS/2 Windows 3.*x* Windows 95 Windows NT Server Windows NT Workstation	Internet Information Server Peer Web Services Personal Web Server
Informix	Linux OS/2 UNIX (several flavors) Windows NT Server	Apache Internet Information Server
Oracle	Linux OS/2 UNIX (several flavors) Windows NT Server	Apache Internet Information Server
SQL Server	Linux OS/2 UNIX (several flavors) Windows NT Server	Apache Internet Information Server
Sybase	Linux OS/2 UNIX (several flavors) Windows NT Server	Apache Internet Information Server

Table 12-1.   *Some of the Web's Most Widely Used Databases*

This database	will present this information to users	and will be manipulated by them in this way
Application software concepts	as many PC- and other platform-related definitions as we can squeeze in; presented as single-sentence explanations; will range from the very simple, such as "The term bit stands for binary digit, and represents the form of numerical notation which is a computer's native 'alphabet.'" to the fairly advanced, as in "Recursive modules can call other modules, including themselves."	not at all; that is, information here is read-only
Hardware concepts	ditto	ditto
Operating system concepts	ditto	ditto
"Meet and consult the experts"	A directory of data processing professionals who are willing to accept and respond to email questions from users	almost ditto; will be modifiable by the experts themselves. That is, if Guru A changes her email address, she will be able to update it directly through the same form users employ to view it.

Table 12-2. *Databases for the Project Web Page*

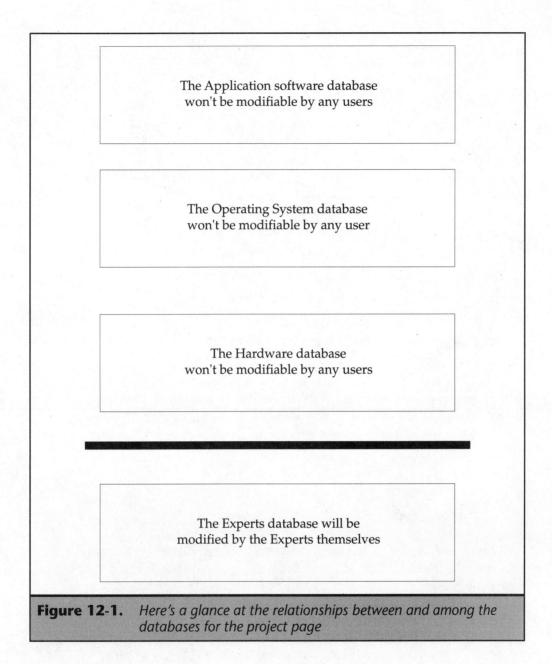

Figure 12-1. *Here's a glance at the relationships between and among the databases for the project page*

It's a simple process. Any of the DBMSs we ticked off in Table 12-1 would recognize a statement of the form:

```
Select * from HWareDB
```

What this line says is, "Dump out all the records in the database called HWareDB." But what if you want to be more selective? It's unlikely, for instance, that any users of our project's page will, in effect, say "Tell me everything you know about hardware." So let's assume that Mr. or Ms. NewUser has keyed in the search string *SDRAM*. The SQL query that would deliver this request to the DBMS could be phrased

```
Select * from HWareDB Where Subject = "SDRAM"
```

You've probably already picked up on the fact that adding even this simple qualifying argument to the SQL query constitutes a form of filtering.

SQL and More Complex Queries

By definition inquisitive, users of the project page will also become more knowledgeable, and therefore able to ask ever more discriminating questions, as they continue to visit the page. What do we do when faced with a search string like *PCs with advanced sound capabilities and Pentium MMX processors*? Once again, standard SQL syntax makes the job an easy one. Consider this example:

```
Select * from HWareDB WHERE Characteristics = "advanced sound capabilities" AND
Subject = "Pentium MMX processors"
```

What this generic SQL command says is, "Dump out all the records in the database called HWareDB that have a value of advanced sound capabilities in the Characteristics field, and a value of Pentium MMX processors in the Subject field."

Once again, the filtering of results to be returned to the user is done at the point of database access. No massaging will be needed at the client end; the information can simply be displayed by the browser. However, although SQL is skilled at retrieving data, it is not the brightest *parsing* bulb around. Any *dissection* of a user-entered search string, as Figure 12-2 points out, must be controlled either through:

- refining field definitions within a Web page's forms
- programming in a non-database-linked language, such as C++, JavaScript, Perl, and so on

Sidebar

We thought it time to bring Perl back into the DHTML discussion for a couple of reasons. First, as mentioned, Perl is an extremely capable scripting language, which excels at tasks like our search-string dissection, referred to in computerese as parsing. Second, Perl holds this distinction because it is in effect a derivative of another UNIX-based programming language called awk. awk is a dynamite little language, designed specifically to manipulate text easily. Because so many Web sites still rely on UNIX, despite the inroads made by Microsoft operating systems like Windows NT, and because the Web server with the largest installed base world-wide remains the freeware UNIX-based Apache, we thought it appropriate to digress about Perl and awk. Besides, UNIX and everything associated with it rank, along with Star Trek, Jackie Chan movies, and cats, among our favorite pastimes.

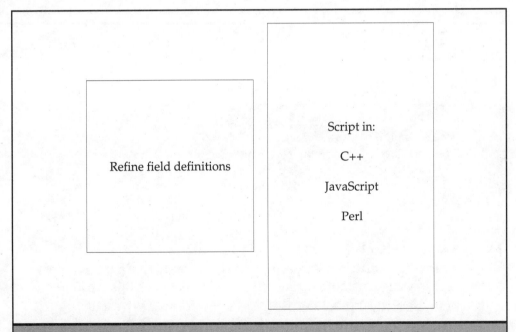

Refine field definitions

Script in:

C++

JavaScript

Perl

Figure 12-2.　*These are the only two ways to parse a search string*

SQL and Conditional Queries

The perspicacity of Web surfers grows at a rate second only to the speed at which software releases succeed one another. Or, as one of our editors noted, "A month in data processing is like a century in anything else." So mere weeks or even days may elapse before we must deal with still more complex inquiries from users of the NWU page.

Take this search string, for example: *artificial intelligence software from 1987 through 1991 inclusive*. Properly processing this inquiry will require more complex code, not so much on the SQL side as in the programming associated with it, as in this Visual Basic example:

```
Dim HWareDB As Database, Results As Recordset, FiltrdResults As
Recordset
' Define the arrays HWareDB, results, and FiltrdResults to hold,
respectively,
' the database object and methods, and two recordsets.
Dim MySpace As WorkSpace
Set MySpace = DBEngine.Workspaces(0)
' Set up a workspace and open it.
Set HWareDB = OpenDatabase("C:\PROJECT\SOURC_IN\HWAREDB.MDB")
' Open the appropriate database and associate it with the variable
HWareDB.
Set Query = Select * from HWareDB WHERE Subject = 'artificial
intelligence software'
' Define a variable and store the appropriate SQL command in it.
Set Results = HWareDB.OpenRecordset(Query, _ dbOpenDynaset)
' Retrieve records that correspond to the basic search condition.
If (Results.Date >= "1987" && Results.Date <= "1991")
Set FiltrdResults = Results
' Filter the results depending upon whether or not the retrieved
records satisfy
' the additional search condition.
```

Sorting Results

As a venerable and wise man said centuries ago, "Put things in order before they exist." Other than its potential as a bad pun, what does this mean in the context of database manipulation? Just this: As was the case with filtering, it makes sense to sort results at the point of inquiry, rather than later, through more complicated programming. Or, to put it another way, wouldn't you rather write a line or two of simple SQL commands than a code block like the one we just walked through? Luckily, SQL in any of its dialects makes that possible, through the keywords INDEX and ORDER BY.

The Pop Quiz shows an example of their use. The Pop Quiz's answer at the end of the chapter will explain it more fully. (Hint: SQL commands like INDEX ON and ORDER BY may vary from DBMS to DBMS, but not by much.)

Pop Quiz   USE HWareDB INDEX ON Subject

Select * from HWareDB WHERE Subject = 'SDRAM' ORDER BY Subject

How DBMSs Recognize SQL

Most of the database management systems listed in Table 12-1 would be able to accept queries or other SQL commands in any of three ways:

- through direct interaction, that is, SQL commands forwarded to the database by means of some DBMS-supplied tool such as a command window

- through embedded SQL, that is, by means of code like that in the section "SQL and Conditional Queries," in which SQL commands are contained in a program written in a language such as C++ or Visual Basic. Consider this more brief Visual Basic example:

```
Query = "SELECT * WHERE Subject = 'SDRAM' "
' Says "I want every record that contains the value SDRAM in the
field Subject.
HWareDB.Execute Query
' Uses the built-in Visual Basic method Execute on the database
HWareDB to run
' the SQL query we've packed into the variable called,
surprisingly enough, Query.
```

- through SQL presented by means of what are frequently called stored procedures—in effect, library modules that carry out common database manipulations. Stored procedures might be as simple as the preceding two-line example, or might consist of dozens of lines of code.

Answer to Pop Quiz

The generalized SQL syntax INDEX ON and ORDER BY mean, respectively, that:

■ the database will be sorted according to the values contained in the field
Subject, before any inquiries are processed or records retrieved

■ retrieved results will be sorted again, also based on values in the field Subject

Thumbnail Review

1. You can query databases of all kinds by means of commands following standard Structured Query Language (SQL) syntax.

2. You can filter query results within the query itself.

3. Queries can range from simple to more complex to conditional.

4. You can use SQL commands to sort query results at the point of record retrieval.

5. SQL commands can be delivered to DBMSs in any of three ways:

■ direct interaction

■ embedded SQL

■ stored procedures

Looking Ahead

Ok, ok; so we lapsed briefly into a bout of coding. The example in the section "SQL and Conditional Queries" is as heavy-duty as things will get from here on out, because our remaining database discussions will build on the code in Chapter 11 and in this chapter.

Although it won't happen too often, at least a few users of the our project's page—its team of experts—will also be editors of one of its databases. We need to link HTML to database update operations. We'll learn how to hook them up in Chapter 13.

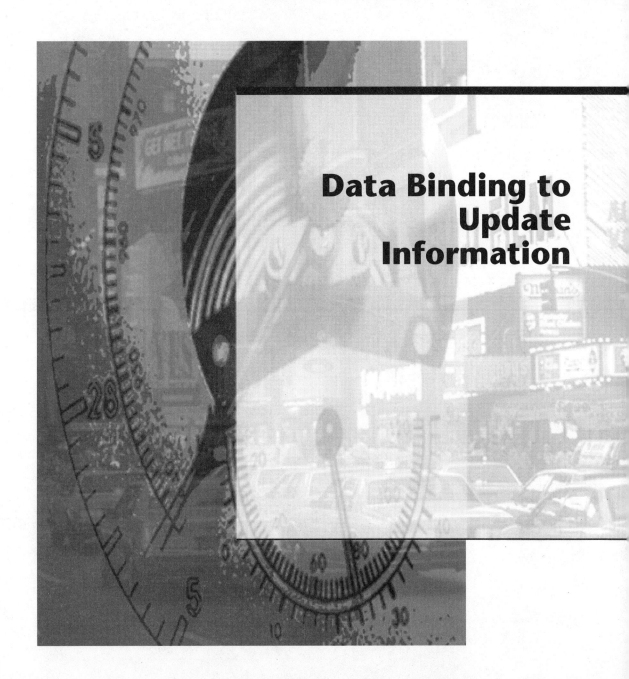

Chapter Thirteen

Data Binding to Update Information

Although, in the context of our sample application, users will rarely update related databases through the Web page, such updates are a common function of Web applications at large. This chapter scrutinizes the means by which these updates can be accomplished. And as in Chapter 12, we'll rely primarily on standardized SQL syntax during our examination.

SQL Keywords and Data Binding

SQL offers three keywords that allow you to deal with various aspects of updating a database. Table 13-1 examines these keywords.

Table 13-2 provides examples of each update-related SQL command.

Pop Quiz Neither ALTER nor UPDATE allow you to delete a column from a database. In fact, there is no keyword, and not even any simple technique, in SQL to let you do this. So, put your thinking caps on, and see if you can come up with the workaround that's commonly used in such situations. As always, the answer is at the end of the chapter.

This keyword	manipulates	by	and is available in these DBMSs, among others
ALTER	a database's schema, or *blueprint* (also sometimes referred to as a *data dictionary*)	defining a new field, or *column*, as it's also known	DB2 Oracle Sybase
INSERT	the data in a database	add data	Access Oracle
UPDATE	the data in a database	modify data	Oracle Sybase

Table 13-1. *SQL's Update Keywords*

Use this keyword	like this
ALTER	ALTER TABLE HWareDB ADD new_column char(20) NULL This line of code tells the DBMS to: add a new field to the table called HWareDB set the data type that that field will be permitted to accept to Character define the field as being able to extend to a length of up to 20 characters make the initial value of the new field NULL, or empty
INSERT	INSERT INTO HWareDB (ItemType, ModelFamily, Vendor, Reputation) VALUES ('Chip Set', 'Tritan', 'Intel', 'top quality') This line of code tells the DBMS to: modify the values stored in the fields whose names are contained within the first set of parentheses use the values contained within the second set of parentheses to do the modification match up values with field names in the order in which the items appear in their respective lists, thereby, for instance, placing the value top quality in the field Reputation
UPDATE	UPDATE HWareDB Set ItemType = 'Sound Card' WHERE ItemType = 'Audio Connector'

Table 13-2.   *Using SQL's Update-Related Keywords*

Updating the Project's Databases

You'll recall from Chapter 12 that the page we're developing as a contribution to the members of the NWU will link to only one database that may be modified by users of the page. That database, a directory of data processing professionals who are willing to accept and respond to email questions from users, will be modifiable only by the experts themselves. And even those folks will not be able to change the database's blueprint.

The table housing this Experts Directory contains the fields outlined in Table 13-3.

Let's talk now about how our panel of experts might carry out the database modification that is open to them. We'll begin with the more obvious task—changing existing data.

Changing Data

Let's assume that Tom Expert, a programmer, system administrator, and manager of a project the goal of which is the complete automation of a college library, has consented to sit on the project page's panel of experts on occasion. Let's assume further that, shortly after sending us his biographical information, Tom changes Internet service providers, and therefore email addresses. Because we've set up such a crackerjack page, Tom just needs to go to that page, and display the Experts Directory in the main text-display frame, as Figure 13-1 illustrates.

Because we've coded the database interaction portion of the page to be sensitive to the point-of-origin of update attempts, and because that code is aware that Tom is authorized to carry out updates, his doing so won't set off any alarms. Rather, it will activate SQL code like this:

```
Select * from ExpertsDB Where Guru='Tom Expert'
UPDATE ExpertsDB SET ISP = 'BigNet.com'
UPDATE ExpertsDB SET emailaddr = 'TExpert@BigNet.com'
```

name	street	city	state	zip	ISP	email	work/home	backgrd
Tom Espert	12 Third St	Oldtowne	PA	15555	Slownet.com	TE@Slownet.com	home	17 years in data processing

Figure 13-1. *Here's what an entry in the Experts Directory might look like*

This field	contains	of data type	and can be
Guru	the expert's first and last name	char	up to 35 characters long
StreetAddr	the expert's home or work address, as he or she prefers	char	up to 25 characters long
City	pertaining to the expert's home or work address	char	up to 15 characters long
State	pertaining to the expert's home or work address	char	up to 3 characters long
Zip	pertaining to the expert's home or work address	char	up to 10 characters long, to provide for zip codes such as 19342-0186
ISP	pertaining to the expert's home or work address	char	up to 20 characters long
emailaddr	pertaining to the expert's home or work address	char	up to 20 characters long
work_or_home	indicates whether the above six fields apply to work or home	char	1 character; only possible values are W or H
Backgrd	a brief description of the expert's skills	char	up to 80 characters long

Table 13-3.   *A Closer Look at the Schema of the Experts Table*

name	street	city	state	zip	ISP	email	work/home	backgrd
Tom Espert	12 Third St	Oldtowne	PA	15555	BigNet.com		TE@BigNetet.com	

home 17 years in data processing

Figure 13-2. *Now Tom's information is up to date*

Once this code has run, any visitor to the page would see what's shown in Figure 13-2 upon accessing Tom's entry in the Experts Directory.

Inserting New Data

Tom has passed the word about the project page's Experts Directory among friends and coworkers. Several of those folks have also been kind enough to volunteer for the panel. Among them is Sarah Ng, an engineer of 15 years.

Once we tweak the programming that controls access to the Experts Directory database, Sarah can key in her biographical information at her leisure. When she does so, code like the following will be kickstarted.

```
INSERT INTO ExpertsDB (Guru, StreetAddr, City. State. Zip, ISP,
emailaddr,
work_or_home, Backgrd)
VALUES ('Sarah Ng', '123 Fourth Street', 'North Braddock', 'PA',
'15104-1234',
'munch.com', 'W', '15 years as an electronics engineer and C
programmer')
```

Another way that SQL can express what Sarah is trying to do is this:
```
INSERT INTO ExpertsDB VALUES ('Sarah Ng', '123 Fourth
Street', 'North Braddock', 'PA',
'15104-1234', 'munch.com', 'W', '15 years as an
electronics engineer and C programmer')
```
But be careful. You can only use this syntax if you are lacing values into every field in a record.

Answer to Pop Quiz

The workaround most frequently used to delete fields from a schema goes like this:

- Create a database that is an exact duplicate of the one that needs a column pulled, except for the fact that the column you're trying to get rid of is absent from the copycat database.

- Run a SELECT that retrieves all data but that in the no-longer-needed column.

- Run an INSERT or UPDATE that places this retrieved data in the newly created, properly-structured database.

- After verifying the structure and contents of that new database, blow away the old file in whatever way is most convenient.

Here's how this procedure might go if we were trying to delete the YrIntroduced field of the HWareDB database. Assume that this database contains these fields:

- ComponentType
- ComponentUse
- ComponentModelSeries
- ComponentMfr
- YrIntroduced
- StillAvailable
- StillSupported
- Characteristics

```
CREATE TABLE HWareDB2 (ComponentType char(10), ComponentUse
char(20),
ComponentModelSeries char(8), ComponentMfr char(15),
StillAvailable Boolean,
StillSupported Boolean, Characteristics char(30) )
SELECT ComponentType, ComponentUse, ComponentModelSeries,
ComponentMfr,
StillAvailable, StillSupported, Characteristics from HWareDB
'Syntax of the While loop sort needed here; we'll use a
```

```
generalized version
WHILE NOT EOF 'for the recordset into which you've placed the
results of the SELECT
INSERT INTO HWareDB2 'name of the recordset containing the values
you want to insert
```

Thumbnail Review

1. Standard SQL offers three keywords that allow you to modify a database's schema or contents: ALTER, INSERT, and UPDATE.

2. ALTER changes a database's blueprint by adding a column (field).

3. INSERT puts data into a record or records in a database.

4. UPDATE changes values already present in a database.

Looking Ahead

Three database interaction topics down, and only one to go. In Chapter 14, we'll investigate what you must do through SQL to create databases, and the data stored there, on the fly.

Chapter Fourteen

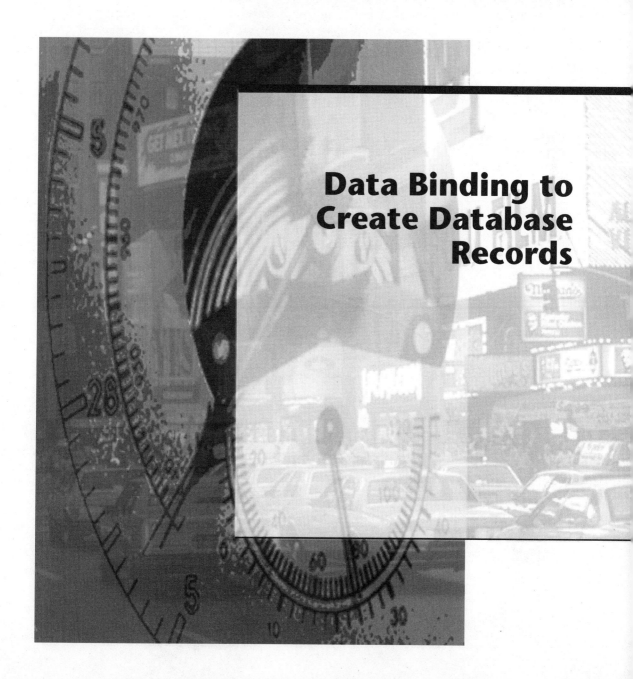

Data Binding to Create Database Records

W e've covered a fair amount of SQL ground since beginning our discussion of the interaction of Dynamic HTML-based Web pages with databases. At this point, you're probably a bit fuzzy on the structural details of the one project database that can be manipulated through such a page. So before we begin walking through the maneuvers we'll need to create new data, we'll briefly review the database's definitions. Then, we'll introduce the SQL keywords and concepts by means of which data will be added to the Experts Directory. Finally, we'll present code samples to accomplish such an addition.

The Directory of Experts

To reinforce the decisions we made in the previous chapter, we'll once again present the structure of the Directory of Experts database in Table 14-1.

The field	represents	is stored as	and can be
Guru	the expert's first and last name	char	up to 35 characters long
StreetAddr	the expert's home or work address, as he or she prefers	char	up to 25 characters long
City	pertaining to the expert's home or work address	char	up to 15 characters long
State	pertaining to the expert's home or work address	char	up to 3 characters long
Zip	pertaining to the expert's home or work address	char	up to 10 characters long, to provide for zip codes such as 19342-0186
ISP	pertaining to the expert's home or work address	char	up to 20 characters long

Table 14-1. *The Structure of the Experts Directory*

The field	represents	is stored as	and can be
emailaddr	pertaining to the expert's home or work address	char	up to 20 characters long
work_or_ home	indicates whether the above six fields apply to work or home	char	1 character; only possible values are W or H
Backgrd	a brief description of the expert's skills	char	up to 80 characters long

Table 14-1. *The Structure of the Experts Directory (continued)*

SQL Keywords and Data Binding

In Chapter 13 you learned that SQL, at least as it's implemented by leading DBMSs such as Oracle and Sybase, provides three keywords that allow you to modify a database's schema or contents. These are

- ALTER
- INSERT
- UPDATE

Of this trio, we'll need only INSERT to create database records. To it, we'll add a new term—the keyword CREATE. Table 14-2 recaps the keywords we'll use to create data for the Experts Directory.

Next, Table 14-3 offers examples of using each data-creation-related SQL command.

This keyword	is used to
CREATE	create a new database table
INSERT	put data into a record or records in a database.

Table 14-2. *SQL Keywords and Creating Data*

Use this keyword	like this
| CREATE | ```
CREATE TABLE Experts
Guru char(35),
StreetAddr char(20),
City char(15),
State char(3),
Zip char(10),
ISP char(20),
emailaddr char(20),
work_or_home char(1),
Backgrd char(80),
``` |
| INSERT | ```
INSERT INTO Experts(Guru, StreetAddr, City,
State, Zip, ISP, emailaddr,
work_or_home, Backgrd)
VALUES('Bob Gean', '', '', '', '',
'voicenet.com',
'Gean@voicenet.com', 'h', Several years'
experience in Web page design and coding')
``` |

Table 14-3. *Using SQL's Data-Creation-Related Keywords*

Pop Quiz #1 Why are there so many empty pairs of single quotes in the last example in Table 14-3? As always, the answer is at the end of the chapter.

Keywords

Create Table

The phrase CREATE TABLE tells any SQL server that supports it several things:

- a new table is about to be built
- that table will contain the fields named as arguments to CREATE TABLE

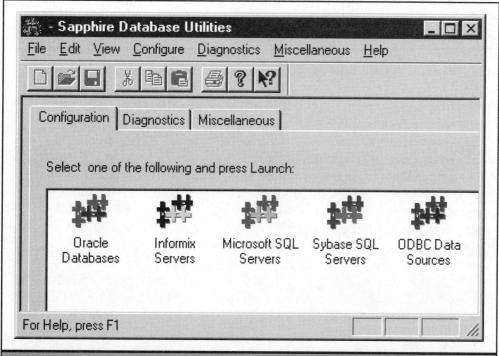

Figure 14-1. *The Web development suite Sapphire, from Bluestone Software, provides a full-function SQL arm*

■ the fields so named will be of the data types and lengths defined in the argument list

Many database management systems offer tools that help you carry out tasks such as the one outlined in Table 14-3; Figure 14-1 shows one of these. That's the good news. Less favorable is the fact that these tools, as you might expect, are suite-specific. What's more, they teach you little if anything about what's going on behind the admittedly impressive user interfaces. So, although such tools can be handy in a crunch, they're not something to rely upon all the time. Look at it this way: If you did so, what would you do if the tools were no longer available? We strongly urge you to persevere, and to learn a little SQL. It's sure to stand you in good stead.

Keys

Although it's stating the obvious, it behooves us to remind you just what a database record is. Such a record is *a single unique occurrence that contains values for previously defined units of information*. The pivotal point of this definition is, of course, the word *unique*. For reasons both logical and physical, databases are duplicate-phobes. Repetitive storage of information offers no benefits in terms of querying or reporting upon that information. And hard-disk drives, although they are a lot bigger than they once were, are still finite. (We have in mind the example of a friend who had to compress his 3.2 gigabyte drive because it wouldn't accept his most recently acquired game.) In other words, when creating records on the fly, or in any other circumstances, you must ensure the uniqueness of each record.

Once again, the SQL syntax needed to do so is largely, if not entirely, DBMS-independent. That syntax involves defining and assigning a primary key to each and every record in a table.

A *primary key* is the field that makes a record unique. Perhaps the best example of a primary key is social security number. However many John Smiths and Jane Does there might be in the United States, each one has his or her own SSN. Therefore, each one can be assured of the uniqueness of the information regarding his or her payments, benefits, and so on.

SQL systems use a variety of techniques to designate a field or fields as the primary key of a table. For instance, Sybase, in its data manipulation language Transact SQL, uses the following syntax:

```
sp_primarykey Experts, [field name]
```

This phrasing tells the Sybase SQL server that the table Experts will have a single primary key. In this example, though, we've not yet defined that key, for a good reason.

Although it's unlikely, it is at least possible that, within our panel of Web authorities, we might have more than one sharing a last name and even a last name/first name combination. We can deal with this situation in either of two ways.

We might create an arbitrary, randomly generated, has-no-meaning-other-than-its-role artificial key. As a matter of fact, that's how social security numbers came into existence. Such a method would indeed provide us with a single field that would be unique, no matter how large our Experts database might grow. However, this technique has drawbacks, too. Chief among them is the fact that, as each record is generated, a call must be made to a library module of some sort, either internal to the database manipulation language or linkable to it. For instance, the 4GLs with which we used to work—Unify/Accell, Informix, and Oracle, all on UNIX platforms—each permitted the use of modules written in C and then hooked into the DBMS's code. In the jargon of programming, such calls would make code that creates records more *processor-intensive*. In English, this means that such code will take longer to run and/or draw off CPU time from any other applications that happen to be executing alongside it. In other words, your server can slow down, perhaps not even perceptibly to users, but certainly appreciably if considered over a long enough period. Add to this the fact that database applications of any sort are *I/O intensive*, or heavy producers and users of intersystem and interprocess communications (particularly so if the database in question is a large one), and you've got the potential for system lags to which even the most tolerant user might take exception.

An alternative, in Sybase at least, to the possibility of gumming up your server by generating keys as you go, is to designate several fields in combination as the primary key. This technique is not without its shortcomings either. Processing time can once again suffer, a wee bit or more, depending upon how many fields you include to produce a unique key. But such additional CPU time will only pertain to database searches, since these require seeking out a match to one or more key field values. The multi-field key technique will not affect record generation as significantly as on-the-spot key generation can.

So, how do you decide which means of producing keys to use? Table 14-4 has the answer.

The technique of	is best used with	and follows syntax like	which tells an SQL server
| randomly generating unique keys | databases that are small, grow infrequently, or both | ```
sp_primarykey
Experts,
gen_key()
which in turn
relies upon the
C code
int gen_key();
#include
"stdlib.h"
main()
int I, key_prim;
for
(i=1;1<NUM_REC;i++
)
key_prim=rand();
return
(key_prim);
``` | to call the C routine gen_key, which will in turn generate a series of random numbers to serve as unique primary keys |
| designating multiple contiguous fields as a key | databases that are large, that can be expected to grow by leaps and bounds, or whose fields readily present unique combination possibilities | ```
sp_primarykey
Experts,
Guru#,
StreetAddr#,
City#, State#,
Zip#
sp_primarykey
Experts,
Guru#>
``` | to use the combination of fields Guru, Street Address, City, State, and Zip as each record's primary key or to designate Guru and every field that follows it as the combination that will make up the primary key |

Table 14-4. *Creating Primary Keys*

Pop Quiz #2 In the lower-right cell of Table 14-4, what is the significance of the pound sign (#) character? You get extra points if you also know which character tells a Sybase SQL server to use all fields, in combination, as the primary key.

Sybase and possibly a few other DBMSs offer another handy key-related tool, which permits you to check that a primary key has been correctly defined. Under Sybase, the syntax for such a check, run on our Experts database, would be

```
sp_helpkey Experts
```

In response to this inquiry, the Sybase SQL server might produce something like this:

```
keytype   object          related_object  object_keys
primary   Experts_table   none            Guru#, StreetAddr#,
                                           City#, State#,Zip#
```

What Sybase is trying to say here is that our Experts table has a primary key that consists of the combination of the fields Guru, StreetAddr, City, State, and Zip, in that order.

Answers to Pop Quizzes

1. As is the case in any programming language, argument lists in a 4GL must contain the same number of parameters as the entity they reference. Because the INSERT statement contains nine field names, we must supply nine values, even null ones, as indicated by the empty quotes. Those values will be inserted into the fields we've indicated in the order in which we specify them.

2. To identify one or more fields as a primary key or part of such a key, you must follow every field name with a pound sign (#); this tells Sybase that you've said all you have to say about that particular field. To tell this DBMS to use every field after a named one as part of a primary key, you must use the greater-than (>) symbol.

Thumbnail Review

1. Only two SQL keywords, CREATE and INSERT, are involved in creating database records.

2. Every DBMS requires that records in a table each contain a unique key field, or primary key. Most such systems also permit the use of secondary keys, which function as additional bases for searching and sorting.

Looking Ahead

If the job of building and publishing a dynamic Web page is beginning to look daunting to you, take heart. In the next three chapters, we'll do more than review the role of multimedia in such pages. We'll introduce you to three tools—two commercial application suites and one simple but efficient shareware package—that automate many of the page design and implementation tasks this book covers.

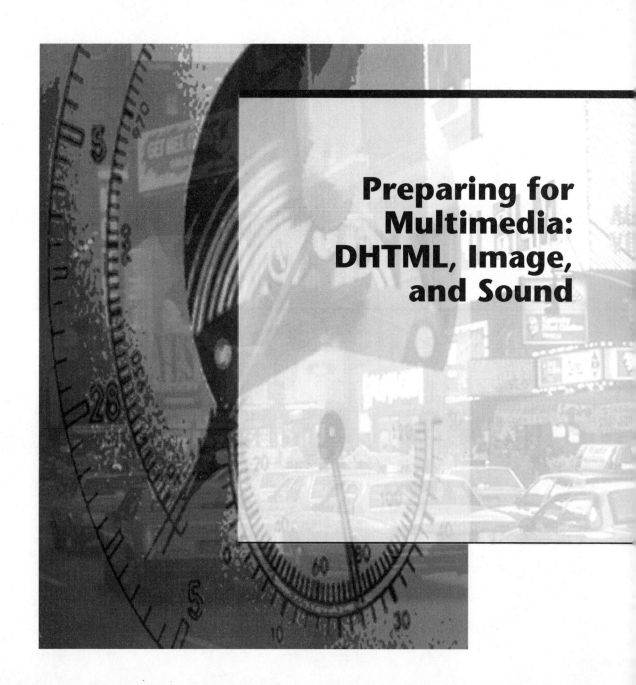

Chapter Fifteen

Preparing for Multimedia: DHTML, Image, and Sound

Y ou wouldn't start out on a long trip, even in familiar terrain, without consulting a map. And you wouldn't (at least, we hope you wouldn't) step out into a busy intersection without first looking in all directions. In similar fashion, it's always a good idea to investigate carefully before venturing into New Software Territory.

Building a dynamic Web page certainly qualifies as such a region. So far, we've introduced and discussed several standards, scripting languages, and techniques. Now, in beginning our review of multimedia and DHTML, we're faced with the prospect of looking at several more. Is there any way to streamline our studies?

As a matter of fact, there is. There are now many tools that not only automate building a dynamic Web page but also greatly facilitate including multimedia features in that page. Several have received the blessing of Microsoft and Netscape Communications, including:

- Backstage, from Macromedia
- Internet Studio, also known as Visual InterDev, from Microsoft
- IntraBuilder, From Borland Corporation
- Sapphire, from Bluestone Inc.

In this chapter, we'll introduce you to Internet Studio as a means of familiarizing you with the multimedia capabilities of such tools in general. In Chapter 16, we'll work with Sapphire as we examine embedding sound in a DHTML page. Then, in Chapter 17, we'll use still another suite to deal with incorporating high-res images into the page.

Microsoft's Internet Studio was specifically designed for the development of dynamic Web applications. As such, it has a number of features of interest to us, such as:

- a complete set of Web site management tools
- an integrated, visually oriented development environment
- full support for interaction with any Open Database Connectivity (ODBC) database
- support for all significant Web-related standards, including not only ODBC but also HTML, HTTP, COM, and Java

Platforms Underlying Internet Studio

The Internet Studio will run under a number of operating system/hardware combinations. Let's discuss the operating systems first.

Operating Systems

The Studio can have, as its underlying operating system, either Windows NT Server 4.0, Windows NT Workstation 4.0, or Windows 95. All of these are 32-bit systems, but the resemblance stops there. Each of these operating systems has distinct characteristics that will affect any LAN and Web site based upon it.

Windows NT Server 4.0

The attributes of Windows NT Server 4.0, the most recent incarnation of Microsoft's Network Operating System (NOS), that are most germane to Internet Studio are

- The availability of a number of Wizards that simplify network administration. NT Server 4 offers these Wizards:

  - Add Printer

  - Add User Account

  - Add/Remove Programs

  - Group Management

  - Install New Modem

  - License

  - Manage File and Folder Access

  - Network Client Administrator

- As this list demonstrates, you can forego much of the drudgery involved in network administration, and therefore have more time to devote to Web site development, if you install the Internet Studio on a NT Server 4.0 platform. NT Server 4.0 gives you the ability to strictly control the conditions of user access, through network-wide user policies and user-specific profiles. NT Server 4.0 allows you to specify, for individual users or workstations, such session characteristics as directories that may be accessed or time frames during which an individual may not log in.

- The ability to administer the server from a client station.
- Improved TCP/IP functionality, and full support for NetWare subnets.
- An extensive and flexible set of administrative tools, through which you can eyeball atypical or ongoing network conditions and events.

Windows NT Workstation 4.0

Although it offers far fewer network administration and security features than NT Server 4.0, the most recent release of Windows NT Workstation can be an adequate LAN host in very small environments. NT Workstation 4.0 shares some of NT Server 4.0's architecture, such as the Hardware Abstraction Layer (HAL), an element of software structure that effectively isolates, and thereby protects the operating system from, inadvertent corruption by clumsy applications. NT Workstation 4.0 also includes some of the most significant NT Server network administration tools: Event Viewer, Performance Monitor, and User Manager. So, if your Web site, and therefore your Internet Studio implementation, resides in a LAN made up of a dozen or fewer stations, NT Workstation 4.0 is a reasonable operating system alternative.

Windows 95

Like Windows NT Workstation 4.0, Windows 95 is capable only of peer-to-peer networking. Unlike NT Workstation, however, Windows 95 does not include the New Technology File System (NTFS) as an additional means of providing file system security. Windows 95's networking capabilities, like those of most peer-to-peer network operating systems, are more nearly those of a workgroup than a client/server environment. This means that, other than defining file and directory sharing, there's little you can do to secure a Windows 95-based LAN.

Windows 95 has another drawback that's particularly relevant to implementing Internet Studio. It lacks not only NT's HAL, but also its multikernel architecture. The multikernel software structure is the feature of NT that segregates various levels of operating system functionality, allowing better prioritization and therefore more efficient functioning of such basic network software components as device drivers. Multikerneling has been particularly effective in improving the performance of graphics and sound. Enough said.

Hardware Requirements

To paraphrase Douglas Adams, in his book *The Hitchhiker's Guide to the Galaxy*, "32 bit operating systems are picky. I mean, they're really, really picky." We'll end our brief discussion of the OS platforms supported by Internet Studio with a review of the hardware requirements of those platforms. Be aware that the specs detailed in Tables 15-1, 15-2, and 15-3 are realistic, not bare bones, and reflect our own experience in installing and configuring these systems. So,

For this component	provide at least
Memory	32MB. EDO or SD RAM, because of its speed, is preferable.
Processor	a Pentium 133 MHz. Don't even think of using anything slower or older. For instance, Microsoft's online NT Server documentation says that the OS will run on any 32-bit processor as fast/recent as a 486 25 MHz. We tried it (with a 486/66 DX, to be precise), with no success.
Motherboard chip set	full Intel only. Once again, although Microsoft doesn't specify this, we found it to be needed in our NT Server installation attempts.
Hard drive	although the OS itself can scratch by with as little as 120MB of hard disk storage, Web content is a hog and then some. You'd be making a mistake if you try to implement NT Server and Internet Studio on any hard drive smaller than 1.2GB.
CD-ROM drive	once again, personal experience mandates a CD-ROM drive no slower than 8x. The CD drive we originally tried to use in installing NT Server was an older Philips, which took over six hours to copy (just copy, not configure) operating system files. Think what havoc a drive like this could wreak on a Web service!

Table 15-1. *Windows NT Server 4.0 Hardware Requirements*

For this component	provide at least
Memory	32MB. Once again, we recommend EDO or SD RAM. And although Microsoft tells us that NT Workstation can function with a minimum of 12MB of RAM, we stick with our suggestion of 32. Remember, you're configuring a Web platform here.
Processor	a Pentium 133 MHz. Again, don't even think of anything slower or older.
Motherboard chip set	full Intel only
Hard drive	at least 1.2GB.
CD-ROM drive	here, you might be able to get by with a 6x.

Table 15-2. *Windows NT Workstation 4.0 Hardware Requirements*

For this component	provide at least
Memory	32MB EDO or SD RAM.
Processor	a Pentium 133 MHz.
Motherboard chip set	full Intel only.
Hard drive	1.2GB.
CD-ROM drive	minimum 6x drive, since by definition an NT Workstation-based LAN will be a small one. However, if you anticipate including a high percentage of dynamic content in the Web pages you'll be building with Internet Studio, go for an 8x.

Table 15-3. *Windows 95 Hardware Requirements*

if there's a difference between what we're about to recommend and what, for example, Microsoft recommends on its Web site, we say—stick with us. We learned these parameters the hard way.

Web Servers

Given their varying natures, it's not surprising that the three operating systems we just examined have similarly varying Internet service and server capabilities. In this section, you'll learn more about those capabilities and their impact on an Internet Studio implementation.

Internet Information Server 3.0

Internet Information Server 3.0 (IIS) is, to say the least, a full-feature Internet server. It offers not only Web services but also FTP, Gopher, and multicast (Internet multimedia broadcast) elements.

IIS 3.0 has a number of other features that can significantly affect and improve Internet Studio performance. Let's look at these features now.

Fully Integrated Internet Publishing

Internet Information Server 3.0 allows you to structure your Internet publishing directories as a single file system whose content may be shared by all IIS 3.0 services, or as a series of related file subsystems. Either of these storage architectures may contain virtual directories, which are in effect nicknames or aliases for existing physical folders.

Management Tools

In addition to NT Server's Performance Monitor and Event Viewer, IIS 3.0 offers two administrative tools of its own: Internet Service Manager (ISM) and Key Manager (KM).

Through Internet Service Manager, you can define, view, or modify the operating characteristics of all Internet services running under IIS 3.0. For instance, you can set custom wording for messages to be displayed to users who are unsuccessful in carrying out anonymous logons.

Key Manager, on the other hand, allows you to establish and manage a high degree of access security, by acting as a vehicle for Secure Sockets Layer (SSL) encryption and decryption of network traffic.

Multimedia Internet Broadcasting

The most recent versions of IIS include NetShow On-Demand and NetShow Live! (exclamation point provided at no extra charge by Microsoft), the MS multimedia Internet broadcasting applications.

NetShow is definitely the star of IIS 3.0. It carries out one-to-many multimedia communications and information distribution over Internet or intranet, offering both live and on-demand audio and video distribution. According to Microsoft, implementing NetShow can actually improve network bandwidth hits. This latter claim is a bit hard to accept, since NetShow is not only impressive but also very demanding of server resources. Even according to Microsoft, NetShow should be run under a Pentium 200 and 48MB RAM to perform adequately (as opposed to just barely).

Index Server

Despite any confusion its name might cause, Index Server is a search engine designed to allow full-text indexing and searching of information in intranet or Internet formats such as HTML or simple text. That information can be in Dutch, English, French, German, Italian, Spanish, or Swedish. Once installed, Index Server automatically builds an index of your Web service. You can search this index from any Web browser.

Crystal Reports

Crystal Reports, the last new feature of IIS 3.0, is a report writer that allows you to create presentation-quality reports and integrate them into database applications, all through an HTML interface. Crystal Reports for Internet Information Server 3.0 (the version of the application specific to and bundled with this release of IIS) also includes preformatted Web log reports for analyzing Web log files.

Crystal Reports has its own versions of Wizards called Experts. Specifically, Crystal Reports provides Experts for:

- Database table selection
- Graphing
- Report creation
- Report distribution
- Style
- Visual linking of reports

Peer Web Services and Personal Web Server

Peer Web Services and Personal Web Server are both peer-to-peer intranet/Internet servers that can do the following:

- publish Web pages with ActiveX controls
- provide FTP services
- support Internet Server API (ISAPI) and Common Gateway Interface (CGI) scripts
- interact with ODBC data sources
- support the Secure Sockets Layer

But of the two, only Peer Web Services can interact securely with Windows NT Server and Novell NetWare, provide local-user security if file and print sharing are not installed, permit remote administration of your Web site, and offer a Gopher service.

Internet Studio Warp and Weave

The Internet Studio has many built-in components, and will interact with many more that it doesn't provide directly. This section examines the ways in which the Studio knits all these pieces together.

User Interface

Internet Studio's user interface is graphically oriented—and then some. The Studio, in a single window, presents you with:

- project management information
- a global workspace in which you can open or work on not only Internet Studio-generated files, but also tasks running under such tools as VBScript and Visual J++
- more buttons and tools than you can shake a Web server at

For example, it offers a file display at the left of its window, and, among other things, a display of multimedia tools currently available on its right.

Live Web Sites

Microsoft might have code-named Internet Studio *Live Web Sites Are Us*. When you work with the Studio, every project you work with is displayed as it will appear on your Web server. What's more, the Studio will happily display multiple Web projects simultaneously. And Internet Studio's workspace includes an Explorer-based navigation capability for all such active projects.

Multiuser Capabilities

Related to its ability to manipulate a number of Web projects simultaneously is Internet Studio's multiuser, or perhaps more specifically multideveloper, support. The Studio allows more than one developer to work on the same Web project at the same time. Even spiffier, it allows its own users and users of FrontPage 97 to do so.

In a slightly different spin on its multiuser features, Internet Studio allows developers to designate a third-party browser such as Netscape Navigator, or even versions of Internet Explorer other than the bundled-with-the-Studio one, as the browser of choice for previewing Web projects.

Themes

As one of Microsoft's Internet Studio White Papers puts it, *a theme, in the Visual InterDev sense, is a collection of graphic images, formatting, fonts, and colors that look good together. When you apply a theme to your Web site, these elements are applied to all the pages in your site, making them all look good together.*

Although Internet Studio provides a library of canned themes, it also allows you to install those supplied by third-party vendors. It even helps you create your own themes, by allowing you to set up a directory with the theme's name that acts the parent for all theme element files. We've summarized the Studio's themes feature in Table 15-4.

Templates

Unlike themes, which more nearly resemble word processor styles, Internet Studio templates are blueprints or models for Web pages. Templates are themselves HTML or ASP files that have a mandated structure and into which you must insert predefined information.

Templates can contain any or all of these elements: HTML layout, HTML text, server scripting, client scripting, and placeholders known as Replaceable Parameters (RPs).

The Element	requires the name	and does the job of
Style sheet	Style1.css	controlling alignment, font, and font attributes for HTML tags.
	Style2.css	like Style1, but with the emphasis on formatting tabular material.
Background	Back1.jpg	Ensuring a smoother appearance for background images.
	Back2.jpg	like Back1, but not allowing left side image effects.
Graphic header	Header1.gif	serving as the beginning of default.htm, a Web site's home page.
Navigation	Nav1.jpg	tiling images horizontally behind navigation table.
	Button1.gif	providing a large blank button for text.
	Button2.gif	providing a small blank button for text.
	Down.gif	providing a Down button.
	Left.gif	providing a Left button.
	Right.gif	providing a Right button.
	Up.gif	providing an Up button.
Horizontal rules	Rule1.gif, Rule2.gif	providing rulers whose sizes can be varied.
Bullets	Bullet1.gif, Bullet2.gif, Bullet3.gif	providing bullets whose sizes can be varied.
Preview bitmap	Preview.bmp	providing a 256-color Windows palette.

Table 15-4. *Internet Studio Themes*

What's more, templates can be made up of just one file, or up to three related files. If you group files in this way in constructing a template, any of the members of the group can be any of the following:

- HTML
- ASP
- Active Layout (ALX)

When you apply a multifile template to a project, only one file is opened, but the information in all member files is used, based upon the contents of the opened file. And there's a pattern to what is opened when, as outlined in Table 15-5.

Why use multifile templates? That's easy. If you need to combine HTML text or tags with either ActiveX controls (for instance, to place active objects) or with Active Server processing (to accomplish, perhaps, database input), you need a multifile template.

More About Replaceable Parameters

Table 15-6 summarizes the roles of Internet Studio's RPs.

A template made up of	will be applied based upon this file being opened
ASP, ALX, HTM	ALX
ASP, HTM	HTM
HTM, ALX	ALX
ASP, ALX	ALX
HTM	HTM
ASP	ASP
ALX	ALX

Table 15-5. *Internet Studio Templates*

The Replaceable Parameter	must be placed in this template file	and represents
<%#THEMENAME#%>	HTM or ASP	the theme name, and therefore the project name. When Internet Studio's Template Wizard encounters this RP, it will prompt you for the actual theme name.
<%#DATACONNECTION#%>	ASP	a live data connection. When Internet Studio's Template Wizard encounters this RP, it will prompt you for the actual connection name.
<%#FILENAMEWITHOUT EXTENSION#%>, <%#FILENAMEWITH EXTENSION#%>	HTM or ASP	allows you to set up a point at which the template's name can be inserted into any documents created by the template.

Table 15-6. *Internet Studio Template Replaceable Parameters*

Internet Studio Ingredients

Now that you have seen some of the ways Internet Studio weaves its components together, it's time to scrutinize those ingredients more closely.

Active Server Pages

ActiveX Server's basic constituent is the Active Server Page (ASP) file, one example of which the following code (which includes HTML code that will display the phrase "Beat 'em, Bucs!" three times, each time in a larger type size) illustrates. An ASP file contains ASCII text formatted as either HTML tags and directives, script (that is, server-executable commands), or text that will be displayed literally.

```
<HTML>
<p>
<% For I=3 TO 6 %>
<FONTSIZE=<%=i%>
Beat 'Em, Bucs!<BR>
</FONT>
<%NEXT%>
</HTML>
```

Pop Quiz The sample ASP file just shown includes not only HTML tags for page formatting, but also HTML that is associated with server scripting logic. Can you distinguish between these elements? (Answer at the end of the chapter; don't peek.)

ASP script is not, as the name might suggest, a separate executable file. Rather, in an ASP context, script refers to commands made up of ActiveX or HTML tags that will be processed by the ActiveX Server engine.

COM and DCOM

In the context of ActiveX and Internet Studio, the acronym COM refers, not to a port, but rather to the idea of the Component Object Model, Microsoft's paradigm for the modular design of ActiveX tools. DCOM simply means Distributed Component Object Model. Figure 15-1 depicts a DCOM-based Web service.

What is the impact of COM and DCOM on your Web development and services? Simply this: Any components that are processor hogs (and with today's Web aesthetics, that means almost all components) can be distributed to secondary servers to increase the efficiency of user request processing. Such distributed processing is transparent to the developer, since it is ActiveX Server scripting on the Web server that manipulates the remote component.

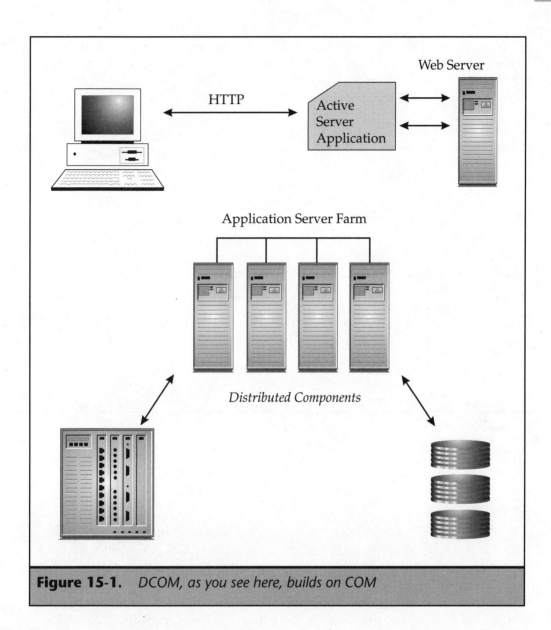

Figure 15-1.   *DCOM, as you see here, builds on COM*

Database Tools

As you might expect, Internet Studio's database connectivity features rely on Microsoft's ODBC standard. Therefore, the Studio's visual tools support any ODBC-compliant Database Management System (DBMS), including but not limited to IBM DB/2, Informix, Microsoft Access, Microsoft SQL Server, Microsoft Visual FoxPro, and Oracle.

Internet Studio's most significant database tools are

- Data View
- design-time ActiveX controls
- database Wizards
- Query Designer
- Database Designer

All these tools rely on Microsoft's concept of Active Data Objects. Active Data Objects (ADO) provide flexible database connectivity within Internet Studio applications, by accomplishing manipulation of database-defined data types. Such data types can even include images such as GIF and JPG. On demand, these and other database-related objects can be retrieved and written into Web pages.

As important, if not more so, the ADO model includes object properties that let you carry out tasks such as:

- configuring query timeouts
- customizing error handling
- defining cursor options
- fine-tuning result set scrolling
- setting locking levels
- setting up login timeouts

Data View

Internet Studio's Data View is a visual interface to all databases within a Web site that are being used by a given Web project. Data View does more than just display these links. It establishes a live connection to each active database. For this reason, developers work directly with real-world data when they design Web applications under Internet Studio. Data View can even supply details about objects and properties within these live databases. Such information includes stored procedures related to specific tables, table definitions, table field types, and table key structures. Internet Studio can present you with information on a variety of ODBC datasources. Such displays are presented in the classic file system tree manner.

Data View is available to both Query Designer and Database Designer, and can converse with any ODBC-compliant database.

Design-Time ActiveX Controls

Now we're getting into really neat stuff. Design-time ActiveX controls are a new subset of this ActiveX feature that automatically generate server-side scripting, including even such relatively sophisticated commands as those that connect to databases within a Web site, query connected databases, or present query results.

An example of a design-time control is the Data Command control, which allows you to:

- connect to an ODBC data source

- visually build a query against that connection, with Internet Studio's Query Designer

- sit back and relax, since a properly used Data Command control will generate all query-related ActiveX Server scripting and automatically add the scripting to the appropriate Active Server Page

Database Wizards

Internet Studio's database Wizards help a developer to create custom, database-driven HTML forms. One example of these database Wizards is the Data Form Wizard shown in Figure 15-2; we chose this step from the Wizard's sequence of tasks at random.

The Data Form Wizard automatically spawns HTML and ActiveX Server scripting, which in turn generate HTML forms directly linked to databases. And since Internet Studio's database Wizards produce standard HTML and ActiveX Server scripting, you can customize that HTML or scripting as needed.

Query Designer

Query Designer is sure to be one of the Internet Studio components you'll rely on most heavily. Query Designer:

- allows you to visually construct complex SQL statements

- creates Data Manipulation Language (DML) for SELECT, INSERT, UPDATE, and DELETE queries

- works with any ODBC data source

For instance, Query Designer can generate inqueries that employ the Boolean operators AND, OR, and NOT.

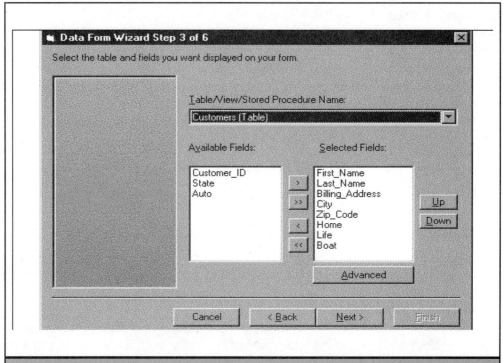

Figure 15-2. *Internet Studio's Data Form Wizard allows you to use HTML to manipulate an ODBC database*

Here's a walkthrough of the general steps involved in using Query Designer:

1. Open a live data source.

2. Drag one of its tables directly into a design pane of the Query Designer window.

3. Select fields from the table.

4. View the SQL statement, as it is being constructed, in the SQL pane.

5. If need be, modify this SQL statement, and view the changes in the query design pane.

6. As we all should but often don't, test your work by executing, once again by means of the query design pane, the SQL statement just generated.

7. View test results in results in Query Designer's results pane.

You can also use the SQL pane to carry out Database Definition Language (DDL) commands against an ODBC data source, create stored procedures, and execute SQL queries.

Database Designer

If you're running SQL Server 6.5, you've come a long way, baby, from the days of laborious, pencil-at-the-ready design and definition of databases and their schemas. Internet Studio provides a Database Designer for SQL Server 6.5.

With this Designer you can

- Create databases
- Define relationships between tables
- Generate DDL scripts
- Modify the data and database properties of existing databases
- Modify the structure of existing databases
- Perform such tasks as changing the data type of fields to be retrieved or manipulated by an SQL query

Database Designer hopes to add support for other DBMSs in the near future.

Management Tools

According to an engineer of some renown, *The more you over-tech the plumbing, the easier it is to stop up the drains.* Internet Studio may be one of the few technologies of which this is not true, because of its built-in management tools. Let's look at these more closely now.

The Project System

Internet Studio's project system is reflected in and used through its Project window.

This Project window offers you a number of Web site management tools, such as the ability to select, and then create databases on, a specific Web server; through its File View, the ability to add, copy, delete, edit, or rename any file on a selected Web site; and the ability to import content files and directories into a selected Web site, through the Import File and Import Folder commands.

The Project window also lets you use the Copy Web command to move an entire Web (you read that right) from one server to another. It even gives you, through a simple right-click on any object in a selected Web site, the means to view property information for that object. Such details include

- all of a file's incoming and outgoing links
- date when file was most recently modified
- file size

Automatic Link Repair

Internet Studio's ability to automatically track and manage links is surely one of its greatest strengths.

Let's suppose, for instance, that you've renamed a content file. Internet Studio will, with no instruction needed from you, automatically search out all pages on your Web site whose URLs include that file. Then, Internet Studio will repair such references to reflect the new file name, thereby preventing broken links. The Studio will also automatically prevent or repair damage to links due to deleted files or pages, moved files or pages, or the restructuring of any Web site it has generated.

Link View

Link View is the Internet Studio tool that gives you a graphical look at your Web site, visually presenting the logical relationship of pages within it. Link View can

- alert you to broken links by displaying these in red
- expand or collapse a view to show as many pages as needed
- filter a view to display any combination of documents, executable components, external files, HTML pages, multimedia files, primary links, or secondary links
- present icons that depict file type, such as HTML, ASP, GIF, or JPG, and more
- show external as well as internal links
- show links from an HTML page to other such pages in or outside your Web site

When you remember that all this information is available at design time and in the context of a live data connection, you can appreciate the value of Link View.

Visual SourceSafe

Programmers and developers who have had any contact with UNIX-based applications will feel right at home with the Internet Studio management tool Visual SourceSafe. It can be considered a GUI descendant of the UNIX Source Code Control System (SCCS).

Under Visual SourceSafe, file check-in and check-out controls can be applied to all files in a Web site. Visual SourceSafe also provides revision tracking and merging, thereby allowing you to accomplish such administrative tasks as reinstating an earlier, or moving to a later, version of a file, or comparing the differences between two versions of a file.

Internet Studio and Visual SourceSafe are fully and transparently integrated. And since SourceSafe runs on the Internet Studio server, you can put any Web project created with the Studio under SourceSafe control without even having to load SourceSafe to development workstations. Table 15-7 summarizes the capabilities of Visual SourceSafe.

Content-Manipulation with FrontPage 97

Internet Studio includes its own version of Microsoft's FrontPage 97 HTML editor. This common ground for content editing allows teams developing Web projects to use a variety of scripting and controls tools, and at the same time maintain homogeneity in the look and feel of the information manipulated by those tools.

Client-Side Script Wizard

Internet Studio's client-side Script Wizard, which made its debut in the ActiveX Control Pad, is driven by a visual interface that allows you to connect user-initiated events such as mouse clicks with appropriate actions, such as playing a video clip.

Script Wizard allows you to:

- associate multiple actions with a single user-initiated event
- select an event from the Event Pane to associate it with an action selected from the action pane
- view all events associated with an ActiveX Control, in Script Wizard's Event Pane

Using this SourceSafe feature	provides you with
automatic creation of SourceSafe projects	transparent generation and maintenance, on your Web server, of all projects
file check-in and check-out	upon requests by developers to edit individual files from a Web project, the explicit check-out of the file in the SourceSafe database, before the developer can actually open the file
	automatic notification to a developer who attempts to check out a file which is already open and in use
automatic generation of a read-only file for developers who request a file already checked out	explicit check-in of files upon their being released by a developer, thereby marking them as available to other members of the design team
automatic addition of elements to a SourceSafe-monitored project	the transparent placing of new content, HTML, or ASP files under SourceSafe control

Table 15-7. *An Overview of Visual SourceSafe*

Script Wizard accomplishes all this by automatically generating script code to be added to specific HTML pages. Script Wizard can produce either VB Script or JScript code, depending on what you tell it you prefer. And Script Wizard doesn't prevent you from churning out such code yourself; its code-entry window is included for just that purpose.

HTML Layout Editor

Like its client-side Script Wizard, Internet Studio's 2.5D, or frame-based, HTML Layout Editor was introduced in the ActiveX Control Pad. This editor resembles a Visual Basic form, and allows you to place multiple ActiveX controls very precisely within a Web page. And we mean *very* precisely. The

Studio's HTML Layout Editor gives you close control over x-coordinate, y-coordinate, and z-coordinate placement of controls. Such precision is especially useful in DHTML, which emphasizes depth and texture in a page.

What distinguishes Internet Studio's HTML Layout Editor from other, earlier such tools is its ability to incorporate, into the pages it helps create, World Wide Web Consortium (W3C) compliant syntax for placement and layering control of Web pages.

This syntax relies on style sheet attributes defined in a W3C draft specification for cascading style sheets.

You can review this specification at the URL:

```
http://www.w3.org/pub/WWW/TR/WD-layout.html
```

Image Composer

Image Composer, one aspect of which is shown in Figure 15-3, allows you to create and customize images which are to be included in a Web site.

Image Composer doesn't mind if your experience as a graphic artist is limited to the occasional nervous doodle. It is friendly and full-featured enough to permit even the most all-thumbs among us to create, modify, and place images. Any Web site developed and maintained in Internet Studio can take advantage of Image Composer.

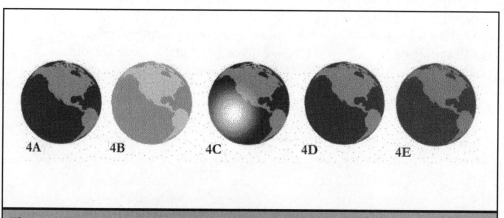

4A   4B   4C   4D   4E

Figure 15-3.   *Image Composer's Web site includes examples like the one on alpha channeling illustrated here*

In addition, Image Composer:

- can automatically save images to a project
- can be started from Internet Studio by clicking a toolbar icon, or by clicking images within the Studio
- handles most popular image file formats
- includes a gallery of Web-ready images, like the one shown in the following illustration:

Saturn.mic
(17K)

- reads Adobe PhotoShop files without any intervening filtering

Music Producer

Today, flashy Web images; tomorrow, sound. Internet Studio includes not only Image Composer but also Music Producer, a tool that allows you to create sound effects for your Web site. Music Producer shouldn't be confused with MIDI-based technologies. It will not, for example, permit you to plug your guitar or harmonica into your PC to create tablatures for the ditties you play. Rather, Music Producer relies on another Microsoft technology, named, in a flash of inspiration by the folks in Redmond, Microsoft Music Technology (MMT).

Music Producer, shown in Figure 15-4, streamlines the creation of Web-related sound effects by providing you with dozens of musical styles such as samba and swing, a collection of musical moods such as up-tempo,

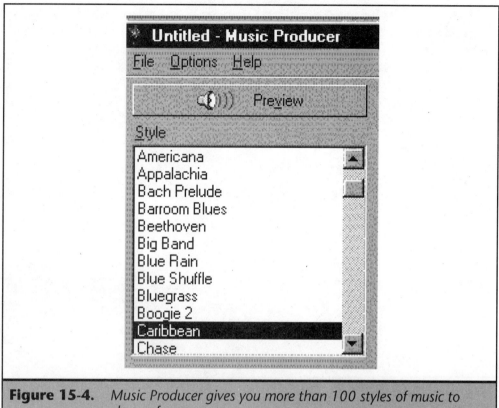

Figure 15-4. *Music Producer gives you more than 100 styles of music to choose from*

and even a set of simulated musical instruments. All this is presented to and used by you through a single screen.

Media Manager

After you've cut and pasted with Image Composer and marimba-ed with Music Producer, how can you keep the fruits of all that creativity straight? Use Media Manager.

Media Manager helps you track and manage Web components, including HTML files, image files, sound clips, and video clips. Media Manager, which uses Windows NT/95 Explorer navigation of the file system, also offers thumbnail previews of images, like the one shown in Figure 15-5.

Media Manager can also preview such material as sound and video clips in its Explorer pane.

Answer to Pop Quiz

The ASP file shown in Figure 15-2 has three lines of server scripting logic. Table 15-8 explains these scripting elements.

Figure 15-5. *Among other things, Media Manager can produce thumbnails of files of a number of formats, including the video file whose thumbnail is shown here*

The scripting element	tells the server to
`<% For I=3 TO 6 %>`	do whatever you're about to tell it to do three times
`<FONTSIZE=<%=i%>`	make the font size equal to the current value of the parameter I
`<%NEXT%>`	go back to the beginning of the loop, that is, to the line that reads <% For I=3 TO 6 %>, and run through the whole process again, as long as the parameter I hasn't reached the value 6 yet

Table 15-8.   *Logic in ASP Script Files*

Thumbnail Review

1. Several application suites can make it easier for you to create and implement multimedia Web pages.

2. Microsoft's Internet Studio is an integrated Web development environment.

3. Internet Studio can run under Windows 95, Windows NT Server 4.0 and up, and Windows NT Workstation 4.0 and up.

4. Internet Studio provides several tools that make it easier to build interaction with databases into a Web page.

5. Internet Studio provides several tools that facilitate building multimedia content into a Web page.

Looking Ahead

In Chapter 16, we'll investigate another Web development suite—Sapphire. We'll work with Sapphire to incorporate sound into the page we're developing as a contribution to the members of the NWU.

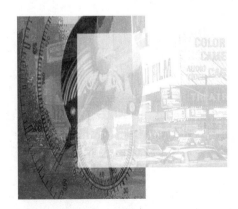

Chapter Sixteen

Using DHTML to Incorporate Sound in a Web Page

In a page such as the one we're building as a gift to the members of the NWU, sound serves as a backdrop or an accent, but no more. In some environments, though, sound can be one of the major forms of information presentation of the page. What spans these scenarios is this—whatever role sound plays in a Web document, you can deal with it, like everything else in that document, as a file that you manipulate through standard syntax.

In this chapter, we'll discuss

- the file types available to audio content
- the HTML tags that you can apply to these files
- tools that expedite that application

Audio File Formats

Files that contain sound effects, music, and so on, and that can be distributed across the Web, fall into several categories, based upon the format used to store the material and the standards upon which that formatting in turn rests. Among the most significant standards and formats are

- 8-bit sample
- AIFF and AIFF-C, Apple's Audio Interchange File Format and Audio Interchange File Format-Compressed, respectively
- Amiga IFF, Interchange File Format
- MIDI, or Musical Instrument Digital Interface
- MPEG, the Moving Picture Expert Group standard (not format) for audio
- RIFF Waveform, the Reserved Interchange File Format employed by Windows-of-whatever-stripe sound files
- SND, or sound (really) format files, which can be found on UNIX, DOS, MAC, and Windows systems
- Sun/NeXT, the sound file format used by Sun Microsystems and NeXT workstations

Table 16-1 summarizes these formats.

This format	involves	can be encoded as this MIME type	samples an audio stream at about this rate	and uses this degree of compression
8-bit sample	no coding or compression, just raw sound	none	8 KHz, or 800 samples per second	
AIFF	the audio formatting scheme developed and used by Apple, and also used by Silicon Graphics	audio/x-aiff	either 8 or 16 KHz	none
AIFF-C	the compression-enabled version of AIFF	audio/x-aiff	either 8 or 16 KHz	about 6 to 1, meaning that a 36,000-byte file would end up as a 6,000-byte unit
Amiga IFF	an 8-bit format peculiar to Amiga	audio/basic	8 KHz	none
MIDI	can be used on any computer equipped with the appropriate synthesizer and/or player; has the extension .mid	none	not sampled	none
MPEG	many vendors of audio software and hardware have developed algorithms and programs that follow this standard; files that adhere to it have the extension .mp2, and can be found in DOS, Widows, MAC, and UNIX environments	audio/mpeg	about 44 KHz	about 20 to 1, bringing a file of 100,000 bytes down to 5,000

Table 16-1. *Common Audio Formats*

This format	involves	can be encoded as this MIME type	samples an audio stream at about this rate	and uses this degree of compression
RIFF Waveform	Windows' sound format; files using it have the extension .wav	audio/x-wav	either about 44 KHz or 8 KHz, depending upon whether the sound is being presented and received as static (mono) or streamed (stereo)	none
SND	a platform-unspecified format; files using it most frequently have the extension .snd			
Sun/NeXT	the audio format employed by Sun workstations, which can accommodate either 8- or 16-bit samples, and which supplies the file name extension .au			

Table 16-1. *Common Audio Formats* (continued)

Each of these formats, in its own way, relies upon three parameters:

■ The number of bits each sample includes, most frequently 8 or 16.

■ The number of channels across which output will be distributed, most frequently one or two, analogous to mono or stereo home sound systems. A mono sound system sends its single channel or stream of output to both its speakers; a stereo system splits its output into two streams, and directs each to a separate speaker, in order to simulate the sound's being all around or "right there in the room with you."

- The rate at which an audio stream is sampled; for instance, 8000 samples taken per second (you read that right).

Similarly, each of these audio formats can be presented as

- what might best be termed static sound—that is, audio that is downloaded as any other file would be, and for which a user must wait as he or she would for any other download

- streamed sound, which emulates listening to a radio broadcast, in that the audio file is downloaded so the user can experience it as if he or she were hearing it live

There's much more involved, of course, but we needn't go into the methodology or physics of audio files. Instead, we'll simply manipulate such files. But before we do that, we'll examine Sapphire Web, the tool that will allow us to jazz up our pages.

Sapphire Web

Sapphire Web/Server, from Bluestone Software of Mount Laurel, New Jersey, was developed to address the need for an alternative to CGI-based Web client/server relationships. Such relationships have a number of shortcomings, including

- lack of scalability to high-volume, highly interactive environments
- poor performance in such environments
- failure to retain connections to data sources

Let's explore these problems a little further.

CGI's Lack of Scalability and Performance

For every http request a CGI-based Web server receives, a CGI process must be executed. Such processes are not memory paupers. Far from it, in fact; CGI code tends to chew up an appreciable amount of RAM. This appetite bodes no good to Web sites that anticipate a large number of simultaneous users. If those users are treated to such multimedia delights as audio or video, RAM-hungry CGI will devour memory even more quickly. It is even possible, under such circumstances, that a server might simply run out of memory, and hang.

CGI's Failure to Retain Connections to Databases

CGI scripts are known as *nonpersistent executables*. What this means is that they do something, and then leave memory until the next time they're called upon. For a dynamic Web page, this may not be a good idea. Recall that we just spent several chapters discussing the intricacies of Web page/database interaction. In a strictly CGI-driven page, every time a user wished to query a database, even if those inquiries were related and done one after another, three things would have to occur:

- A connection with the database would have to be established.
- The user would then carry out the single query.
- The application would then have to disconnect from the database.

Not the height of efficiency, to say the least.

Sapphire and CGI

Sapphire/Web's Application Server lacks CGI's limitations. Sapphire is rather like the Battery Bunny—it keeps going and going, executing without interruption regardless of the number of user requests to which it has responded. To the administrator or programmer, this means that CPU and memory are used more efficiently. To users, Sapphire's ability to forego the connect/query/disconnect cycle common to CGI means quicker production and display of results.

Sapphire Features

Before we walk you through loading and using Sapphire, let's take a moment to tick off its most important features:

- exists as a compiled C, C++, or Java executable, thereby providing efficient processing
- can generate 100% Java-based applications
- can specify behavior particular to an individual application

- automatic start/stop and load balancing
- can specify, programmatically, server timeout and clean-up

Now let's present a scenario that illustrates Sapphire's software architecture. Imagine that you're using Netscape Communicator to view the project page, and you click the page object that offers display of the Experts directory. Imagine further (would it were true; we'd love to have such a machine) that the Web server on which the page is housed is a DEC Alpha running Windows NT Server 4.0 as its operating system, and Internet Information Server as its Web server. IIS would accept the request that your click represents, and then query a Sapphire configuration file that had previously been cached in memory. This file would then tell IIS where to find the Sapphire process that must handle the incoming request.

As we've seen, such requests often involve some sort of database interaction. Whatever that interaction consists of, once it is complete, Sapphire passes its result back to IIS, which in turn hands it off to Communicator.

Sapphire's Web Application Server can even support multiple Web servers.

Sapphire Platforms

Sapphire is nothing if not versatile. Table 14-2 summarizes the range of environments in which it can run.

Installing Sapphire Under Windows NT 4.0

Loading Sapphire was simplicity itself. We didn't even have to click a thing; the CD that contained the release we worked with also included an autorun feature that started the installation process as soon as we placed the CD in the drive. Sapphire presented the Welcome screen illustrated in Figure 16-1, and then led us through the usual sequence of Wizard-based installation instructions.

As we loaded Sapphire, we were also able to configure it to a large degree. For instance, as Figure 16-2 shows, we had the chance to choose C/C++, Java, or both as a development environment.

The install routine also gives you the option, as depicted in Figure 16-3, of loading the Java Developers Kit (JDK) immediately, or at another time.

In this area	Sapphire can work with
Operating system	■ DEC Alpha (NT and UNIX) ■ Hewlett Packard Series 9000 ■ IBM RS/6000 ■ Pyramid ■ SGI ■ Siemens Nixdorf ■ SUN ■ Windows 95 ■ Windows NT
Databases	■ DB2 ■ Informix ■ JDBC ■ Microsoft SQL Server ■ ODBC ■ Oracle ■ Sybase
Browsers and client-side scripting languages	Netscape Navigator, Microsoft Explorer, any HTML version 2.0 or higher, VRML, Java, ActiveX
Web servers	Netscape, Microsoft, Apache, CERN, NCSA, Open Market, Process, or any http, shttp, or ssl server
HTML editors	FrontPage, Netscape Navigator Gold, Hot Dog, Hot Metal, Notepad, vi, emacs, or any editor that supports HTML version 2.0 or higher
Code management applications	PVCS, Visual Source Safe, MKS Source Integrity, ClearCase, SCCS, RCS, or any source code control system

Table 16-2.   *Platforms Supported by Sapphire*

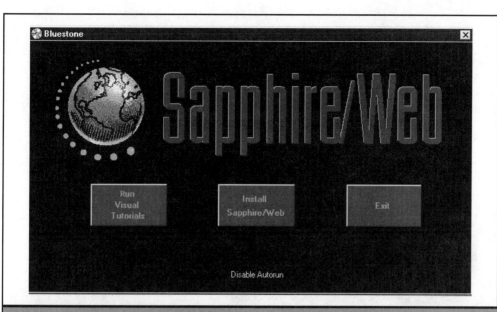

Figure 16-1. *Sapphire's opening reinforces the product's name by using a sapphire-blue foreground*

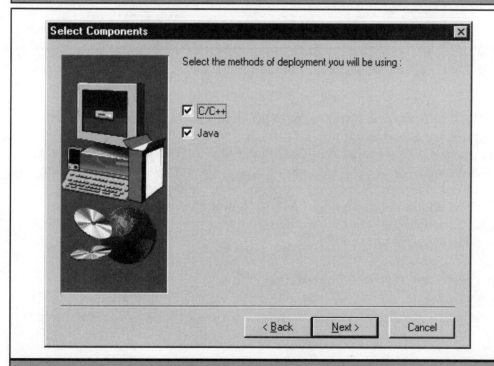

Figure 16-2. *Sapphire offers the best of two worlds*

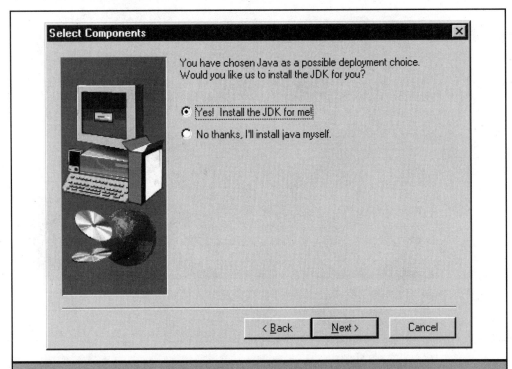

Figure 16-3. *We liked the chatty tone of Sapphire's messages and prompts as much as we liked what they represented*

The product's install routine gives you many other options, such as which components to load; Figure 16-4 shows the list of available components.

After we indicated that we wanted everything it had to offer, and made a few more installation decisions, Sapphire's load completed with the screen illustrated in Figure 16-5; the whole process took about seven minutes.

After rebooting (which under NT can take almost as long as it took us to install Sapphire), we saw the new program group shown in Figure 16-6 when we clicked Programs from the NT Start menu.

Getting to Know Sapphire

There was absolutely nothing organized, let alone scientific, about our initial work with Sapphire. We simply wandered around, clicking program group

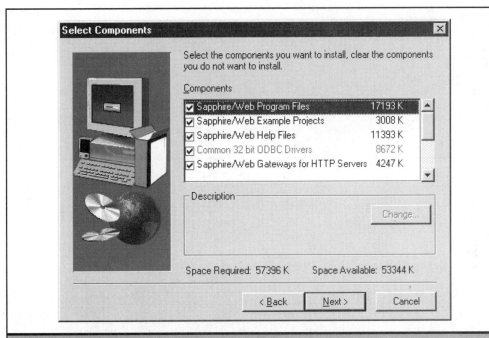

Figure 16-4. *While it lists available components, Sapphire won't allow you complete control of them. For instance, you must include ODBC.*

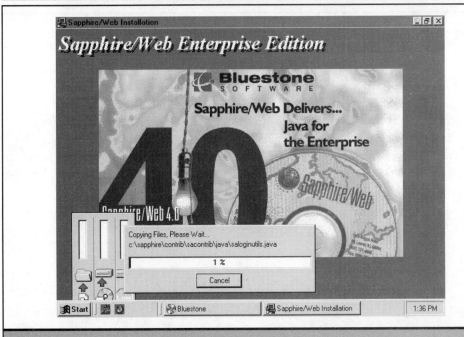

Figure 16-5. *Sapphire indicates how its installation progresses*

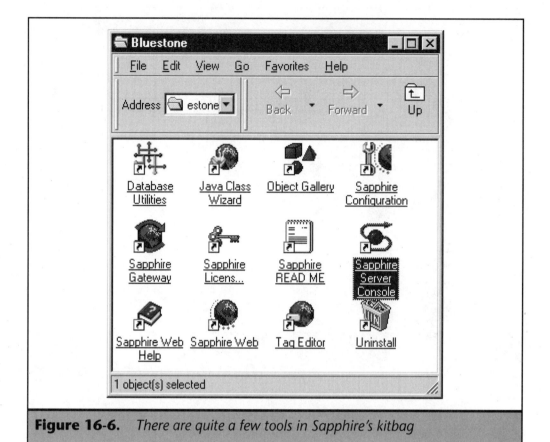

Figure 16-6. *There are quite a few tools in Sapphire's kitbag*

icons at random. Curious about its potential as an HTML editor, we looked at Tag Editor, shown in Figure 16-7.

Then, wondering what there could be left to do after the very thorough installation process, we tried Sapphire Database Utilities, whose main screen Figure 16-8 illustrates.

We found that, among other things, we could define database interaction parameters, as Figure 16-9 shows.

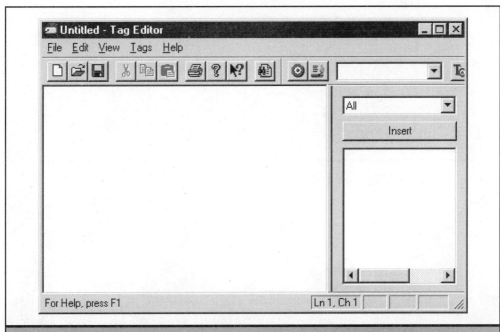

Figure 16-7. *Sapphire's Tag Editor allows you to create, delete, modify, and otherwise massage HTML tags*

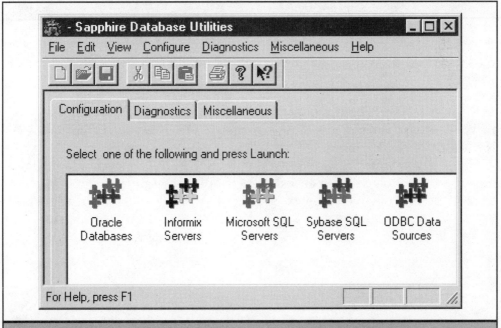

Figure 16-8. *The suite provides tools to manage a number of the most important RDBMSs*

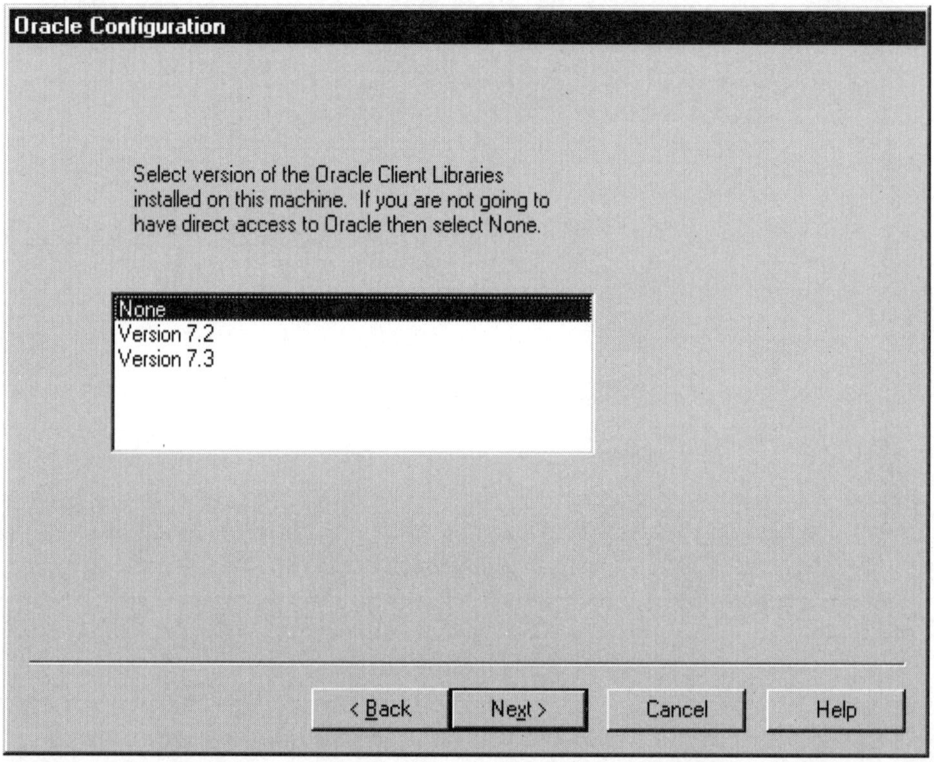

Figure 16-9. *You can define database interaction parameters for any of the databases that Sapphire supports, as we did here*

We kibitzed a little longer, setting up the HTTP server parameters Figure 16-10 illustrates.

Then, remembering that we were supposed to be building sound into the project page, not playing, we checked out Sapphire's sample applications, about 25 percent of which are shown in Figure 16-11, thinking there might be

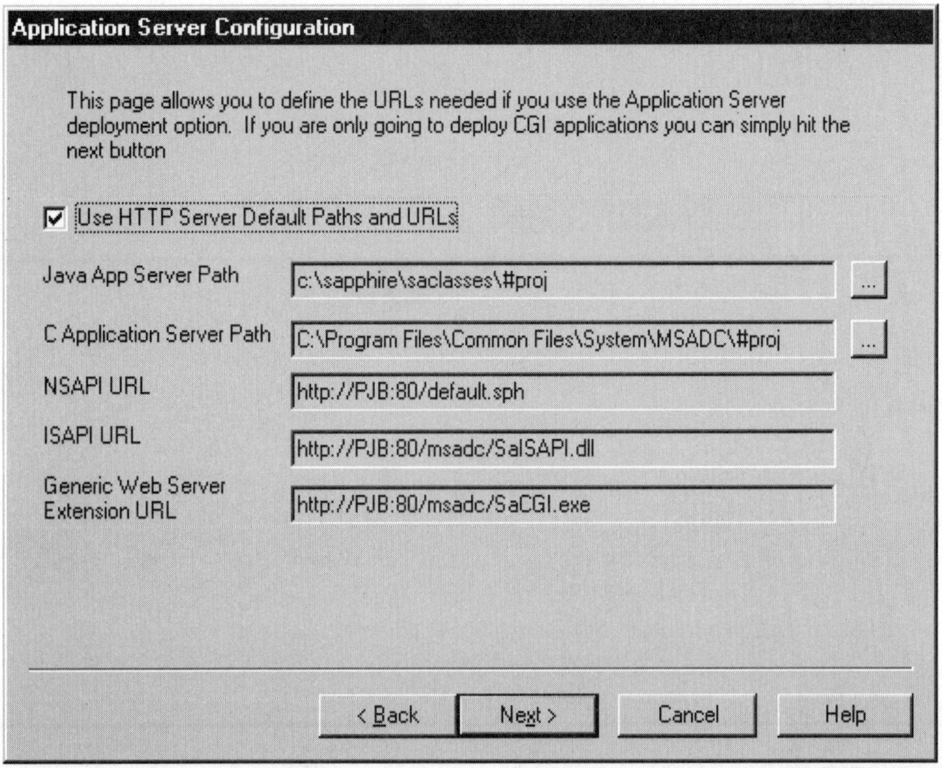

Application Server Configuration

This page allows you to define the URLs needed if you use the Application Server deployment option. If you are only going to deploy CGI applications you can simply hit the next button

☑ Use HTTP Server Default Paths and URLs

Java App Server Path	c:\sapphire\saclasses\#proj
C Application Server Path	C:\Program Files\Common Files\System\MSADC\#proj
NSAPI URL	http://PJB:80/default.sph
ISAPI URL	http://PJB:80/msadc/SalSAPI.dll
Generic Web Server Extension URL	http://PJB:80/msadc/SaCGI.exe

< Back   Next >   Cancel   Help

Figure 16-10. *We defined HTTP server parameters for Sapphire that included almost all of the application's defaults*

one in this list titled *Here's How to Do Audio for the Page You're Designing.* (So we tend to over-optimism. So what?)

Finding no ready sample from which to work, we turned to the techniques outlined in the remaining sections of this chapter.

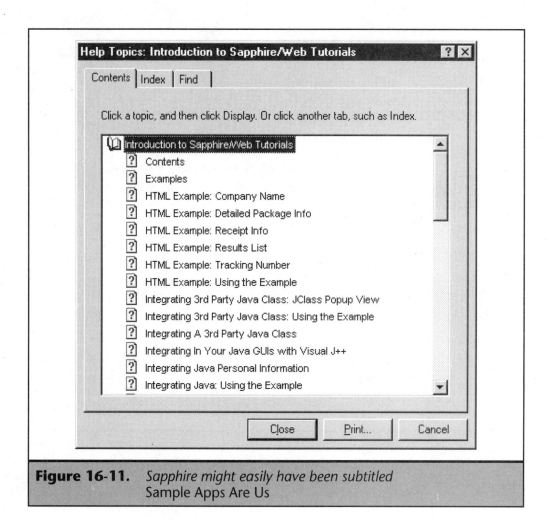

Figure 16-11. *Sapphire might easily have been subtitled Sample Apps Are Us*

Sapphire and Sound

However well-organized and professionally implemented, Sapphire—like Internet Studio, IntraBuilder, and many others—is only a tool, and you can only use it effectively if you understand what you want to do with it. This section, therefore, recaps our work with Sapphire to include static sound in the project page. Then it reviews Sapphire's audio streaming capabilities, for those of you who must implement more sophisticated sound distribution than that page requires.

Static (Unstreamed) Sound

In Chapter 2, in the section "Defining the Activity of Dynamic Elements," we used a WAV file containing the sound of a cat yowling as the only audio element of the page. Although this file can be considered dynamic in that it will only be presented to users as an emphasis of and a warning against attempts to take some unauthorized or nonexistent action, it can more correctly be thought of as static, since the file

- will always be physically present in the page
- will be distributed as a single distribution of a short sound clip—that is, no streaming will be needed

By keeping the sound clip short, we not only avoid subjecting users to the fingernails-on-blackboard jitters a cat's yowl can produce, we also keep them from growing impatient while waiting for the clip to download and play. Bear in mind that sound files equal image files in their voracious disk storage appetites. Even a one-minute 8-bit (mono) recording can use about 150KB; a stereo sound sample of the same length can devour as much as 10MB of your drive. So, unless there's a good reason to do otherwise, keep your sound files simple and short. When incorporating static sound into a page, there's rarely any good reason to do otherwise.

Because we don't want users to be aware of the audio clip unless there's an error situation, we can't simply place a link to it in the code for the project page. (As you'll see in Chapter 17, however, this technique does suffice for many scenarios in which image files must be embedded in or accessed from a page.) Rather, we must code the page to reference the file automatically in those situations. The next two sections present such code.

Including Sound with JavaScript

We pulled up Sapphire's Tag Editor, opened the file that contains the HTML code for the project page, and added lines that follow the general JavaScript syntax

```
<TAG eventHandler="JavaScript Code">
```

In this syntax, TAG can be any HTML tag, while eventHandler is the name of some existing, or user-defined, JavaScript function or method that you want to kickstart in a given situation.

More Complete Sound-Related JavaScript Code

In our case, we want to display a message, and accompany it with the yowling sound clip, in any circumstances that constitute an error. Which is to say we must use the JavaScript method

```
document.write
```

as well as an anchor tag to reference our WAV file. Here's the code in more detail:

```
<HTML>
<!--Some intervening code, then...-->
<BODY>
<!--Some more intervening code, then...-->
<SCRIPT LANGUAGE="JavaScript">
var numframes = 1;
for (i=1; i<9; i++) {
<!--By beginning our loop at 1, we avoid messing with the overall window.-->
<!--What's more, we confine ourselves to those frames that have been
defined to-->
<!--forego any dynamic behavior, and in which, therefore,-->
<!--any keyboard or mouse input is superfluous.-->
if (( i = 1) || (i = 4) || (i = 5)) {
if (i=1)
{
 <P ALIGN=CENTER>
 BANNERIMG = parent.frame[i].open ("BANNERIMG.HTM" }onAbort =
 document.write (Please allow the image to finish loading.";
 <A> HREF= " ~/nwu_home/cat_yowl.wav" </A>
 </P>
break;
}
 <!--The condition onAbort encompasses a number of circumstances,
including-->
 <!--a user's clicking a browser's Stop icon.-->
if (i=4)
< !--Now we repeat the same sequence for Frame 4...-->
if (i=5)
<!--and again for Frame 5...-->
}
for (i=1; i<9; i++) {
```

```
if (( i = 2) || (i = 3) || (i = 6) || (i = 7) || (i = 8) {
<!--Now we can deal with the frames that are capable of dynamic behavior.-->
break;}
</SCRIPT>
</BODY>
</HTML>
```

Streaming and Sapphire

Although, at least at this stage of its evolution, the page we're building for the members of the NWU does not stream sound, many Web pages might benefit from such steady, quasi-live audio presentation. For example, the text displayed in the Milton Reading Room in Chapter 8 would certainly be enhanced if accompanied by a voice-over of the same text. Such a soundtrack would lose all effectiveness if it arrived at the user's ear in fits and starts, as would most likely happen if you simply referenced it with a link like that in the preceding section.

To stream James Earl Jones or some other sonorously voiced reader's rendering of Milton, the Reading Room's designers, working now in Sapphire, decided to add another tool to their kit. Operating under the limited budget common to academic institutions, they chose the shareware package Internet Audio Publisher version 2.4, a multiformat streaming audio tool that supports all Windows 3.x and 32-bit Windows operating systems. With this new tool, the Reading Room's designers could handle several fairly sophisticated publishing tasks, such as

- compressing or expanding as a means of converting to or from WAV or AU

- playing sound files in formats including AU, Sun/NeXT, and WAV

- recording in AU, SunNeXT, WAV, and more, at sample rates of 8000, 11000, 22000, and 44000 Hz

- streaming an audio file in Microsoft's GSM format, whether that file is sampled at 8000, 11025, 22050, or 44100 Hertz

- streaming audio files in formats such as TrueSpeech from any HTTP/1.0 or higher server

- uploading audio files and their accompanying metafiles or indices/playback instructions

▮ Thumbnail Review

1. Sound file formats include

- ▮ Amiga IFF, Interchange File Format
- ▮ MIDI, or Musical Instrument Digital Interface
- ▮ MPEG, the Motion Picture Experts Group standard (not format) for audio
- ▮ RIFF Waveform, the Reserved Interchange File Format supported by all versions of Windows
- ▮ SND, or sound format files, supported by UNIX, DOS, MAC, and Windows
- ▮ Sun/NeXT, the format used by Sun Microsystems and NeXT workstations

2. Sound file formats all represent, among other things, the rate at which a sound stream is sampled and the quality of sound reproduction—that is, mono or stereo.

3. You can incorporate audio into Web pages as downloadable clips or as streamed soundtracks.

4. Sapphire/Web, like other similar tool suites, can incorporate sound into Web pages through additions to the HTML code of a page, or through other scripting languages, such as Java or C++.

▮ Looking Ahead

In Chapter 17, we'll investigate another Web page development tool. We'll work with the shareware package Anansi to incorporate high-resolution images into the project page.

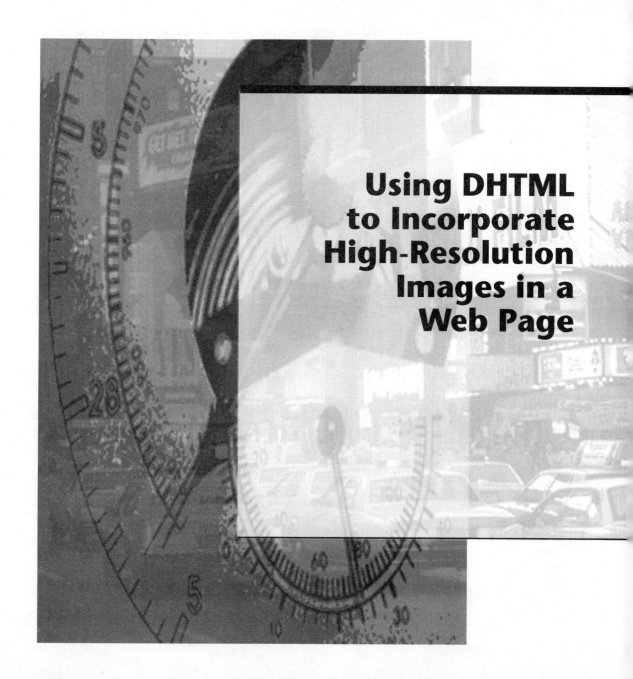

Chapter Seventeen

Using DHTML to Incorporate High-Resolution Images in a Web Page

Although the NWU page can do without streaming audio, it cannot forego images. High-resolution images can help the page better serve its audience. For instance, a user who queries the page for a definition of a term would better understand the nature of that term if explanatory text were accompanied by a photograph.

Like streaming audio, streaming video doesn't form part of the NWU page design at the moment. However, if the page evolves into anything like a full-function distance learning site, streaming video might have to be incorporated into it.

So, in this chapter, we'll investigate

- the file types available to high-resolution image content
- the HTML tags that you can apply to these files
- a simple tool called Anansi that can help you incorporate these images into your page

High-Resolution Image File Formats

Like Web sounds, the great majority of Web images fall into one of six categories, according to their format:

- AVI, that is, Microsoft's Video for Windows
- GIF, or Graphics Interchange Format, files
- JPEG, a standard for image compression from the Joint Photographic Expert Group
- MPEG-1 and MPEG-2, standards developed by the Moving Pictures Expert Group that differ from one another primarily in the compression ratios they can achieve
- QuickTime, originally Apple-specific, but now available for both UNIX and Windows platforms

Table 17-1 outlines the most widely used of these formats.

This format	delivers this number of frames per second	at this resolution	can be encoded as this MIME type	carries the file extension	and compresses at
AVI	about 30	about 320x240	video/ x-msvideo	.avi	about 7 to 1
GIF	not framed; that is, GIF applies only to still images	expressed not in pixels, but in the number of colors that can be represented; for the original GIF specification, 256	image/gif	.gif	about 4 or 5 to 1, resulting in images that require only 1/4 or 1/5 the storage
JPEG	not streamed, but rather still	supports full 24-bit color, which means that each of the 300,000+ pixels on a PC monitor can have 24 bits dedicated to specifying its hue	image/ peg	.jpg	from a low of about 7 to 1, to a high of over 20 to 1
MPEG	about 30	about 350x240 for MPEG-1; as much as 720x480 for MPEG-2	video/ mpeg, for both MPEG-1 and MPEG-2	.mpe, .mpeg, and .mpg for both MPEG-1 and MPEG-2:	as high as 200 to 1

Table 17-1.   *High-Resolution Image Formats*

Pop Quiz Although there are about the same number of commonly used image formats on the Web as there are sound formats, what characteristic, other than the nature of the content they deal with, separates these two format types?

As we did with sound files, we'll sidestep any discussion of the methodology or physics of image files. Instead, we'll just work with them. But before we do that, we'll introduce the tool we'll use: Anansi.

Anansi

The freeware application Anansi is at the far end of the complexity spectrum from suites like Sapphire/Web or Internet Studio. For example, as Figure 17-1 shows, Anansi has only one significant user interface to its authoring arm.

For a brief look at how Anansi came to be, and a message from its author, go to the URL http://www.xs4all.nl/~hbosma/ anansi/help/man_intr.html

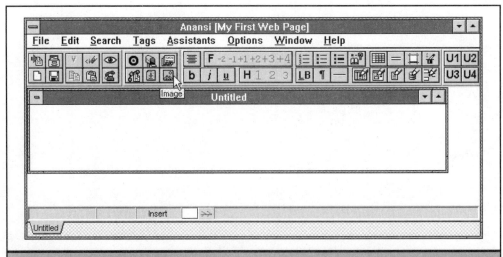

Figure 17-1. *From this single simple screen, you can do quite a bit with Anansi*

Now take a look at Figure 17-2; it gives you a glance at one part of Anansi's project management capabilities.

Anansi has other project management tools, like:

- a multi-part project manager, shown in Figure 17-3, and

- a palette editor, as Figure 17-4 illustrates.

Don't mislead yourself into thinking that Anansi is not to be taken seiously. In small or nascent Web sites, its simplicity could be a strength rather than a disadvantage. As Figure 17-5 shows, the application can generate syntactically correct, HTML 3.0-compliant code, which is a large part of what professional (and expensive) suites like Internet Studio are used to do.

To someone who's never dabbled in HTML, the automatic production of even this tiny bit of code would be impressive, and helpful.

Anansi even has its own sort of wizard; anyone wanting to add to a page but uncertain of the HTML needed could still accomplish the modification through the dialog box shown in Figure 17-6.

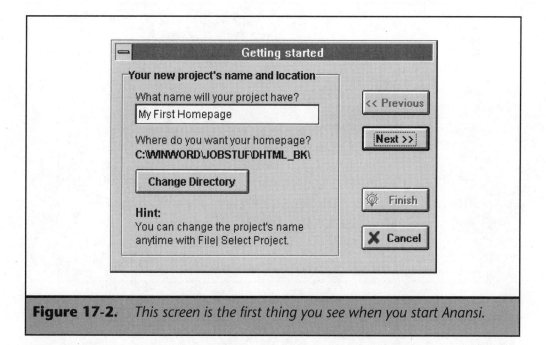

Figure 17-2. *This screen is the first thing you see when you start Anansi.*

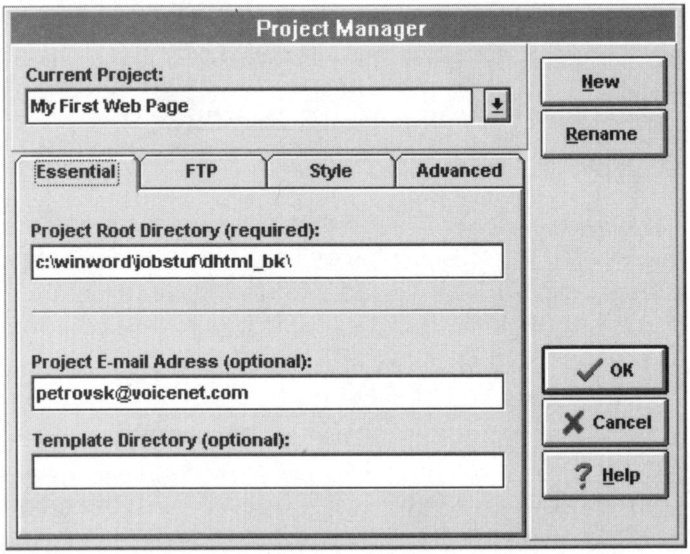

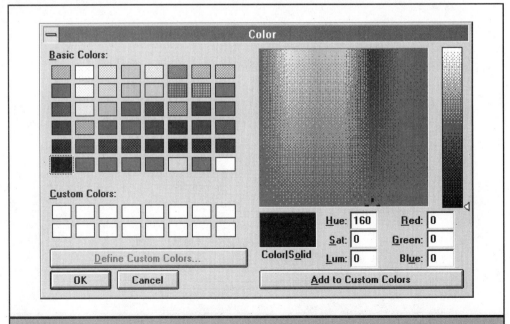

Figure 17-3. *Anansi's project Manager is compact but capable*

Figure 17-4. *This Anansi tool could be particularly useful in working with images*

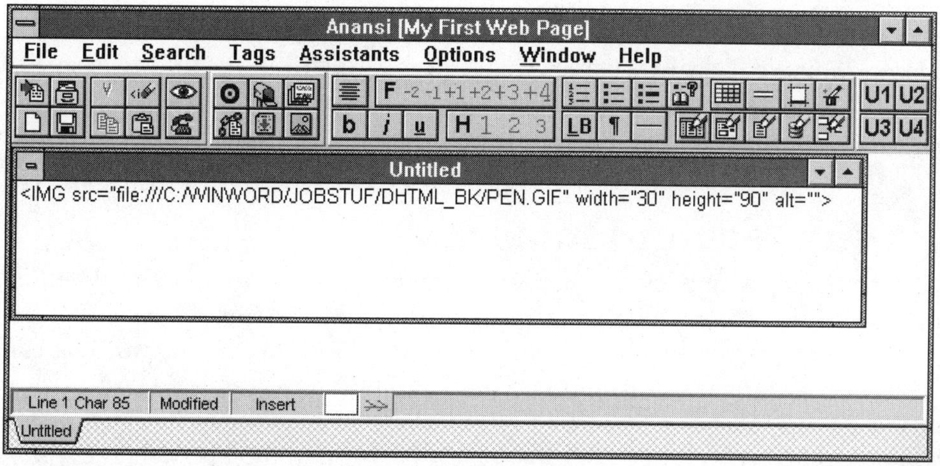

Figure 17-5. *Remember, more (interface, icons, and so on) is not necessarily better*

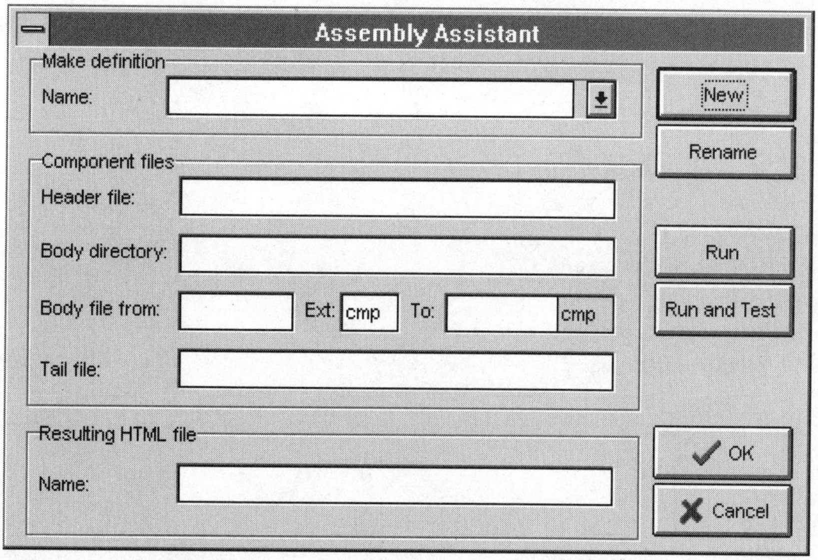

Figure 17-6. *With Anansi's Assembly Assistant, you can piece together HTML documents from other files*

Anansi and High-Res Images

In this section we'll explore using Anansi to include high-resolution images in the NWU page. We'll also research its role in incorporating streamed video images into Web pages.

Static (Unstreamed) Images

Once again, let's turn back to Chapter 2 for a moment. In the section "Defining the Activity of Dynamic Elements," we decided upon a banner image that would be dynamic in the context of containing changing content, but that can be considered static when its method of presentation is examined. We envisioned this image as consisting of the image of a quill pen initially imposed upon that of a PC; with the PC transparent to the user when the page is first displayed. This is a nice visual touch, but it doesn't constitute streaming.

As proved true with static audio page elements, static images, however high their resolution, require no cutting-edge code to implement; the scripting logic and DHTML tags we've become so familiar with will more than suffice.

Including High-Res Images with JavaScript

Anansi doesn't generate scripting code; it is, after all, a pared-down package. But through its HTML editor, you can incorporate code like the following into pages you've created with the application.

```
<HTML>
<!--Some intervening code, then...-->
<BODY>
<!--Some more intervening code, then...-->
<SCRIPT LANGUAGE="JavaScript">
var numframes = 1;
for (i=1; i<9; i++) {
<!--By beginning our loop at 1, we avoid messing with the overall
window.-->
<!--What's more, we confine ourselves to those frames that have
been defined to-->
<!--forego any dynamic behavior.-->
if (( i = 1) || (i = 4) || (i = 5)) {
if (i=1)
{
 <P ALIGN=CENTER>
 BANNERIMG = parent.frame[i].open ("HI_RES.JPG" }";
```

```
<!--With this single change, we've substituted a high-resolution copy of-->
<!--our banner image.-->
</P>
break;
}
if (i=4)
 <--! Now we can carry out similar sequences for Frame 4...-->
if (i=5)
 < !--   and again for Frame 5...-->
}
for (i=1; i<9; i++) {
if (( i = 2) || (i = 3) || (i = 6) || (i = 7) || (i = 8) {
 < !--Now we can deal with the frames that are capable of dynamic behavior.-->
break;}
</SCRIPT>
</BODY>
</HTML>
```

Streaming Video in JavaScript

To provide visitors to the NWU page with streamed video—that is, with videos whose size exceeds the capacity of local disk storage and that are presented as if they were being played on a VCR—new data communications software must enter the picture. We need special real-time protocols like the Video Datagram Protocol (VDP). VDP is what's known as an *adaptive protocol*. This means that it uses only available bandwidth while running over an IP network. VDP can adjust its data rates to accommodate the needs of the moment, and at the same time use efficient video formats and compression algorithms, such as MPEG1and MPEG2. So, by using scripting code like that in the section "Including High-Res Images with JavaScript" in combination with add-on tools like Vivo Streaming Video to handle protocol-related tasks, we can

- create video footage and digitize it with the appropriate equipment
- use already digitized video in a format like.avi
- use Vivo to convert our video file to an uploadable format
- upload the file to the appropriate part of a Web server's file system
- reference the video clip with code that sets parameters such as
- the name of the video player software to be used by client browsers

■ the size of the window to be devoted to the video, for example, `WIDTH=176 HEIGHT=144`

■ whether to autostart the video playback

■ whether to autostart the browser's video controls

Of course, you'll also have to ensure that users have the Vivo Player available.

Answer to Pop Quiz

The significant organizational distinction between Web audio and Web image formats is that image formats specifically take into account the differences inherent in static and streamed presentation, while the audio files do not.

Thumbnail Review

1. Widely-used Web mage file formats include

   ■ AVI

   ■ GIF

   ■ JPEG

   ■ MPEG-1

   ■ MPEG-2

   ■ QuickTime

2. The Web's image file formats, unlike its audio formats, take into account whether the content they represent will be static or streamed.

3. Like its audio elements, a Web page's images can be distributed as downloadable clips or as streamed—that is, progressively displayed—sequences.

4. Anansi, a freeware, can help simplify including images in Web pages through its ability to recognize a variety of image formats and to generate HTML code appropriate to those formats.

Looking Ahead

To paraphrase Gladys Knight and the Pips, "We've *almost* come to the end of our road." In Chapter 18, we'll pull together everything we've learned to this point.

Chapter Eighteen

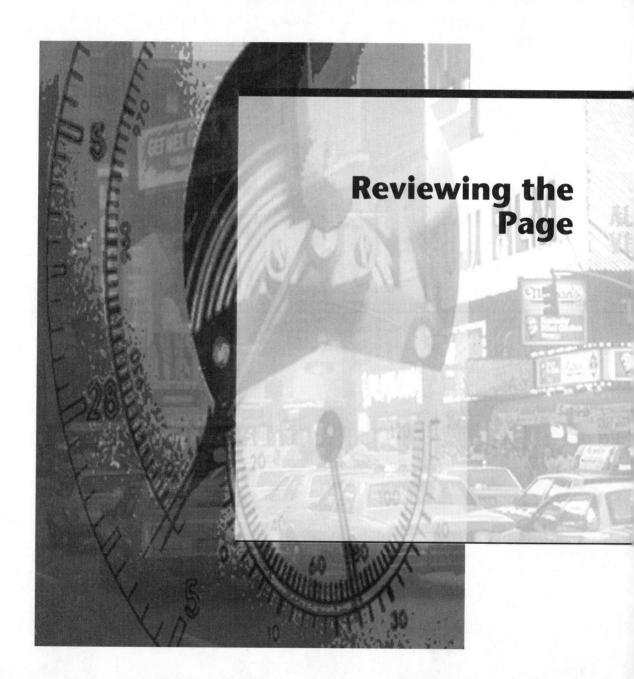

Reviewing the Page

This last chapter, unlike its predecessors, contains very little discussion of concepts. Rather, it consists primarily of code, in three categories:

■ the HTML source for the basic NWU page

■ a second level of HTML and scripting that the basic page draws upon

■ a number of HTML/scripting examples that present possible ways of implementing the page's more sophisticated dynamic behaviors

First, we'll take a moment to review the page's design requirements. Then we'll jump into the code.

Design Requirements

Here is a summary of the design requirements for the page we're building as a contribution to the membership of the NWU.

1. The page must:

   ■ act as a source of information on technical writing and editing for anyone seeking to break into those fields, but lacking a technical background

   ■ therefore supply information not only on writing and editing for technical, and in particular for computer-related topics, but also on the topics themselves

2. The page will contain only two visual elements, one of which will act as illustration of text-based information, and the other as a means of conveying the friendly feel we want the page to have.

3. The page will have three groups of elements that will remain static:

   ■ the page's banner—its content, font characteristics, and placement

   ■ the first paragraph of body text, which explains the page's purpose

   ■ the placement and composition of links, navigation buttons, and feedback/email prompts

4. The page will have three elements that will exhibit at least some degree of dynamic behavior:

   ■ the link to other sources of information on PCs

 ■ the image, in the page's banner, of a quill pen superimposed upon a PC

 ■ the WAV file linked to the page's navigation

Figure 18-1 depicts all the page's design requirements.

The Page's Code

Keep in mind that the code examples that make up the remainder of this chapter were created and tested locally—that is, on the PC, on which this book was written, rather than at a remote site. All the code works. But to implement it in your environment, you will have to tailor two of its most important factors to that environment:

 ■ the path names of all subsidiary HTML and content files

 ■ the path names of all referenced URLs

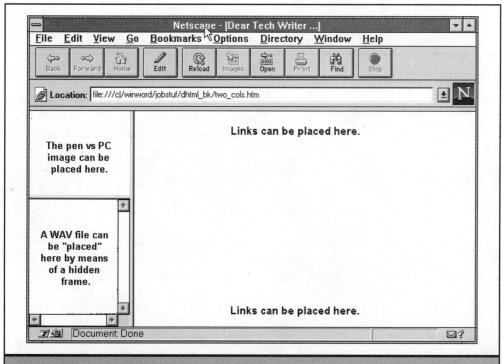

Figure 18-1. *This page satisfies all the requirements just noted*

Also, you should be aware that all the code in this chapter was tested and functioned under several versions of Netscape Navigator, including 1.2, 2.0, 3.0, and 4.0. However, if you're running Internet Explorer in any of its incarnations, or some other browser such as NCSA Mosaic, you may want to tweak this code slightly to get the same results we did. For example, we did all our scripting in JavaScript. So, if you're trying to port this code to an Internet Explorer 4.0 environment, the lines that read

```
SCRIPT LANGUAGE="JAVASCRIPT"
```

could be changed to

```
SCRIPT LANGUAGE="JSCRIPT"
```

We'll present the code for the NWU page in three categories:

- the basic page
- the second level
- more sophisticated dynamic behaviors

The Basic Page

As in any effective coding or programming, you should implement the design of a dynamic HTML page in a modular fashion. The file nwu_dtwr is in effect a *main* module that *calls* other modules functioning at greater levels of detail.

```
<HTML>
<HEAD>
<TITLE>Dear Tech Writer...</TITLE>
<!--Since the phrase you include within the TITLE container will be
--displayed in a browser's status bar when the file is opened, make
--sure that phrase is something meaningful to others.-->
</HEAD>
<FRAMESET COLS=21%,79%>
<!--Create two columns for the page, one occupying 21% of the screen,
--and the other taking up 79%.-->
<FRAMESET ROWS=29%,71%>
<!--In the page's first column, create two rows, one occupying 21% of the
--column's height, and the other taking 71% of that height.
-->
```

This building-the-frames level of the page's development is shown in Figure 18-2.

In Figure 18-2, you can take a peek at one of the many simple tests we did during the development of the project page.

As Figure 18-3 shows, almost any image can be used for testing purposes.

```
<FRAME
<!--Define the frame that will house the page's banner image.-->
<!--In testing this frame, we used the static TIFF shown in Figure 18-3.-->
NAME="BANNERIMG"
SRC="movement.htm"
<!--The file movement.htm, which we'll present later in this
--chapter, provides rudimentary animation of the banner image.-->
MARGINHEIGHT = 1
MARGINWIDTH = 1
SCROLLING = "NO"
NORESIZE>
```

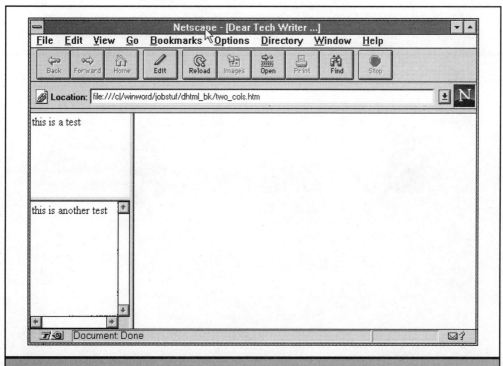

Figure 18-2.   *It's important to test at every stage of development. That's what we did here.*

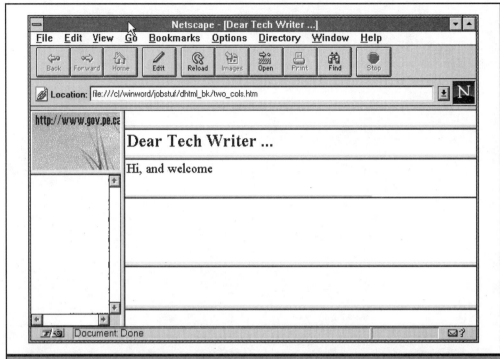

Figure 18-3. *This image in the upper-left corner of the screen was only a placeholder*

```
<FRAME
NAME="NAVIGATE"
SRC="navigate.htm"
<!--The file navigate.htm, which we'll present later in this
--chapter, provides dynamic behavior in the form of links.-->
--It also provides the means by which the user can query
--one of the page's associated databases.-->
MARGINHEIGHT = 1
MARGINWIDTH = 1
SCROLLING = "YES"
NORESIZE>
</FRAMESET>
<!--The two frames in the left column have now been defined.-->
<FRAMESET ROWS=8%,14%,18%,32%,20%,8%>
<!--In the right column, we set up six rows, and six frames.-->
<FRAME
NAME="TOPLINKS"
```

```
SRC="javsimap.htm"
<!--The file javsimap.htm, which we'll present later in this
--chapter, provides more rudimentary dynamic behavior in the form of
--an image map offering links to remote sites.-->
-->
```

Figure 18-4 shows one part of the verify-every-frame stage of the project page's development.

```
MARGINHEIGHT = 1
MARGINWIDTH = 1
SCROLLING = "NO"
NORESIZE>
<FRAME
NAME="BANNERTEXT"
```

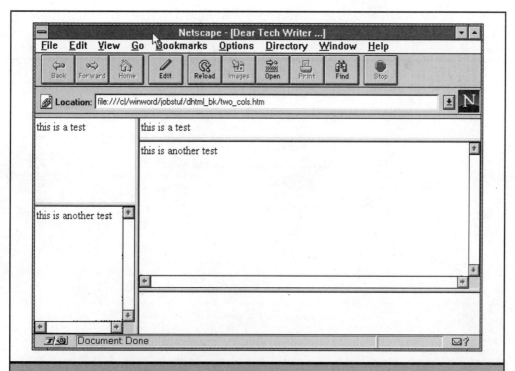

Figure 18-4. *As this look at another of our simple tests shows, development must proceed and be verified one frame at a time*

```
SRC="banner.htm"
MARGINHEIGHT = 1
MARGINWIDTH = 1
SCROLLING = "NO"
NORESIZE>
```

Figure 18-5 shows an early version of this frame, with which we weren't completely satisfied.

```
<FRAME
NAME="PURPOSETEXT"
SRC="purpose.htm"
MARGINHEIGHT = 1
MARGINWIDTH = 1
SCROLLING= "NO"
```

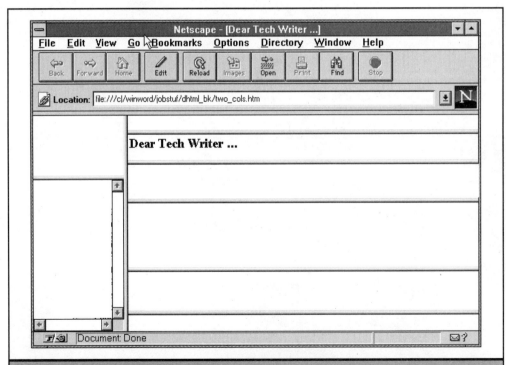

Figure 18-5.   *As is often the case during development, this presentation was unimpressive. Let's be blunt; it's bland.*

```
NORESIZE>
<FRAME
NAME="DISPLAYTEXT"
SRC="dsplytxt.htm"
MARGINHEIGHT = 1
MARGINWIDTH = 1
SCROLLING="YES"
NORESIZE>
<FRAME
NAME="DISPLAYFIGS"
SRC="dsplyfig.htm"
MARGINHEIGHT = 1
MARGINWIDTH = 1
SCROLLING="YES"
NORESIZE>
<FRAME
NAME= "BOTMLINKS"
SRC="javsimap.htm"
MARGINHEIGHT = 1
MARGINWIDTH = 1
SCROLLING ="NO"
NORESIZE>
</FRAMESET>
</FRAMESET>
<NOFRAMES>
<!--In order to accommodate users working with older,
-- frames-incapable browsers, we've included this section.-->
To use this page to best effect,
you need a 32-bit Web browser, such as Netscape 2.0 or higher,
or Internet Explorer 3.0 or higher, that allows you to view frames.
<A HREF="c:\winword\jobstuf\dhtml_bk\src_info\noframes.txt"
<EM><STRONG>Click here
</EM><STRONG>
</A>
if you wish to continue without the ability to see frames.
</NOFRAMES>
</HTML>
```

Let's wrap up this presentation of the basic project page with a look at two more files—those that will create the shells into which retrieved text and figures will be placed.

First, we'll show you dsplytxt.htm.

```
<HTML>
<BODY BGCOLOR="#FFFFFF" BACKGOUND="3whtbkg.gif"
<P>
<IMG SRC="undercon.htm" WIDTH="490" HEIGHT="70">
</P>
</BODY>
</HTML>
```

Now, here's dsplyfig.htm.

```
<HTML>
<BODY BGCOLOR="#FFFFFF"
<P>
<IMG SRC="3whtbkg.gif" WIDTH="490" HEIGHT="28">
</P>
</BODY>
</HTML>
```

The Second Level

This section presents the code for the page's more simple dynamic behaviors.

Dynamic Behavior in the Banner Image Frame

The file movement.htm, shown below, causes the image of a quill pen to shoot across that of a PC. This module makes use of layers, and some elementary JavaScript.

```
<HTML>
<HEAD>
<TITLE>Pen and PC</TITLE>
</HEAD>
<BODY onLoad="movePen">
<!--The opening BODY tag makes use of the built-in JavaScript
--method onLoad to begin to move the image of the quill pen
--across that of the PC as soon as the frame loads.-->
<LAYER ID="firstpc" LEFT="10" TOP="8">
<IMG SRC="wallpapr.jpg">
</LAYER>
```

```
<LAYER ID="pen" LEFT="10" TOP="8" ABOVE="firstpc">
<IMG SRC="pen.jpg" >
</LAYER>
<!--The LAYER tag is specific to more recent versions of Netscape.
--However, layers can also be implemented through the use of CSS1
--style sheets.-->
<SCRIPT>
<!--Simple move function-->
function movePen() {
var penPlace = document.layers["pen"];
<!--The variable penPlace is assigned a value derived from the
--built-in JavaScript document attribute document.layers.-->
if (penPlace.left < 140) {
<!--If the pen layer's upper-left corner is at a point less than 140
--pixels from the left of the frame, we'll move it...-->
pen.moveBy(1,0);}
<!--one pixel at a time...-->
else {penPlace.left = 10;}
<!--Otherwise, we'll place it at the 10-pixel point.-->
setTimeout(movePen, 700);}
<!--Then we'll wait 700 milliseconds before starting the whole
--process over again.-->
</SCRIPT>
</BODY>
</HTML>
```

Dynamic Behavior in the Local Navigation Frame

This section presents two files:

- navigate.htm, which enables the user to send email to Dear Tech Writer, to send email to an Expert, and to query the page's database of technical terms
- search.htm, which allows the user to enter a query.

Here is the content of navigate.htm.

```
<HTML>
<BODY BGCOLOR="#A6CAF0" LINK="#000000" ALINK="#800000">
<!--The hexadecimal value A6CAF0 sets the frame's background color
--to sky blue. The value 000000 sets the color of unvisited links
--to black. The hex number 800000 sets the color of visited links
```

```
--to dark red.-->
<P>
<STRONG>
<FONT SIZE="2">
Links to Other Information:<BR><BR>
</STRONG>
</FONT>
<FONT SIZE="2">
<A HREF="mailto:petrovsk@voicenet.com">
Send mail to Dear Tech Writer.<BR><BR></A>
```

Being overzealous in defining this link by providing too lengthy a file name produced an error and the message Figure 18-6 depicts.

```
</FONT>
<FONT SIZE="2">
<A HREF="mailto:tpark@voicenet.com">
Send mail to an Expert.<BR></A>
</FONT>
</P>
<P>
<A HREF="search.htm">
<STRONG>
<FONT SIZE="2">
<I>Search our database of technical terms.</I></A>
</FONT>
</STRONG>
</P>
</BODY>
</HTML>
```

Next we present the content of the file search.htm.

```
<HTML>
<HEAD>
</HEAD>
<BODY BGCOLOR="#FFFFFF" TEXT="#000080">
<P>
<FORM NAME="queryForm" ACTION=" METHOD="GET">
<!--Define the form into which the user will enter queries.-->
```

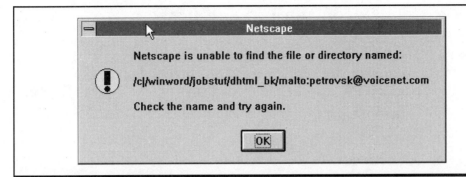

Figure 18-6.   *In this case, a full path name wasn't needed*

```
<STRONG>
<FONT SIZE="2">
<I>Hi! I'm Dear Tech Writer.<BR><BR></I>
Click in the box below, and enter the term you want me to define.
Then click the Submit button.<BR><BR>
</FONT>
</STRONG>
<INPUT TYPE="text" NAME="inputbox" VALUE="">
<INPUT TYPE="button" NAME="submtbtn" Value="Submit"
onClick="dbsearch(queryForm)">
<!--When the user clicks the Submit button, the JavaScript routine
--dbsearch will execute.-->
<SCRIPT LANGUAGE="JAVASCRIPT">
function dbsearch(form) {
var searchString=document.queryForm.inputbox.value;
<!--Set the variable searchString equal to the phrase the user
--entered.-->
<!--Code here to pass the search string the user has entered to your
--database/SQL server; the section "The Dynamic Display of Text and
--Figures" later in this chapter gives one example.-->
window.open("peaceful.jpg","NAVIGATE");
<!--Clear the frame by using the built-in JavaScript method
--window.open to display the canvas in the JPEG file peaceful.-->
}
</SCRIPT>
</FORM>
</P>
</BODY>
</HTML>
```

Dynamic Behavior in the Top and Bottom Navigation Frames

The JPEG file links.jpg is the source for the image map displayed in both the top and bottom navigation frames. The HTML document shown below, javsimap.htm , controls this map, in part through the use of a CSS1 style sheet and in part through more complex scripting than we've needed to this point.

```
<HEAD>
<STYLE TYPE="text/css">
<!--Define the type of style sheet used.-->
#elMenu { position: relative }
<!--The element defined as Menu will be positioned relative to
--other elements.-->
    #elMenuUp {
<!--The element defined as MenuUp will be positioned absolutely
--within the frame.-->
        position: absolute;
        top: 0;
        left: 0
    }
    #elMenuOver {
        position: absolute;
        visibility: hidden;
<!--The element defined as MenuOver will be positioned absolutely
--within the frame and will be hidden, or transparent.-->
        top: 0;
        left: 0
    }
-->
</STYLE>
<SCRIPT LANGUAGE="JavaScript">
<!--
ver4 = (document.layers || document.all) ? 1 : 0;
    if (ver4) {
<!--Find out the version of Navigator being used
--If it's Communicator, that is, version 4, do the following.-->
        secondIm = "<IMG SRC='links.jpg' USEMAP='#linksMenu'
        WIDTH=500 HEIGHT=22 BORDER=0>";
<!--Define the image to be used as the basis of the image map.-->
        arPopups = new Array()
<!--Create the array that will index the image map.-->
    }
```

```
        else { secondIm = "" }
<!--If you're not dealing with Communicator, these features will
--be defined later.-->
        function setBeginEnd(which,from,to) {
<!--This function tracks the coordinates of the portion of
--the image map being activated or deactivated.-->
            if (!ver4) { return };
<!--Since we've already dealt with Communicator, we can
--bypass this code if that's the version running.-->
            arPopups[which] = new Array();
            arPopups[which][0] = from;
            arPopups[which][1] = to;
        }
        function mapOver(which,on) {
<!--This function takes actions specific to the part of
--the image map being activated or deactivated.-->
            if (!ver4) { return };
<!--Since we've already dealt with Communicator, we can
--bypass this code if that's the version running.-->
            if (document.all) { whichEl = document.all.elMenuOver.style;
<!--if the cursor is in the periphery of the image map,
--apply transparency to the entire image map.-->
            else { whichEl = document.elMenu.document.elMenuOver };
<!--otherwise, only apply transparency to the current area
--of the image map.-->
            if (on) {
                whichEl.clip.left = arPopups[which][0];
                whichEl.clip.right = arPopups[which][1];
<!--If one of the linkable areas of the image map is being moused
--over, grab the coordinates of that area.-->
whichEl.visibility = "visible"
<!--Also, make sure the area is visible.-->
            }
            else { whichEl.visibility = "hidden" }
        }
-->
</SCRIPT>
</HEAD>
<BODY>
<DIV ID="elMenu">
<!--The DIV tag was introduced in HTML 3.0 to allow you to specify
```

```
--logical divisions in a page. Using this capability also lets you
--do such things as align all the text in such a section with a
--single command.-->
    <DIV ID="elMenuUp">
    <IMG SRC="links.jpg" USEMAP="#mpLinks" WIDTH=500 HEIGHT=22
     BORDER=0>
    </DIV>
    <DIV ID="elMenuOver">
<!--Now we're defining the behavior to be associated with
--style sheet elements.-->
    <SCRIPT LANGUAGE="JavaScript">
    document.write(secondIm)
    </SCRIPT>
    </DIV>
</DIV>
<MAP NAME="mpLinks">
<AREA SHAPE="RECT" COORDS="0,0 145,15" HREF="http://www.nwu.org"
 TARGET="_blank">
<AREA SHAPE="RECT" COORDS="160,0 305,15"
 HREF="http://www.altavista.digital.com"
 TARGET="_blank">
<AREA SHAPE="RECT" COORDS="320,0 465,15"
 HREF="http://www.opentext.net"
 TARGET="_blank">
</MAP>
<!--The coordinates in this map definition agree precisely with
--the size of the JPEG file that is its source image.
--Note also that this definition uses the attribute TARGET and the
corresponding value "_blank"
--to cause activated links to open a new, blank browser window.-->
</BODY>
</HTML>
```

The Static Banner Text Frame and Purpose Text Frame

Surely the simplest of the many HTML files that make up the NWU page, these frames employ no scripting of any kind. Nor do they require any but the most basic tags.

The files in question are banner.htm and purpose.htm.

Now take a look at the content of the file banner.htm.

```
<HTML>
<BODY BGCOLOR="#FFFBF0"BACKGROUND="3whtbkg.gif">
<P ALIGN=CENTER>
<FONT
SIZE=5
<EM>
<STRONG>
Dear Tech Writer...
</EM>
</STRONG>
</FONT>
</P>
</BODY>
</HTML>
```

The next file whose content we present is purpose.htm.

```
<HTML>
<BODY BGCOLOR="#A6CAF0"> BACKGROUND="3whtbkg.gif"
<P>
<FONT SIZE=-1>
Hi, and welcome to
<B>
Dear Tech Writer.
</B>
We hope, through this page, to help those of you who wish to learn
more about technical writing,
and especially about writing on data processing-related subjects.
</FONT>
</P>
</BODY>
</HTML>
```

More Sophisticated Dynamic Behaviors

One of the design requirements of the NWU page is that it have sound linked to the local navigation frame defined by navigate.htm. This audio is to be played only as part of a warning generated if the user attempts unauthorized or ill-advised actions.

The second example of more sophisticated dynamic behavior in the project page is the ability to query one or more databases, which we plan to incorporate in it as part of the project's ongoing evolution.

This section presents code that you might use to accomplish these behaviors in JavaScript-capable environments.

Sound Linked to Alerts

The file js_sound.htm shown below uses a hidden frame that can be referenced by and will then in effect be superimposed upon navigate.htm to present sound. A number of events, including onLoad, onClick, and onUnload might be used to trigger execution of js_sound.htm.

```html
<HTML>
</A>
<FONT COLOR = "#0000DF">
<PRE>
<FRAMESET ROWS="0,*" FRAMEBORDER=0 BORDER=0>
<!--Note that the sound-frame has no rows, columns, or border.-->
<FRAME
SRC="blank.htm"
<!--The file blank.htm is truly empty; it serves only to
--allow us to embed sound.-->
NAME="SOUNDFRAME"
SCROLLING=NO
MARGINHEIGHT=0
MARGINWIDTH=0
NORESIZE>
</FRAMESET>
</PRE>
</FONT>
<!--The JavaScript routine presented next controls the playing of
the WAV file housing the alert sound.-->
function play_sound(file)
{
 with (parent.sound_frame.document)
<!--The line above defines the parent document of the sound frame,
--in this case, the local navigation frame, as that with which
--the sound will be associated.-->
 {
   open ("blank.htm");
   writeln ('<EMBED SRC="..." WIDTH=2 HEIGHT=2
<!--Place the name of the source file containing the sound
```

```
--you want to play within these quotes.-->
    CONTROLS=console VOLUME=100 LOOP=10 AUTOSTART=TRUE
    NAME="music_embed">;');
<!--By writing this HTML line to blank.htm, we also specify
--parameters, such as volume and number of repetitions,
--that will be applied to the sound to be played.-->
    close ();
}
</HTML>
```

The Dynamic Display of Text and Figures

The file get_quer.c shown here is CGI-compliant, and uses C++ to extract user
input to be forwarded to a server-side database. You'll notice, in scanning
through this example, that writing such code requires a degree of
programming sophistication, as well as an understanding of C and C++.

```
#include <stdio.h>
/* Tell the compiler to include the library stdio, or standard I/O,
in your executable.*/
#ifndef NO_STDLIB_H
#include <stdlib.h>
#else
char *getenv();
#endif
/* If the constant NO_STDLIB_H hasn't been defined, tell the compiler
to include the library stdlib in your executable.  Otherwise, tell it
to grab characteristics of your operating environment.*/
typedef struct {
    char name[128];
    char val[128];
} entry;
/*Create and define the compound variable called entry, which will
store user input.*/
void getword(char *word, char *line, char stop);
char x2c(char *what);
void unescape_url(char *url);
void plustospace(char *str);
/*Create variables that store pointers to such aspects of user input
as the words, lines, and end-of-line it includes.*/
main(int argc, char *argv[]) {
    entry entries[10000];
```

```
    register int x,m=0;
    char *cl;
    printf("Content-type: text/html%c%c",10,10);
  if(strcmp(getenv("REQUEST_METHOD"),"GET")) {
        printf("This script should be referenced with a METHOD of GET.\n");
        printf("If you don't understand this, see this ");
        printf("<A
HREF=\"http://www.ncsa.uiuc.edu/SDG/Software/Mosaic/Docs/fill-out-
forms/overview.html\">forms overview</A>.%c",10);
        exit(1);
/*This program is kind enough to point those who employ it
inappropriately to sources of further help before bailing out.*/
    }
cl = getenv("QUERY_STRING");
/*Then the code gets down to business, and grabs the query.*/
    if(cl == NULL) {
        printf("No query information to decode.\n");
        exit(1);
/*If nothing's been entered, it responds appropriately, and exits.*/
/*Otherwise, it parses the user's entry, and prints results with
appropriate HTML tags.*/
    }
    for(x=0;cl[0] != '\0';x++) {
        m=x;
        getword(entries[x].val,cl,'&');
        plustospace(entries[x].val);
        unescape_url(entries[x].val);
        getword(entries[x].name,entries[x].val,'=');
    }
printf("<H1>Query Results</H1>");
    printf("You submitted the following name/value pairs:<p>%c",10);
    printf("<ul>%c",10);
for(x=0; x <= m; x++)
        printf("<li> <code>%s = %s</code>%c",entries[x].name,
                entries[x].val,10);
    printf("</ul>%c",10);
}
```

Current-Record Binding in Internet Explorer 4.0

Current-record binding is the name given by Microsoft to their
recently-developed technique for sorting and filtering retrieved data solely

through the client browser. This technique thereby spares the user the finger-drumming that often accompanies waiting for the results of server-based sorts and similar operations. As important, by reducing the number of calls to the server, current-record binding improves overall throughput and reduces bandwidth demands.

To illustrate current-record binding, we will use:

- a hypothetical database that we'll assume was created in Microsoft Access
- VBScript code
- the existing HTML tags <OBJECT>, <SPAN>, and <TABLE>
- the new attributes, proposed by Microsoft to the W3C as extensions to HTML, <DATAFLD> and <DATASRC>

We'll assume further that the schema for the data file we've created in Access defines the fields described in Table 18-1.

Here are a few sample records from our fictitious file.

```
Flower, Light, Soil
Zinnia, full sun, acid
Portulaca, full sun, poor
Nierembergia, shade, clay
```

This field	is of this data type	and represents
Flower	string	a type of flower
Light	string	the type of light the flower in question needs in order to thrive; for example, "full sun"
Soil	string	the type of soil in which the flower in question is most likely to thrive; for instance, "acid"

Table 18-1. *Partial Schema of a Gardening Database*

Because our data includes a header line that defines field names, VB will be able to use its Tabular Data Control to read our data and prepare that data for being bound to HTML-based forms controls. But in order to complete this process of making VB's life easier, we must add appropriate code to an HTML document. That is, we must incorporate the Tabular Data Control into the HTML page with the <OBJECT> tag.

Remember, from some of our earlier discussions, what object-oriented programming—and objects—allow us to accomplish. An object can be thought of as a composite variable that enables us to define or deal with a number of characteristics of a single entity.

In the sample <OBJECT> tag below, for example, we've defined

- an overall object that happens to be a Tabular Data Control
- the name of the file from which we'll draw the source data that the control will help us manipulate
- the nature of the delimiter that will separate units within a record from that file
- the fact that we want VB to use the header that's included in our data file

```
<OBJECT ID=TDC>
<PARAM NAME=DataURL Value="GardenInput.txt">
<PARAM NAME=TextQualifier Value=",">
<PARAM NAME=UseHeader Value=True>
</OBJECT>
```

Table 18-2 explains this code fragment in more detail.

A number of standard HTML elements can be used in conjunction with both DATASRC and DATAFLD. Among these are

A	LABEL
DIV	MARQUEE
FRAME	OBJECT
IMG	SPAN
INPUT	TEXTAREA

This line of code	**means**
`<OBJECT ID=TDC>`	the object we're creating will act as a tabular data control, that is, a template which can be used to pass data back and forth between client and server
`<PARAM NAME=DataURL Value="GardenInput.txt">`	the source of the data against which we'll match this template is the file called GardenInput.txt, at the URL we've defined elsewhere in our HTML document
`<PARAM NAME= TextQualifier Value=",">`	fields within our data records will be indicated and separated by commas
`<PARAM NAME= UseHeader Value=True>`	we want to use the header line of the file as the means of identifying individual fields within retrieved records
`</OBJECT>`	we're done setting up our template/object

Table 18-2.   *Coding to Create a Tabular Data Control*

In addition to these and other tags, you may also use the tag <TABLE>, but only with DATASRC, not DATAFLD.

How does Internet Explorer 4.0 field all this? Here's an introduction of the team. IE4 includes two agents, or specialized software components, which exist specifically to handle record and field binding. The first is the binding agent, which moves data from the appropriate database fields into the HTML fields or other elements with which that data has been associated, or, to put it another way, to which that data has been bound. The second agent is the repetition agent, which repeatedly searches tables or data files for records that meet specified criteria.

Now that you've met the players, let's move onto the play-by-play.

1. When an HTML document is parsed, that is, dissected to determine the meaning of its codes and directives, IE4's binding agent tracks all elements that have been coded with the DATAFLD attribute.

2. Then, the binding agent fills these fields or elements with data from the field within the data source object with which the HTML field has been associated.

3. At the same time, the binding agent monitors and records any changes the user might make to this bound data, and sends the modified data, if any, back to the server for re-incorporation into the data source.

4. Backing up the binding agent on every play it makes is IE4's table repetition agent. This second specialized software component applies the record template that we have supplied through the <OBJECT> tag to every record in our data source file. The table repetition agent does this by:

   ■ searching out any <TABLE> tag that contains the DATASRC attribute in an HTML document

   ■ successively applying the template our <OBJECT> tag represents to record after record of the indicated data source and sending records derived from that source according to that template to the HTML page, where the data is available to and actually displayed by the binding agent

That's current-record binding in a nutshell. But in order to use this technique to either sort or filter retrieved data, we must write code; Internet Explorer 4.0 is bright, but it's not a mind-reader. So, let's show you some code that might execute when our user indicates, by clicking the button we've labeled Flower, that he or she wants to see information on posies we might plant in a shade garden. We'll begin with a section of code that could sort data retrieved from the server.

```
<INPUT TYPE=BUTTON VALUE="Flower" ONCLICK=flower_sort()>
<SCRIPT>
function "flower_sort()" {
TDC.SortAscending=true;
TDC.SortColumn="Flower";
TDC.Reset(); }
</SCRIPT>
```

Now let's use Table 18-3 to elaborate upon this code.

Filtering, of course, is another matter. Recall that, in setting up this example, we said we wanted to gather data on flowers that would be good

This line of code	means
`<INPUT TYPE=BUTTON VALUE="Flower" ONCLICK=flower_sort()>`	clicking this button tells HTML, through the VBScript code we've embedded, that we want to see data on flowers, rather than on soil or water conditions, for instance
`<SCRIPT>`	here's where the script we've embedded begins
`function "flower_sort()" {`	here's where the function that will sort the names of flowers retrieved from our data file begins
`TDC.SortAscending=true;`	sort the data retrieved from the file represented by the object TDC in ascending order
`TDC.SortColumn="Flower";`	run that ascending-order sort on the contents of the file Flower
`TDC.Reset(); }`	start all over again to sort the next set of retrieved records/fields
`</SCRIPT>`	here's where the embedded script ends

Table 18-3. *Coding to Sort Retrieved Data*

candidates for a garden in a shady spot. That type of conditional retrieval and presentation fairly screams *filter*. So, we must expand the code we just wrote. Here's that extended code.

```
<INPUT TYPE=BUTTON VALUE="Flower" ONCLICK=flower_sort()>
<SCRIPT>
function flower_filter() {
TDC.FilterColumn="Light";
TDC.FilterValue=flower.value;
TDC.FilterCriterion="Shade";
```

```
TDC.Reset(); }
function "flower_sort()" {
TDC.SortAscending=true;
TDC.SortColumn="Flower";
TDC.Reset(); }
</SCRIPT>
```

Once again, we'll turn to a table, Table 18-4, to explain this sample code.

You may be wondering: "A Tabular Data Control without a table?" Yes and no. Had we completely fleshed out our sample code, we would have included many lines of standard or very-nearly-standard HTML, like

```
<TABLE ID=GardenTable DATASRC=#TDC>
<TBODY>
<TR>
<TD><SPAN DATAFLD=Flower></SPAN></TD>
</TR>
```

in which we would have specified the nature and structure of the table our HTML document will use as the carton, so to speak, for the data we retrieve. But TABLE, TR, TD, and SPAN belong to standard, not Dynamic, HTML. They certainly don't pertain directly to current-record binding. So, for the purposes of this discussion, we've foregone them.

If the explanations in this section on current-record binding seem a little stiff, just be thankful we haven't given them to you in formal data processing jargon. In that style of speech, "filling elements" would be called "populating," and "sending data back" would be called "propagating changes back." We think the meaning is as clear, if not more so, when conveyed in English. And there's something more important for you to understand here than differences in phrasing. The basic principles of programming will always apply, no matter the language used to describe them. So, current-record binding can legitimately be seen simply as the association of values contained in variables, that is, pigeonholes in a computer's memory, with external receptacles, such as records in a file somewhere on disk, or, as it happens, areas of an HTML document. While the latter usage is new, the principle has been around for a long, long time. So don't let the jargon throw you.

This line of code	means
`<INPUT TYPE=BUTTON VALUE="Flower" ONCLICK=flower_sort()>`	clicking this button tells HTML, through the VBScript code we've embedded, that we want to see data on flowers, rather than on soil or water conditions, for instance
`<SCRIPT>`	here's where the script we've embedded begins
`function flower_filter() {`	here's where the function that will filter retrieved data begins
`TDC.FilterColumn="Light";`	filter the data retrieved from the file represented by the object TDC on the basis of the field (column) Light...
`TDC.FilterValue=light.value;`	and of the values contained in that field...
`TDC.FilterCriterion="Shade";`	passing to the binding agent only those records that have a value equal to "Shade" in this field
`TDC.Reset(); }`	start all over again to filter the next set of retrieved records/fields
`function "flower_sort()" {`	here's where the function that will sort the names of flowers retrieved from our data file begins
`TDC.SortAscending=true;`	sort the data retrieved from the file represented by the object TabDatCtrl in ascending order
`TDC.SortColumn="Flower";`	run that ascending-order sort on the contents of the filed Flower
`TDC.Reset(); }`	start all over again to sort the next set of retrieved records/fields
`</SCRIPT>`	here's where the embedded script ends

Table 18-4.   *Coding to Both Filter and Sort Retrieved Data*

Conclusion

Finally, we'd like to express the hope that you've learned as much from reading this book as we did in preparing it, and that your learning was as enjoyable as ours was, as learning should, ideally, always be. Given the medium we've been studying, there's little doubt we'll all continue to crack the books.

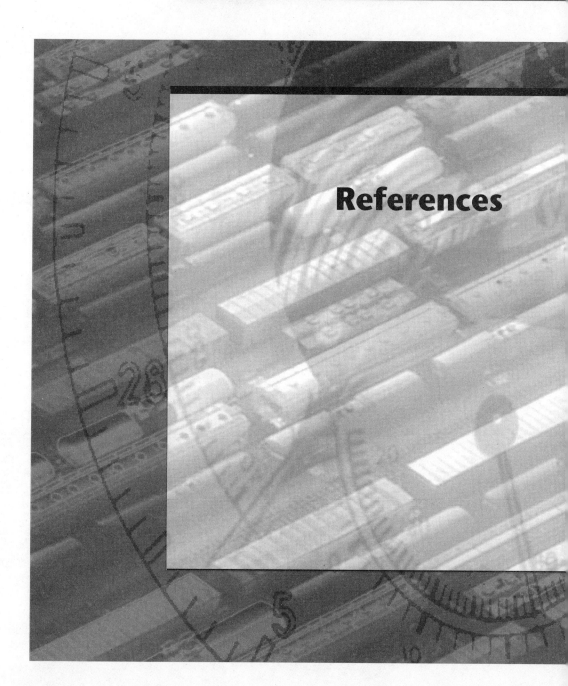

PART THREE

References

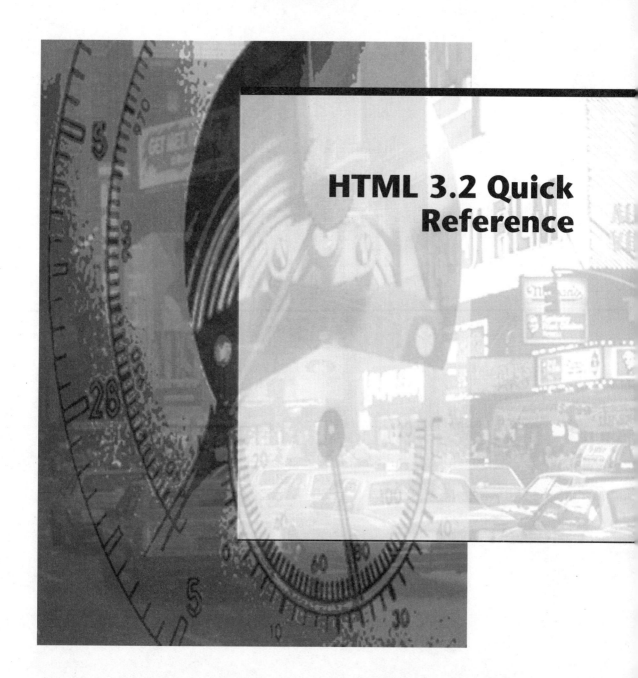

Appendix A

HTML 3.2 Quick Reference

This alphabetized table is a much-streamlined presentation of the World Wide Web Consortium's standard for HTML 3.2.

This concept	can be best understood in this way
additions to HTML 3.2	widely deployed features such as tables, applets and text flow around images
<!DOCTYPE> declaration	distinguishes HTML 3.2 documents from other versions of HTML

<!DOCTYPE> declaration, followed by an HTML element containing a HEAD and then a BODY element	must be at the beginning of every HTML 3.2-compliant document; for example:
	
	`<!DOCTYPE HTML PUBLIC`
	`"-//W3C//DTD HTML 3.2 Final//EN">`
	`<HTML>`
	`<HEAD>`
	`<TITLE>A study of population dynamics</TITLE>`
	`... other head elements ...`
	`</HEAD>`
	`<BODY>`
	`... document body ...`
	`</BODY>`
	`</HTML>`

ADDRESS	requires start and end tags; specifies information such as authorship and contact details for the current document; for example: `<ADDRESS>` `Newsletter editor ` `J.R. Brown ` `8723 Buena Vista, Smallville, CT` `01234 ` `Tel: +1 (123) 456 7890` `</ADDRESS>`

This concept	**can be best understood in this way**
attribute values	may be presented with either double or single quotes
BASE	defines base URL for resolving relative URLs

	BASE also gives the base URL for dereferencing relative URLs, using the rules given by the URL specification, for example:
	`<BASE href="http://www.acme.com/intro.html">`
	`<IMG SRC="icons/logo.gif">`
	The image is thereafter referenced as:
	`http://www.acme.com/icons/logo.gif.`

block level elements	causes paragraph breaks
BLOCKQUOTE	quoted passage; requires starting and ending angle brackets; used to enclose extended quotations and is typically rendered with indented margins
	BLOCKQUOTE also can be used to enclose block quotations from other works; requires starting and ending angle brackets
BODY	contains document body; both opening and closing angle bracket delimiters may be omitted; can contain a wide range of elements, including: headings (H1 - H6) ADDRESS block-level elements text-level elements

This concept	**can be best understood in this way**
	Attributes used with BODY include:
	■ BACKGROUND
	■ BGCOLOR
	■ TEXT
	■ LINK
	■ VLINK
	■ ALINK

	For example:
	`<body bgcolor=white text=black`
	`link=red vlink=maroon`
	`alink=fuchsia>`

CENTER	text alignment; requires starting and ending angle brackets; used to center text lines
CENTER	Netscape introduced CENTER before it added support for the HTML 3.0 DIV element, which also deals with text alignment; CENTER retained in HTML 3.2 due to its widespread deployment

This concept	**can be best understood in this way**
color names and corresponding hexadecimal values	■ Aqua = "#00FFFF" ■ Black = "#000000" ■ Blue = "#0000FF" ■ Fuchsia = "#FF00FF" ■ Gray = "#808080" ■ Green = "#008000" ■ Lime = "#00FF00" ■ Maroon = "#800000" ■ Navy = "#000080" ■ Olive = "#808000" ■ Purple = "#800080" ■ Red = "#FF0000" ■ Silver = "#C0C0C0" ■ Teal = "#008080" ■ White = "#FFFFFF" ■ Yellow = "#FFFF00"
colors	given as hexadecimal numbers (as in COLOR="#C0FFC0"), or as one of 16 widely understood color names
common block-level elements	headers, paragraphs, list items
common text-level elements	EM, I, B and FONT for character emphasis; A for hypertext links; IMG and APPLET for embedded objects; and BR for line breaks
containers	requires both start and end tags; examples are TITLE, SCRIPT and STYLE
contiguous sequences of white space	treated as equivalent to a single space character (ASCII decimal 32)

This concept	**can be best understood in this way**

descriptive title element	must be included in every HTML 3.2-compliant document; for example:
	`<!DOCTYPE HTML PUBLIC`
	`"-//W3C//DTD HTML 3.2 Final//EN">`
	`<TITLE>A study of population`
	`dynamics</TITLE>`

DIR and MENU	part of HTML from the early days; intended for unordered lists similar to UL elements; it's recommended that you render DIR elements as multicolumn directory lists, and MENU elements as single column menu lists
DIV	document divisions; requires starting and ending angle brackets; used with the ALIGN attribute to set the text alignment of the block elements it contains
DL	definition lists; requires starting and ending angle brackets
DTD	SGML-compliant definition of the intended interpretation of HTML 3.2 elements
FORM	fill-out forms; requires starting and ending angle brackets; used to define a fill-out form for processing by HTTP servers; can accept the attributes ACTION, METHOD, and ENCTYPE
HEAD	element that contains the document head; may include an unordered collection of the following elements:

This concept	**can be best understood in this way**
	■ BASE
	■ ISINDEX
	■ LINK
	■ META
	■ SCRIPT
	■ STYLE
	■ TITLE
headings	six levels, from H1 (the most important) to H6 (the least important); all can be used for document headings
HR	horizontal rules; not a container, so closing angle brackets are forbidden; can accept attributes ALIGN, NOSHADE, SIZE, and WIDTH
HTML version 3.2	aims to capture recommended practice as of early 1996; used as a replacement for HTML 2.0
IBM, Microsoft, Netscape Communications Corporation, Novell, SoftQuad, Spyglass, and Sun Microsystems	contributors to the content of HTML 3.2
ISINDEX	pertains to simple keyword searches; indicates that the browser should provide a single-line text input field; can appear in a document's head or body;

This concept	**can be best understood in this way**
LINK	defines relationships with other documents;
	provides a media-independent method for defining relationships with other documents and resources; LINK has been part of HTML since the very early days, but few browsers as yet take advantage of it
META	provides meta information in the form of a name/value pair; can be used to include name/value pairs describing properties of the document, such as author, expiration date, a list of key words, and so on
OL	ordered (in other words, numbered) lists; requires starting and ending angle brackets
P	paragraph element; requires an opening angle bracket, but you can omit the closing one

This concept	can be best understood in this way
PRE	preformatted text; requires starting and ending angle brackets; renders text in a monospace font; preserves layout defined by whitespace and line-break characters; for example, here is "To a Skylark" from Shelley:

```
<PRE>
    Higher still and higher
    From the earth thou springest
    Like a cloud of fire;
    The blue deep thou wingest,
And singing still dost soar, and
soaring ever singest.
</PRE>
```

this is rendered as:

```
    Higher still and higher
    From the earth thou springest
    Like a cloud of fire;
    The blue deep thou wingest,
And singing still dost soar, and
soaring ever singest.
```

PROMPT	attribute of ISINDEX that can be used to specify a prompt string
end of a line of markup immediately following an opening angle bracket	no longer acceptable in HTML 3.2; therefore:

```
<P>Text
```

should be substituted for:

```
<P>
Text
```

| end of a line of markup immediately preceding an ending angle bracket | should be discarded; therefore: |

```
Text </P>
```

should be substituted for:

```
Text
</P>
```

This concept	**can be best understood in this way**
SCRIPT	reserved for use with scripting languages
SGML	HTML 3.2 conforms to the International Standard ISO 8879 Standard

Some proposed relationship values for LINK	rel=top: link references the top of a hierarchy, such as the first or cover page in a collection
	rel=contents: link references a document serving as a table of contents
	rel=index: link references a document providing an index for the current document
	for example:
	`<LINK REL=Contents HREF=toc.html>`
	`<LINK REL=Previous HREF=doc31.html>`
	`<LINK REL=Next HREF=doc33.html>`
	`<LINK REL=Chapter REV=Contents HREF=chapter2.html>`

STYLE	reserved for use with style sheets
TABLE	can be nested; requires starting and ending angle brackets; includes one or more TR elements defining table rows
text level elements	does not cause paragraph breaks
TITLE	tag that defines the document title; required under HTML 3.2
UL	defines unordered lists
XMP, LISTING, and PLAINTEXT	obsolete tags for preformatted text ; these tags predate the introduction of the tag PRE, used to indicate such text

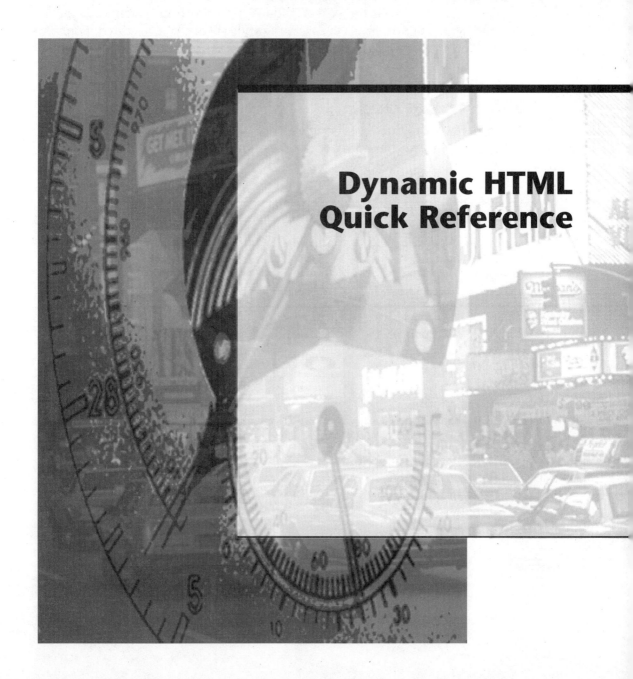

Appendix B

Dynamic HTML Quick Reference

This appendix presents the text of a document called "CSS1-Properties Quick Reference Table," created by Joachim Schwarte of the University of Stuttgart in Germany. Mr. Schwarte is one of many people in the data processing community who freely share and allow the distribution of their work. His document distills the World Wide Web Consortium's standards for the use and syntax of properties in cascading style sheets. We've edited it only to bring its formatting into agreement with the rest of this book.

CSS1 Properties

In this section, we provide an overview of CSS1 properties. Then, in the following sections, we elaborate upon some of the information in Table B-1.

The property	can accept values like	has the initial value	applies to	can be inherited	and can use values formatted as percentages
font-family	[[<family-name> | <generic-family>],]* [<family-name> | <generic-family>]	specific to the user agent (UA), or browser	all elements	yes	N/A
font-style	normal | italic | oblique	normal	all elements	yes	N/A
font-variant	normal | small-caps	normal	all elements	yes	N/A
font-weight	normal | bold | bolder | lighter | 100 | 200 | 300 | 400 | 500 | 600 | 700 | 800 | 900	normal	all elements	yes	N/A
font-size	<absolute-size> | <relative-size> | <length> | <percentage>	medium	all elements	yes	relative to parent element's font size

Table B-1. *Summarizing CSS1 Properties*

The property	can accept values like	has the initial value	applies to	can be inherited	and can use values formatted as percentages
font	[<font-style> | | <font-variant> | | <font-weight>]? <font-size> [/ <line-height>]? <font-family>	not defined for shorthand properties	all elements	yes	allowed on <font-size> and <line-height>
color	<color>	UA specific	all elements	yes	N/A
background-color	<color> | transparent	transparent	all elements	no	N/A
background-image	<url> | none	none	all elements	no	N/A
background-repeat	repeat | repeat-x | repeat-y | no-repeat	repeat	all elements	no	N/A
background-attachment	scroll | fixed	scroll	all elements	no	N/A
background-position	[<percentage> | <length>]{1,2} | [top | center | bottom] | | [left | center | right]	0% 0%	block-level and replaced elements	no	refer to the size of the element itself
background	<background-color> | | <background-image> | | <background-repeat> | | <background-attachment> | | <background-position>	not defined for shorthand properties	all elements	no	allowed on <background-position>
word-spacing	normal | <length>	normal	all elements	yes	N/A
letter-spacing	normal | <length>	normal	all elements	yes	N/A
text-decoration	none | [underline | | overline | | line-through | | blink]	none	all elements	no[**]	N/A

Table B-1. *Summarizing CSS1 Properties (continued)*

The property	can accept values like	has the initial value	applies to	can be inherited	and can use values formatted as percentages
vertical-align	baseline | sub | super | top | text-top | middle | bottom | text-bottom | <percentage>	baseline	inline elements	no	refer to the 'line-height' of the element itself
text-transform	capitalize | uppercase | lowercase | none	none	all elements	yes	N/A
text-align	left | right | center | justify	UA specific	block-level elements	yes	N/A
text-indent	<length> | <percentage>	0	block-level elements	yes	refer to parent element's width
line-height	normal | <number> | <length> | <percentage>	normal	all elements	yes	relative to the font size of the element itself
margin-top	<length> | <percentage> | auto	0	all elements	no	refer to parent element's width
margin-right	<length> | <percentage> | auto	0	all elements	no	refer to parent element's width
margin-bottom	<length> | <percentage> | auto	0	all elements	no	refer to parent element's width
margin-left	<length> | <percentage> | auto	0	all elements	no	refer to parent element's width
margin	[<length> | <percentage> | auto]{1,4}	not defined for shorthand properties	all elements	no	refer to parent element's width

Table B-1.   *Summarizing CSS1 Properties* (continued)

The property	can accept values like	has the initial value	applies to	can be inherited	and can use values formatted as percentages
padding-top	<length> | <percentage>	0	all elements	no	refer to parent element's width
padding-right	<length> | <percentage>	0	all elements	no	refer to parent element's width
padding-bottom	<length> | <percentage>	0	all elements	no	refer to parent element's width
padding-left	<length> | <percentage>	0 .	all elements	no	refer to parent element's width
padding	[<length> | <percentage>]{1,4}	0	all elements	no	refer to parent element's width
border-top-width	thin | medium | thick | <length>	'medium'	all elements	no	N/A
border-right-width	thin | medium | thick | <length>	'medium'	all elements	no	N/A
border-bottom-width	thin | medium | thick | <length>	'medium'	all elements	no	N/A
border-left-width	thin | medium | thick | <length>	'medium'	all elements	no	N/A
border-width	[thin | medium | thick | <length>]{1,4}	not defined for shorthand properties	all elements	no	N/A
border-color	<color>{1,4}	the value of the 'color' property	all elements	no	N/A

Table B-1.   *Summarizing CSS1 Properties* (continued)

The property	can accept values like	has the initial value	applies to	can be inherited	and can use values formatted as percentages
border-style	none	dotted	dashed	solid	double	groove	ridge	inset	outset	none	all elements	no	N/A
border-top	<border-top-width>		<border-style>		<color>	not defined for shorthand properties	all elements	no	N/A
border-right	<border-right-width>		<border-style>		<color>	not defined for shorthand properties	all elements	no	N/A
border-bottom	<border-bottom-width>		<border-style>		<color>	not defined for shorthand properties	all elements	no	N/A
border-left	<border-left-width>		<border-style>		<color>	not defined for shorthand properties	all elements	no	N/A
border	<border-width>		<border-style>		<color>	not defined for shorthand properties	all elements	no	N/A
width [*]	<length>	<percentage>	auto	auto	block-level and replaced elements	no	refer to parent element's width
height [*]	<length>	auto	auto	block-level and replaced elements	no	N/A
float	left	right	none	none	all elements	no	N/A

Table B-1. *Summarizing CSS1 Properties (continued)*

The property	can accept values like	has the initial value	applies to	can be inherited	and can use values formatted as percentages
clear	none | left | right | both	none	all elements	no	N/A
display	block | inline | list-item | none	block	all elements	no	N/A
white-space	normal | pre | nowrap	normal	block-level elements	yes	N/A
list-style-type	disc | circle | square | decimal | lower-roman | upper-roman | lower-alpha | upper-alpha | none	disc	elements with 'display' value 'list-item'	yes	N/A
list-style-image	<url> | none	none	elements with 'display' value 'list-item'	yes	N/A
list-style-position	inside | outside	outside	elements with 'display' value 'list-item'	yes	N/A
list-style	<keyword> || <position> || <url>	not defined for shorthand properties	elements with 'display' value 'list-item'	yes	N/A
position	absolute | relative | static	static	all elements	no	N/A
left	<length> | <percentage> | auto	auto	elements with the 'position' property of type 'absolute' or 'relative'	no	refer to parent element's width; if parent's height is set to 'auto', percentage is undefined

Table B-1. *Summarizing CSS1 Properties* (continued)

The property	can accept values like	has the initial value	applies to	can be inherited	and can use values formatted as percentages
top	\<length\> | \<percentage\> | auto	auto	elements with the 'position' property of type 'absolute' or 'relative'	no	refer to parent element's height; if parent's height is set to 'auto', percentage is undefined
width [*]	\<length\> | \<percentage\> | auto	auto	block-level and replaced elements, elements with 'position' property of type 'absolute'	no	refer to parent element's width
height [*]	\<length\> | \<percentage\> | auto	auto	block-level and replaced elements, elements with 'position' property of type 'absolute'	no	refer to parent element's height; if parent's height is 'auto', percentage of height is undefined
clip	\<shape\> | auto	auto	elements with the 'position' property of type 'absolute'	no	N/A
overflow	none | clip | scroll	none	elements with the 'position' property of type 'absolute' or 'relative'	no	N/A

Table B-1. *Summarizing CSS1 Properties* (continued)

The property	can accept values like	has the initial value	applies to	can be inherited	and can use values formatted as percentages
z-index	auto | <integer>	auto	elements with the 'position' property of type 'absolute' or 'relative'	no	N/A
visibility	inherit | visible | hidden	inherit	all elements	if value is 'inherit'	N/A
page-break-before	auto | allways | left | right	auto	block-level elements outside of tables	no	N/A
page-break-after	auto | allways | left | right	auto	block-level elements outside of tables	no	N/A
size	<length>{1,2} | auto | portrait | landscape	auto	page context	N/A	N/A
marks	crop | | cross | none	none	page context	N/A	N/A

Table B-1. *Summarizing CSS1 Properties* (continued)

Notation for Property Values

In this section, we offer an overview of CSS1 notation.

Brackets

In the CSS1 world, brackets are more than just brackets. The standard distinguishes between three types of brackets, and the uses to which these types may be put. We've summarized the CSS1 bracketing standards in Table B-2.

Bracket type	Meaning
	Words without any brackets are keywords that must appear literally, without quotes. These words may be used directly as values of the respective property.
< ... >	Words between < and > give a type of value.
[...]	Grouping
{ ... }	Curly braces indicate a special modifier.

Table B-2. *Summarizing Bracket Use in CSS1 Style Sheets*

Separators

As it does with brackets, CSS1 distinguishes between types of separators or delimiters that may be used in style sheets. Table B-3 gives an overview of CSS1 separators.

Separator	Meaning
	Several things juxtaposed mean that all of them must occur, in the given order.
|	A bar separates alternatives. One of them must occur.
| |	A double bar (A | | B) means that either A or B or both must occur, in any order.

Table B-3. *Summarizing CSS1 Separators*

Modifier	Meaning
*	The preceding type, word, or group is repeated zero or more times.
+	The preceding type, word, or group is repeated one or more times.
?	The preceding type, word, or group is optional.
{A,B}	A pair of numbers in curly braces indicates that the preceding type, word, or group is repeated at least A and at most B times.

Table B-4. *Summarizing CSS1 Modifiers*

Modifiers

CSS1 style sheets use a sort of shorthand, similar to that found in UNIX, to indicate ranges and types of values. Table B-4 examines these CSS1 modifiers.

Types of Values

Values that may be assigned to parameters in CSS1 style sheets fall into quite a few categories, whose meaning isn't always immediately apparent. Table B-5 elaborates upon the types of parameter values that may be used in CSS1 style sheets.

Type of value	Meaning
<absolute-size>	An <absolute-size> keyword is an index to a table of font sizes computed and kept by the UA. Possible values are: [xx-small | x-small | small | medium | large | x-large | xx-large]
<background-attachment>	Any value of the property *background-attachment*
<background-color>	Any value of the property *background-color*
<background-image>	Any value of the property *background-image*
<background-position>	Any value of the property *background-position*
<background-repeat>	Any value of the property *background-repeat*
<border-bottom-width>	Any value of the property *border-bottom-width*
<border-left-width>	Any value of the property *border-left-width*
<border-right-width>	Any value of the property *border-right-width*
<border-style>	Any value of the property *border-style*
<border-top-width>	Any value of the property *border-top-width*
<border-width>	Any value of the property *border-width*
<bottom>	Possible values: [auto | <length>]
<color>	A color is either a keyword or a numerical RGB specification. The suggested list of keyword color names is: aqua, black, blue, fuchsia, gray, green, lime, maroon, navy, olive, purple, red, silver, teal, white, and yellow.
<family-name>	The name of a font family. Examples are 'helvetica' and 'arial'.

Table B-5.   *Summarizing CSS1 Property Value Types*

Type of value	Meaning
<font-family>	Any value of the property *font-family*
<font-size>	Any value of the property *font-size*
<font-style>	Any value of the property *font-style*
<font-variant>	Any value of the property *font-variant*
<font-weight>	Any value of the property *font-weight*
<generic-family>	The following generic families are defined: 'serif' (such as Times) 'sans serif' (such as Helvetica) 'cursive' (such as Zapf-Cancery) 'fantasy' (such as Western) 'monospace' (such as Courier)
<integer>	Any integer value
<keyword>	Any value of the property *list-style-type*
<left>	Possible values: [auto | <length>]
<length>	The format of a length value is an optional sign character ('+' or '-', with '+' being the default) immediately followed by a number (with or without a decimal point) immediately followed by a unit identifier (a two-letter abbreviation). After a '0', the unit identifier is optional.
<line-height>	Any value of the property *line-height*
<number>	Any numerical value
<percentage>	The format of a percentage value is an optional sign character ('+' or '-', with '+' being the default) immediately followed by a number (with or without a decimal point) immediately followed by '%'.
<position>	Any value of the property *list-style-position*

Table B-5.   *Summarizing CSS1 Property Value Types* (continued)

Type of value	Meaning
<relative-size>	A <relative-size> keyword is interpreted relative to the table of font sizes and the font size of the parent element. Possible values: [larger | smaller]
<right>	Possible values: [auto | <length>]
<shape>	Possible values: [rect (<top> <right> <bottom> <left>)]
<top>	Possible values: [auto | <length>]
<url>	The format of a URL value is 'url', followed by an optional white space, followed by an optional single quote (') or double quote (") character, followed by the URL itself, followed by an optional single quote (') or double quote (") character, followed by an optional white space followed by ')'. Quote characters that are not part of the URL itself must be balanced.

Table B-5. *Summarizing CSS1 Property Value Types* (continued)

Appendix C

JavaScript Quick Reference

This appendix presents a condensed review of JavaScript syntax, as well as several simple examples of complete JavaScript programs. The features are listed alpahbetically and will be discussed individually.

JavaScript Syntax

argument

argument is the item or items upon which a procedure or function operates. This feature can be a variable or a constant.

array

array is a variable that represents a group of contiguous memory locations, all of which contain the same type of data. It is used to represent related data, such as the fertilizer requirements of seven species of flowers. It needs as many values as it has units. It can be placed anywhere in a JavaScript program.
It is used like this:
JavaScript presents you with a number of built-in arrays, including

- anchors: reflects all <A> tags containing a NAME attribute in a document, in the order in which they appear in the document

- applets: reflects all the <APPLET> tags in a document, in the order in which they appear in the document

- arguments: reflects all the arguments to a function

- elements: reflects a form's elements

- embeds: reflects a document's <EMBED> tags, in the order in which they appear in the document

- forms: reflects a document's <FORM> tags, in the order in which they appear in a document

- frames: reflects all the <FRAME> tags in a window that has a <FRAMESET> tag; frames store document data in the order in which the documents appear in the HTML source file

- history: reflects a window's history entries

- images: reflects a document's <IMG> tags, in the order in which they appear in the document; note that images created with the Image() constructor are not included in the images array

- links: reflects a document's <AREA HREF="..."> tags, <A HREF=""> tags, and Link objects created with the link method, in the order in which they appear in the source document

- mimeTypes: reflects all the MIME types supported by the client

- options: reflects all the options in a Select object (<OPTION> tags), in the order in which they appear in a document

- plugins: reflects all the plug-ins installed on the client, in the order in which they are referenced by the source document

call

JavaScript most frequently executes procedures implicitly, that is, without a specific call statement. Further, unlike VBScript, JavaScript relies most heavily on its built-in variables, functions, and methods.

Call is used like this:

```
INPUT TYPE="button" VALUE="Calculate" onClick="compute(this.form)">
```

comment

comment is documentation inside a JavaScript program's source code. It is used to make that code more understandable to the programmer who writes or must modify it. It needs to be preceded by the characters

```
<!--
```

and terminated by the characters

```
-->
```

so as to be distinguished from executable code. *comment* can be placed anywhere in a JavaScript program.

It is used like this:

```
<SCRIPT>
<!--Begin to hide script contents from old browsers.
JavaScript statements...
// Stop hiding. -->
</SCRIPT>
```

This example presents two forms of commenting in JavaScript. Non-JavaScript-capable browsers will ignore the beginning and ending SCRIPT tags. In similar fashion, all statements in between are enclosed in an HTML comment, so they are ignored, too.

event

event is a term used to describe something that takes place during the execution of a JavaScript program, to which the program can be instructed to respond in specified ways. It is used to allow the user and JavaScript to interact. It needs to be detected by JavaScript (which takes place automatically) and to have code attached to it that specifies the actions to be taken when the event is detected. It can be placed in any part of a JavaScript program.

This example of how *event* works, drawn from the JavaScript Programmer's Guide, creates an event handler called compute for a button called Calculate.

```
<HEAD> <SCRIPT>
<!--- Hide script from old browsers
function compute(f) { if (confirm("Are you sure?"))
f.result.value = eval(f.expr.value)
<!-- If the user has indicated yes to the prompt for confirmation,
set f.result.value equal to the result of evaluating the contents
of f.expr.value-->
else
alert("Please come back again.") }
// end hiding from old browsers -->
</SCRIPT> </HEAD>
<BODY>
<FORM>
Enter an expression:
```

```
<INPUT TYPE="text" NAME="expr" SIZE=15 >
<INPUT TYPE="button" VALUE="Calculate"
onClick="compute(this.form)">
<!--   more code    -->
</FORM>
</BODY>
```

If... Then... Else

If ... Then ... Else is a statement block. It is used to make a decision between two alternatives. It needs code to be executed if the test indicated in the *If* portion of the statement is true, as well as code to be executed in all other cases—that is, if the *Else* portion of the statement is correct. It can be placed anywhere in a JavaScript program.

To explain how this feature is used, we will once again offer an example from the JavaScript Programmer's Guide. Note that this example uses the traditional HTML means of indicating comments.

```
// Determine if a checkbox is checked
if (checkboxWin.document.musicForm.checkbox2.checked) {
<!-- Note the use of a Boolean test in the line above.-->
alert('The checkbox on the musicForm in checkboxWin is checked!')}
else
// Check the checkbox
checkboxWin.document.musicForm.checkbox2.checked=true
// Determine if an option in a Select object is selected
if (checkboxWin.document.musicForm.musicTypes.options[1].selected)
{alert('Option 1 is selected!')}
else
// Select an option in a Select object
checkboxWin.document.musicForm.musicTypes.selectedIndex=1
```

operator

operator is a symbol. It is used to indicate a task to be carried out. *operator* can be arithmetical, relational, logical, or unary. It needs an operand, that is, the entity upon which it will act. It can be placed anywhere in a JavaScript program.

operator is used like this:

```
C=A +B
```

C equals A plus B
or

```
D>E
```

Test to see if D is greater than E
or

```
if (HOMERUN)
```

Is the value of HOMERUN true?
or

```
!TRIPLEPLAY
```

In every other case than a triple play, do ...

SCRIPT

SCRIPT is a tag. It is used to indicate the presence within an HTML document of scripting commands. It needs the attribute LANGUAGE. The LANGUAGE attribute must be set to the value JavaScript, as in LANGUAGE= "JavaScript". SCRIPT can be placed in the HEAD section, to carry out tasks that will affect a page as a whole.

SCRIPT is used like this:

```
<HTML>
<HEAD>
<TITLE>JavaScript Tutorial</TITLE>
<SCRIPT LANGUAGE="JavaScript">
`    some code
</SCRIPT>
</HEAD>
```

The SCRIPT tag can also be placed in the BODY section, to carry out more specific tasks such as testing the results of a particular user-initiated operation. To see how SCRIPT is used in that context, see the example for the *event* entry, earlier in this appendix.

variable lifetime

variable lifetime is the length of time for which a variable will maintain its contents. It is used to ensure the validity of variables' values. It needs to be kept in mind. For example, a local variable—that is, one that exists only within a procedure—will be removed from memory when that procedure finishes running.

variable name

variable name is the symbolic representation of data storage. It is used to set aside memory to hold a value of a particular data type. It needs to begin with an alphabetic character; to contain no embedded periods; to be no longer than 255 characters; to be unique in the scope within which it is declared. It can be placed in the early section of JavaScript programs or modules.

variable scope

variable scope is the extent to which a variable name will be recognized. It is used to ensure the uniqueness of variable names. It needs to be applied sensibly. For instance, declaring a variable within a procedure makes it recognizable only within that procedure.

Appendix D

VBScript Quick Reference

T his appendix summarizes Microsoft's Programmers Reference for Visual Basic Scripting Edition, that is, VBScript. It includes a capsulized look at VBScript syntax, as well as several simple examples of complete VBScript programs.

VBScript Syntax

The VBScript feature	is	is used to	needs	can be placed	and is used like this
argument	the item or items upon which a procedure or function operates; can be a variable or a constant				
array	a variable that represents a group of contiguous memory locations, all of which contain the same type of data	represent related data, such as the fertilizer requirements of seven species of flowers	as many values as it has units	anywhere in a VBScript program	`DIM record(10)` (that is, create an array called Record, which has 11 components, since arrays are numbered beginning with zero) or `DIM Square (5,6)` (to create a two-dimensional array with five rows and six columns)
assignment statement	an operation	place a value in a variable	to have a variable name on the left of the equal sign, and a value on the right	anywhere in a VBScript program	`planets=9` or `alien="Kazon"`
Call	a statement	execute a procedure	arguments	anywhere in a VBScript program	`Call UserProc(arg1, arg2)` or `UserProc arg1, arg2` (Note that the first form explicitly uses the Call statement, while the second omits it, but that both forms supply an argument list.)

The VBScript feature	is	is used to	needs	can be placed	and is used like this
comment	documentation inside a VBScript program's source code	make that code more understandable to the programmer who writes or must modify it	to be preceded by a single quote, so as to be distinguished from executable code	anywhere in a VBScript program	`'This tells VBScript that the line that follows is only commentary.` It's important to point out that VBScript instructions are themselves considered as comments when embedded in an HTML document, as in: `<!–` `'    some VBScript code` `-->` Only the <SCRIPT> / </SCRIPT> tag pair itself need not be presented to HTML as a comment.
CONST	a statement	create a symbolic name for a value that will not change during the course of a VBScript program's execution	a symbolic name and associated value, as an argument	the early section of VBScript programs or modules	`CONST Vulcan= "T'Lar"` or `CONST Planets=9`
DIM	a keyword	declare a variable	a variable name, or list of variable names separated by commas, as arguments	any part of a VBScript program	`DIM Bajoran, Betazoid, Trill`
Do ... Loop	a looping construct	repeat an action or group of actions as long as a controlling condition remains in effect	a controlling condition; an action or set of actions to carry out	any part of a VBScript program	`Do While NumPlants > 10` `NumPlants = NumPlants - 1` `counter = counter + 1` `Loop`

The VBScript feature	is	is used to	needs	can be placed	and is used like this
event	a term used to describe something that takes place during the execution of a VBScript program, to which the program can be instructed to respond in specified ways	allow the user and VBScript to interact	to be detected by VBScript (which takes place automatically) to have code attached to it that specifies the actions to be taken when the event is detected	any part of a VBScript program	`EVENT="OnClick"` `FOR="ButtonA"` (code fragment which, when used in a complete line of VBScript code, would specify actions to be taken when a user clicks Button A)
executing functions	a process	cause a function to do its thing	to be on the right side of an equal sign, with the variable that will contain the value the function will produce and return on the left; must not be combined with the Call statement	anywhere in a VBScript program	`CanadaDollars = Convert (USDollars)` (executes the function Convert, which simply multiplies by 1.3, on the value represented by the argument USDollars, and places the result in the variable CanadaDollars)
For ... Next	a looping structure	repeat an action or group of actions	a range of integers that represents the number of times the action or actions are to be carried out; a task or group of tasks to perform	anywhere in a VBScript program	`For x = 1 To 50` `document.write "Beat 'Em, Bucs!"` `Next` (will display the phrase *Beat 'Em, Bucs!* 50 times in the current window or frame)

The VBScript feature	is	is used to	needs	can be placed	and is used like this

For Each ... Next	a looping structure	repeat an action or group of actions	a range of integers that represents the number of times the action or actions are to be carried out; a task or group of tasks to perform	anywhere in a VBScript program	`<HTML>`
					`<SCRIPT LANGUAGE="VBScript">`
					
					`<!--`
					`'    some`
					`code`
					`Counter=A`
					`For Each I in Counter`
					`'    do some stuff`
					
					`Next`
					`-->`
					`</SCRIPT>`
					(will "do some stuff" the number of times indicated by the value in Counter)

Function ... End Function	a program module type	return a value to a calling procedure	to have defined for it the steps it will take to obtain the value	anywhere in a VBScript program	`Function Convert (dollars)`
					`Convert=dollars*1.3`
					`End Function`

If ...Then ... Else	a statement block	make a decision between two alternatives	code to be executed if the test indicated in the If portion of the statement is true, as well as code to be executed in all other cases, that is, if the Else portion of the statement is correct	anywhere in a VBScript program	`If A < Average`
					`Then Average = Average + 1`
					`Else`
					`A = A - 1`
					(If the value in the variable A is less than that in the variable Average, add 1 to Average. Otherwise, subtract 1 from A.)
					Note that when more than one action pertains to an If or Else statement, the block as a whole must end with the statement
					`End If`

The VBScript feature	is	is used to	needs	can be placed	and is used like this
operator	a symbol	indicate a task to be carried out; can be any of these: arithmetical relational logical unary	an operand, that is, the entity upon which it will act	anywhere in a VBScript program	`C=A+B` (C equals A plus B) or `D > E` (test to see if D is greater than E) or `if (HOMERUN)` (is the value of HOMERUN true?) or `!TRIPLEPLAY` (in every other case than a triple play, do ...)
OPTION EXPLICIT	a statement	tell VBScript that you will explicitly declare every variable	no arguments	the first line of a VBScript program	`OPTION EXPLICT`
scalar	a variable that represents only one location in memory	hold a single value	only one value	anywhere in a VBScript program	
SCRIPT	a tag	indicate the presence within an HTML document of scripting commands	the attribute LANGUAGE; The LANGUAGE attribute must be set to the value VBScript, as in LANGUAGE= "VBScript".	the HEAD section, to carry out tasks that will affect a page as a whole	`<HTML>` `<HEAD>` `<TITLE>Sample of the SCRIPT tag</TITLE>` `<SCRIPT LANGUAGE= "VBScript">` `'    some code` `</SCRIPT>` `</HEAD>`

The VBScript feature	is	is used to	needs	can be placed	and is used like this

SCRIPT	a tag	indicate the presence within an HTML document of scripting commands	the attribute LANGUAGE; The LANGUAGE attribute must be set to the value VBScript, as in LANGUAGE= "VBScript".	in the BODY section, to carry out more specific tasks such as testing the results of a particular user-initiated operation	`<BODY>`
					`<FORM NAME="Form1">`
					`<INPUT`
					`TYPE="Button" NAME=`
					`"ButtonButton"`
					`VALUE="Click">`
					`<SCRIPT FOR=`
					`"ButtonButton"`
					`EVENT="onClick"`
					`LANGUAGE=`
					`"VBScript">`
					`MsgBox "Button`
					`Pressed!"`
					`</SCRIPT>`
					`</FORM>`
					`</BODY>`

Select Case	a statement	make a decision between a number of alternatives	to have defined for it the actions it will take in each possible situation	anywhere in a VBScript program	`Select Case`
					`Document.FormA.`
					`Hero`
					`Case "Tubman"`
					`'    do some stuff '`
					`'    such as`
					`'    displaying`
					`'    an image of`
					`'    Harriet Tubman`
					`Case "Truth"`
					`'    do some stuff '`
					`'    such as`
					`'    displaying`
					`'    an image of`
					`'    Sojourner Truth`
					`Case "Blackwell"`
					`'    do some stuff '`
					`Case "Stowe"`
					`'    do some stuff '`
					`End Select`

The VBScript feature	is	is used to	needs	can be placed	and is used like this

Step	a keyword	adjust the number of times a loop will execute	to be supplied an integer that represents the size of the "step" it will take through the loop	anywhere in a VBScript program	`For j = 2 To 10`
					`Step 2`
					`total = total + j`
					`Next`
					(Despite the range of this loop containing 9 values, the loop will execute only five times, because the step keyword will cause it to hop through the range of values of j in units of 2.)

Sub ... End Sub	a program module, usually referred to as a procedure	carry out some task, which does not involve returning a value to the calling procedure	to have defined for it the actions it is to take	anywhere in a VBScript program	`Sub ConvertMoney()`
					`USDol =`
					`InputBox("Please`
					`enter the amount`
					`you wish to`
					`convert from US to`
					`Canadian`
					`dollars.", 1)`
					`End Sub`

variable lifetime	the length of time for which a variable will maintain its contents	ensure the validity of variables' values	to be kept in mind. For example, a local variable —that is, one that exists only within a procedure— will be removed from memory when that procedure finishes running.		

The VBScript feature	is	is used to	needs	can be placed	and is used like this
variable name	a symbolic representation of data storage	set aside memory to hold a value of a particular data type	to begin with an alphabetic character; to contain no embedded periods; to be no longer than 255 characters; to be unique in the scope within which it is declared	the early section of VBScript programs or modules	
variable scope	the extent to which a variable name will be recognized	ensure the uniqueness of variable names	to be applied sensibly. For instance, declaring a variable within a procedure makes it recognizable only within that procedure.		

The VBScript feature	is	is used to	needs	can be placed	and is used like this
Variant	a data type (the only data type available in VBScript)	indicate a variety of data characteristics	to represent one of these: empty null Boolean byte integer long single double date/time string object currency error	any part of a VBScript program	**empty:** 0 for numerics, or a zero-length strring for character data **null:** no value (not even zero) **Boolean:** either True or False **byte:** integers in the range 0 to 255 **integer:** integers in the range -32,768 to 32,767 **long:** integers in the range -2,147,483,648 to 2,147,483,647. **single:** a single-precision, floating-point number in the range -3.402823E38 to-1.401298E-45 for negative values; 1.401298E-45 to 3.402823E38 for positive values **double:** a double-precision, floating-point number in the range -1.79769313486232E308 to -4.94065645841247E-324 for negative values; 4.94065645841247E-324 to 1.79769313486232E308 for positive values **date/time:** a number that represents a date between January 1, 100 to December 31, 9999 **string:** a variable-length string that can be up to approximately 2 billion characters in length **object:** an object **currency:** -922,337,203,685,477.5808 to 922,337,203,685,477.5807 **error:** an error number

VBScript Examples

In this section, we'll look at two simple VBScripts.

Using Script, Sub ... End Sub, and Events

This VBScript uses a very simple document to demonstrate SCRIPT, Sub ... End Sub, and event handling.

```
<HTML>
<HEAD><TITLE>A Taoist Example</TITLE>
<SCRIPT LANGUAGE="VBScript">
<!--Sub ButtonButton_OnClick
' Define a subroutine which in turn defines what's to be done when
' an input button is clicked.
MsgBox "Heaven sends rain without choosing between the thriving
and the withering.  (Xiujing)   "
' Then, in a message box, display appropriate text.
End Sub
-->
</SCRIPT>
</HEAD>
<BODY>
<FORM>
' If we're to have an input button, we must first have a form.
<INPUT NAME="ButtonButton" TYPE="BUTTON" VALUE="Click Here to See
a Quote from A Master.">
' So, after we call for a form, we define our input button.
</FORM>
</BODY>
</HTML>
```

Checking User Input and Sending Legitimate Data to a Server

Our second example not only verifies user input but also then passes that input to a server. In this example, we're offering to give the user the value, in Canadian dollars, of a specified number of US dollars.

```
<SCRIPT LANGUAGE="VBScript">
<!--
```

```
Sub Submit_OnClick
Dim UserEntryForm
' Dimension, that is, define the form into which users will enter
data.
Set UserEntryForm = Document.ValidForm
' Use the built-in VBScript method ValidForm to check the form
we've just defined.
MsgBox "Please enter, as an integer, the number of US dollars you
wish to convert to Canadian dollars."
' Display a prompt to our users in a message box.
If IsNumeric(UserEntryForm.Text1.Value) Then
' If the value the user has entered into the first field in our
form is numeric   ...
    If (UserEntryForm.Text1.Value/10) > 0 Then
' and if we determine that it's not a whole number   ...
    MsgBox "Please enter a whole-number value."
' ask the user to correct his or her mistake.
Else
' Otherwise,
MsgBox "Your entry is being processed."
' Tell the user everything's cool, and   ...
UserEntryForm.Submit
' send the data just entered to the server.
End If
End Sub
-->
</SCRIPT>
```

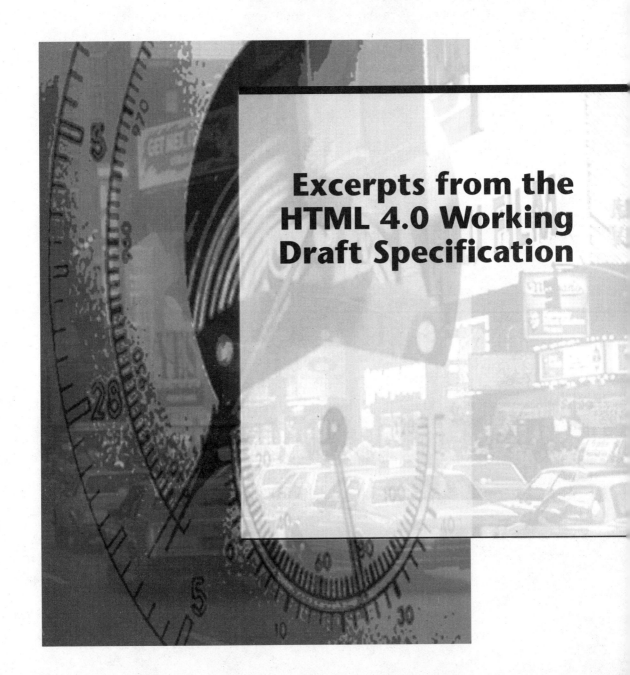

Excerpts from the HTML 4.0 Working Draft Specification

The source of this material is the W3C's most up-to-date (August 1997) effort at standardizing HTML. Given the various definitions of Dynamic HTML still to be found when this book went to print, we wanted to include highlights of the W3C working draft as a means of offering you a view of the subject that transcends vendor- and jargon-specific interpretations.

Changes between HTML 3.2 and HTML 4.0 Working Draft

In HTML 4.0, we find	which include	and indicate
new elements	Q	a quotation
	INS	newly inserted text
	DEL	newly deleted text
	ACRONYM	an acronym, such as WWW
	LEGEND	a label that can be applied to a group of items defined by FIELDSET
	COLGROUP	allows sets of columns to be grouped with different width and alignment properties specified by one or more COL elements; STYLE attribute acts as the means of extending properties associated with edges and interiors of groups of cells; for example: line styles dotted, double, thin, and so on fill patterns cell margins
	BUTTON	used to allow greater variety in the definition of forms buttons
	FIELDSET	groups related form fields together so that they can be referenced and manipulated as a group
deprecated or being phased out	ISINDEX	
	APPLET	
	CENTER	
	FONT	
	BASEFONT	
	STRIKE	

In HTML 4.0, we find	which include	and indicate
	S	
	U	
	DIR	
	MENU	
obsolete elements	XME	
	PLAINTEXT	
	LISTING	
changes to and enhancements of tables	maintained backward compatibility with the Netscape implementation of tables	
	simplified importing tables that adhere to the SGML model	
	made ALIGN attribute compatible with the latest versions of the most popular browsers	
	clarified the role of the DIR attribute when absolute and relative column widths are mixed	
	modified FRAME and RULES attributes to avoid SGML name clashes with each other, and to avoid clashes with the ALIGN and VALIGN attributes	
changes to and enhancements of forms	added ACCESSKEY attribute to provide direct keyboard access to form fields	
	added DISABLED attribute to provide the ability to enable or disable form controls	

In HTML 4.0, we find	which include	and indicate
	added READONLY attribute to provide a means of precluding any changes to a form field	
	defined LABEL element to provide the ability to associate a label with a form control	
	defined FIELDSET element to provide the ability to group related fields together	
	defined LEGEND element to provide the ability to name a group of fields organized by FIELDSET	the new elements FIELDSET and LEGEND are part of the W3C's effort to improve Web accessibility; for example, speech-based browsers would be better able to describe a form that used FIELDSET and LEGEND, because these tags would allow form fields to be described as a group
	added ACCEPT attribute to allow authors to specify a list of valid media types or patterns for input	applicable to INPUT element only
	added BUTTON element	intended to allow the creation of forms that contain buttons other than the basic submit and reset buttons
	added ACCEPT_CHARSET attribute	applicable to FORM element; modeled on the HTTP "Accept-Charset" header; use to specify a list of character sets acceptable to a Web server
closer compliance with SGML	entities	character entities are numeric or symbolic names for characters that you can include in an HTML document; use when authoring tools do not provide for the entry of little-used characters; character entities begin with an ampersand (&) and end with a semicolon (;)
	elements	an SGML-compliant element typically consists of a start tag, content, and an end tag

In HTML 4.0, we find	which include	and indicate
		an SGML-compliant element's start tag is written `<element-name>` where *element-name* is the name of the element
		an SGML-compliant element's end tag is written with a slash before the element name: `</element-name>` for example: `<pre> ... </pre>`
		some HTML elements may not require end tags
		some HTML elements may not include content; for example, the element BR (line break) never carries content and never requires an end tag
	element names	always case-insensitive
	Elements are not tags!	some literature incorrectly calls elements *tags*, as in *the P tag*; elements must be distinguished from the start and/or end tags that may encase them for example, the HEAD element is always present, but both start and end tags for this element can be omitted
	attributes	the term *attributes* refers to properties associated with specific elements
		values may be assigned to attributes
		attribute/value pairs must appear before the final > of an element's start tag

In HTML 4.0, we find	**which include**	**and indicate**

any number of attribute/value pairs may appear in an element's start tag, as long as

the members of the set of attribute/value pairs are separated by spaces
the individual attribute/value pairs are made up of attributes and associated values that are allowed for the element in question

for example, the following code, while it is syntactically correct, contains an illegal attribute/value pair:

```
<A WIDTH=150>
</A>
```

the members of an attribute/value pair list may appear in any order

attribute values must be delimited by either double quotes (" ")
single quotes (' ')

single quotes can be included within an attribute value that has been delimited by double quotes; double quotes can be included within an attribute value that has been delimited by single quotes

ASCII values can be used to represent both double and single quotes

HTML attribute values can be specified without any quotation marks if the attribute value contains only one or more of the letters a-z and A-Z
the digits 0-9
hyphens (ASCII decimal 45)
periods (ASCII decimal 46)

attribute names are always case-insensitive

HTML documents may compress better if you use lowercase letters for element and attribute names; compression algorithms do a better job on repeated patterns, and lowercase letters are more frequent than uppercase ones

In HTML 4.0, we find	**which include**	**and indicate**
	comments	HTML comments must use the following syntax:

```
<!— a single comment —>
<!— a single comment that uses
two lines —>
```

HTML comments must not be written in such a way as to cause browsers to interpret and carry them out as part of a document

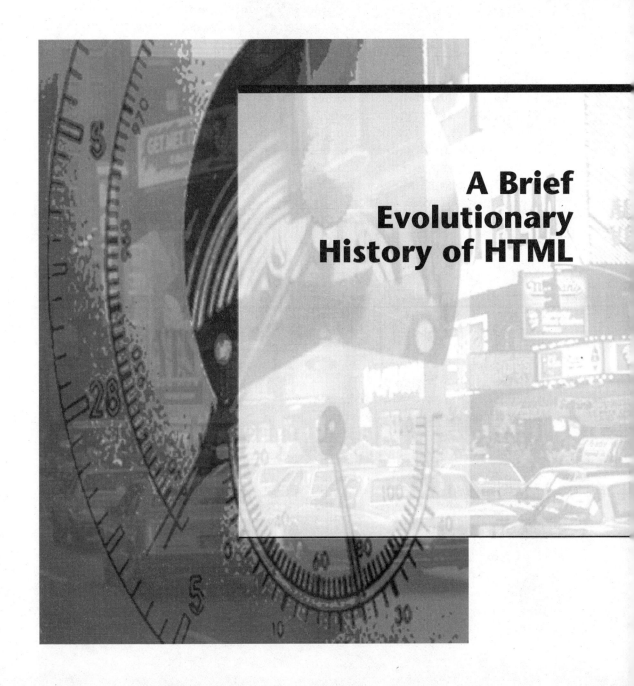

Appendix F

A Brief Evolutionary History of HTML

A Brief History of the Internet

You might say it all began with the invention, by Ray Tomlinson in 1971, of an email program to send messages across a distributed network. Others might choose to date the Big Bang of Internet information distribution from the introduction, in 1972, of a utility called telnet (for *telephone network*). The telnet utility allows a user to establish a session on a remote host. In 1973, a related utility called FTP, or file transfer protocol, was introduced to allow a user to upload files to or download files from a remote host.

Internet information exchange really began to gather steam in 1974, with the publication of a detailed design for the Transmission Control Protocol (TCP). By the early 1980s, the Internet Protocol or IP joined TCP to manage Internet routing. Then, in 1981, data communications burst (no pun intended) into something approaching its modern form with the establishment of BITNET, the Because It's Time NETwork. BITNET started as a cooperative effort between the City University of New York and Yale, and it provided many of the features we've become accustomed to on today's Internet:

- email services
- listserv or newsgroup services
- FTP services

The year 1982 is the true birth date of the modern Internet. It was then that the Department of Defense and the Advanced Research Projects Agency (ARPA) decided that the dynamic duo of TCP and the Internet Protocol (IP), by now commonly known as TCP/IP, should be the default protocol suite for what was then known as ARPANET. This seal of approval led to the first real structure deserving the name *Internet*—a connected set of networks that relied upon the TCP/IP protocols.

By 1983, the Internet had begun to take on some of the characteristics it has today. In that year, for instance, programmers at the University of Wisconsin developed the concept of a *name server* application, which permits users to locate information without knowing the exact path to a remote system. And in 1984, the domain name server (DNS) application was introduced to manage host names. DNS arrived none too soon, because it was also in 1984 that the number of host computers connected to the Internet exceeded 1,000.

The most recent antecedent to the modern Internet, the National Science Foundation Network (NSFNET), was established in 1988. NSFNET boasted a then-blazing speed of 56 kilobits per second (Kbps) along its backbone, or main cable runs. More significantly, NSFNET also involved the creation of five super-computing centers, at Princeton, Carnegie-Mellon, Cornell, the University of California, and the University of Illinois. Connections to these centers burgeoned until, in 1987, the number of host computers on the Internet surpassed 10,000, and in 1989, 100,000.

From 1991 to today, the Internet and the World Wide Web—today the most frequently used of the Internet's means of transferring information—have moved steadily toward becoming synonymous. It was in 1991 that the British researcher Tim Berners-Lee developed the Hypertext Markup Language, or HTML, the basis for structuring documents to be presented via the Web. In order to move documents formatted in HTML between Internet sites scattered around the world, the protocol called Hypertext Transfer Protocol, or HTTP, was in turn invented.

A protocol *is nothing more than a set of rules under which computers will exchange information. HTTP, therefore, defines how hypertext (text that you can access without a precise idea of its location) moves between machines.*

Privacy Issues and Speed of Transfer Come into Play

1991 also saw the introduction of two other Internet features that foreshadowed today's concerns about privacy and speed on Internet:

- Pretty Good Privacy (PGP), a program that allows largely anonymous net surfing by covering a surfer's tracks as he or she moves from site to site

- the upgrade of the Internet (still at that point officially known as NSFNET) backbone to allow it to transfer data at a rate of 44.736 megabits per second (Mbps)

In 1992, the number of hosts on the increasingly visually oriented Internet passed one million, and the multimedia future of the Web was forecast by the first Internet audio broadcast in March, and the first Internet video broadcast in November.

In Internet-ese, broadcasting *is referred to as* multicasting.

InterNIC, the organization that today assigns and oversees Web addresses, was created in 1993. Shortly thereafter, in 1994, the Web became the second most frequently-used Net feature, in terms of the percentage its traffic formed of the total number of packets and bytes moved.

The WWW Comes into Its Own

The Web didn't play second fiddle for long. Early in 1995, it surpassed its only remaining rival, FTP, in the number of packets and bytes it pushed out onto the Internet. And at about the same time, the multicast technique known as streaming was introduced.

Streaming *refers to a method of transmission in which the display of information does not await the complete transfer of that information. Rather, data moves in a continuous stream, and can be presented immediately and continuously upon its arrival at its destination.*

Table F-1 summarizes the growth of the World Wide Web into the dominant Internet service it is today.

At this date	there were about this many Web sites
June, 1993	130
December, 1993	620
June, 1994	2700
June, 1995	23,000
January, 1996	100,000
June, 1996	230,000

Table F-1. *A Thumbnail of WWW Growth*

The Web as a body of software, a set of protocols and conventions, and a collection of information continues to grow and change. However, it still relies on two fundamental underpinnings—HTTP and HTML. It is these which make the Web easy and interesting for anyone to roam and browse. So we'll continue our perusal of the evolution of Web publishing with a discussion of HTTP and HTML.

A Little More Detail on HTTP

The Hypertext Transfer Protocol operates as a client/server process. That is, it passes requests for information originating at your PC (the client) to a beefier machine somewhere on the Internet (the server), which functions as a Web concierge, if you will.

On the server, something known as a daemon (pronounced and tongue-in-cheek-named just like *demon*) actually processes your request. The term *daemon* applies to any program or utility that:

■ runs in the background, unbeknownst to all but the system or network administrator who configured it

■ most frequently handles requests for some sort of service

When you use your browser to enter a request for information in an HTML document on the web, an HTTP service configured as a daemon on the remote machine automatically handles the request.

A Little More Detail on HTML

The HyperText Markup Language (HTML) is a simple method for creating documents that are portable from one platform to another. HTML documents, and HTML itself, in turn rely on another language: the Standard Generalized Markup Language (SGML).

Sidebar

SGML documents have three major sections:

■ a SGML declaration

■ a Document Type Declaration (DTD)

■ marked, that is, format-tagged, content

HTML files are nothing more than SGML documents with generic grammar and symbol sets. The grammar and symbols have been designed to be appropriate for representing textual information from a wide range of sources and of a wide range of appearances.

HTML Standards

As a format for exchanging documents on the Web, HTML must meet a number of criteria. Here are some of them:

- Provide interoperability between a number of products running a gamut of applications, such as word processing, Web authoring, and database-related publishing

- Offer users a consistent view of a diverse, distributed set of information sources

- Meet the common needs of information providers for publishing and delivering their varied information and services over the Web

- Provide a simple user interface for interactive tasks such as completing order forms and database queries

- Have rich expressive power and visual impact (this is important because of the continually expanding variety of materials that it must handle)

- Be simple (this characteristic has been critical to the growth of the Web)

- Be backward-compatible with existing documents

- Take into account the capabilities and constraints presented by a variety of display technologies, such as the Graphical User Interfaces (GUIs) in the various incarnations of Windows; text-only displays such as VT-100 terminals; text-to-speech devices such as voice simulators; Braille devices; and printers

Glossary

L
ike the Bibliography, this Glossary is structured as a simple alphabetized table. Unlike the Bibliography, there's only one table here. But we think it gives you your money's worth, since we've tried to include in it the terms most significant to Dynamic HTML.

This term	refers to	and can be illustrated by
<AU>	the HTML 3.0 tag with which you can specify the author of a document	
Access	Microsoft's relational database management system	
Acrobat	an application suite from Adobe which uses a PostScript-based file format as the foundation for a cross-platform delivery system for documents	
ActiveX	the successor to OLE as Microsoft's scheme for data, method, and object sharing between applications	
AIFF	Audio Interchange File Format	
ALIGN	attribute that can be used in conjunction with a number of HTML tags, such as <CAPTION>, <IMG>, and <MARQUEE>	`<IMG` `ALIGN=BASELINE` `/IMG>` (BASELINE value specific to Netscape 3.0)
anchor	the HTML tag <A>, which points a browser to a linked document	`<A` `HREF="GO2.HTM"` `/A>`

This term	refers to	and can be illustrated by
Apache	a freeware, UNIX-based Web server which, according to many sources, has the largest worldwide installed base of any such application	
APP	a tag included in HTML documents by older releases of Java to indicate that a browser is to execute a Java applet	`<APP    .../APP>`
applet	small Java applications that execute entirely on a client station, without making calls to a server-side program	
APPLET	a tag included in HTML documents by more recent releases of Java to indicate that a browser is to execute a Java applet	`<APPLET    .../APPLET>`

AREA	an HTML tag indicating the screen area that is to be occupied by an image map	`<AREA`
		`SHAPE="rect"`
		`COORDS=20,20,40,40`
		`HREF="somefile.htm"`

attributes	attributes are qualities which can pertain to an HTML tag, for example, arguments, options, switches, or parameters.	

This term	**refers to**	**and can be illustrated by**
AU	audio file format created by Sun Microsystems. Originally found only in UNIX environments. Now available in almost every other environment.	
authentication	security for a Web site. Specifically, refers to verifying such information as user ID and password and workstation IP address	

AUTOSTART	attribute that can be applied to plug-ins for Netscape 3.0 and higher. Has only two possible values: TRUE, indicating that an audio or video file will play as soon as it downloads, without a user's having to start it explicitly FALSE, telling the browser that a user must manually start such a file	`<EMBED`
		`SRC="WHATEVER.AVI"`
		`WIDTH=240`
		`HEIGHT=240`
		`AUTOSTART=TRUE/EMBED>`

AVI	also known as Video for Windows	
background	the aspects of a Web page that seem to recede from the eye	

This term	**refers to**	**and can be illustrated by**
BACKGROUND	attribute added to the <BODY> tag in HTML 3.0 to allow you to specify a color other than the default gray for a page's background	```<BODY BACKGROUND= "snowfield.gif" . . . </BODY>```
bandwidth	the range of frequencies available to data communications; usually expressed in MegaHertz or MHz, which denotes millions of cycles of an electronic signal per second	13.3 MHz
BANNER	tag introduced in HTML 3.0 with which you can define an area of the screen which will not scroll	```<BANNER <P BOLD Overview /P> </BANNER>```
BASE	a tag, permitted only within the HEAD element, which allows you to specify an initial link for a document	```<HEAD> . . . <BASE HREF="somefile.htm" /BASE> </HEAD>```
base font	the default font for a Web page; can be modified with the BASEFONT tag	

This term	refers to	and can be illustrated by
BASEFONT	a tag, supported by both Internet Explorer 3.0 and higher and Netscape navigator 3.0 and higher, which allows you to define a page's default font size; usually used in combination with the FONT tag	`<BASEFONT SIZE=7 /BASEFONT>`

BGCOLOR	attribute, available to the tags BODY, MARQUEE, and tags representing portions of tables in Internet Explorer 2.0 and up, through which you can set the background color of an area of a page; values can be supplied as a color name or as a hexadecimal value	`<MARQUEE`
		`    ... other code ...`
		`BGCOLOR=YELLOW`
		`    ... other code ...`
		`/MARQUEE>`

BGPROPERTIES	an attribute, specific to Internet Explorer 2.0 and up, which allows you to set nonscrolling background areas; must be used within the BODY element	`<BODY`
		`BACKGROUND="gif2.gif"`
		`BGPROPERTIES=FIXED`
		`    ... other code ...`
		`</BODY>`

This term	**refers to**	**and can be illustrated by**

BGSOUND	a tag, specific to Internet Explorer 2.0 and up, which allows you to define background sound for a page; the default is to play the theme once, after the file containing it is fully downloaded	`<BGSOUND`
		`SRC="willy.wav"`
		`LOOP=INFIINITE`
		`/BGSOUND>`
		(treats visitors to your page to a refrain from Credence Clearwater Revival's "Willy and the Poor Boys"; refrain will repeat as long as the page is active)

BIG	a tag introduced in HTML 3.0 that allows you to display the text contained within the tag's delimiters in a large font	`<BIG>`
		`This should get your attention.`
		`</BIG>`

BLINK	a tag specific to Netscape 1.0 and higher that causes text embedded within the tag's delimiters to blink	`<P>`
		`<BLINK>`
		`Do you find this annoying?`
		`</BLINK>`
		`</P>`

bookmark	pointers, kept by every browser known to humanity, which store URLs and act as shortcuts to the sites referenced by those URLs	
broadcast	on the Web, refers to streamed, or continuously displayed, you-don't-have-to-wait-for-the-download-to-finish, audio or video	

This term	refers to	and can be illustrated by
browser	client software that allows the viewing of HTML pages. Among the gazillion-plus browsers available at the time this book was being written are Aficionado Web Surfer Cello CyberJack Fountain Grail Internet Explorer Lynx NCSA Mosaic Netscape Navigator WebSurfer	
button	Web page objects that can be clicked to initiate some action; types of buttons available include check box, navigation, and radio	
C	the successor to B (really); a programming language that combines the logical constructs available to high-level languages with the down-on-the-metal control usually associated with assembly language	
C++	a superset of C that implements Object-Oriented Programming	

This term	refers to	and can be illustrated by
capture	most frequently, screen capture; taking a snapshot of the current display. Accomplished through applications like Collage (which snapped all the screen shots contained in this book) and HiJack	
case-sensitive	distinguishing between upper- and lower-case letters; most frequently pertains to references to file systems in UNIX environments	
CDF	Channel Definition Format; Microsoft's proposed alternative/ successor to traditional netcasting push/pull methods; relies largely upon XML	
CERN	European Laboratory for Particle Physics (from its original French name, Conseil Européen pour la Recherche Nucleaire); where http, HTML, and the Web were invented	

This term	refers to	and can be illustrated by
CGI	Common Gateway Interface; a set of standards for the exchange of data between applications across a client/server network. CGI programs can be written in a variety of languages	
CGM	Computer Graphic Metafiles; a standard for Web graphics variously defined by such organizations as American National Standards Institute (ANSI) International Standards Organization (ISO) National Institute of Standards and Technology (NBS; we don't know why) and as such occasionally producing unexpected results. Still worthwhile in spite of this shortcoming, since it is a documented international standard which supersedes formats like GIF or JPEG	

This term	**refers to**	**and can be illustrated by**
character set	The set of characters most frequently used in Web pages is ISO-Latin 1, which includes not only the usual ASCII characters, but also such internationalizing additions as umlauts grave accents circumflexes diphthongs	
channel	in Web parlance, a preferred or frequently-visited site or set of sites	
class	in a Java context, and as defined on Sun Microsystems' site http://www.javasoft.com: "A class is a blueprint or prototype that you can use to create many objects. The implementation of a class is comprised of two components: the class declaration and the class body.

classDeclaration {classBody} | |

This term	refers to	and can be illustrated by
	The class declaration component declares the name of the class along with other attributes such as the class's superclass, and whether the class is public, final, or abstract. The class body follows the class declaration and is embedded within curly braces. The class body contains declarations for all member variables for the class. In addition, the class body contains declarations methods for the class.	
crawler	a type of Web-searching software that indexes site content as a means of expediting searches; not to be confused with a browser	
CreativeVoice	SoundBlaster's audio file format; carries the extension .voc	
CSS	Cascading Style Sheet; the term used by the W3C as an umbrella for its stylesheet definitions	

This term	refers to	and can be illustrated by
daemon	used most frequently in UNIX environments, indicates a process which runs in the background, completely invisible to a user; a bit of data processing punning	
DDL	SQL-ese for Data Definition Language; those commands through which you define a database and its characteristics, including field data types and lengths and record lengths	
defaults	values assigned to HTML tags unless you tell a browser otherwise	
dialog, dialog box	points or areas within a Web page that allow a user to do such things as choose an item or items from a displayed list or enter text in response to a prompt	

This term	refers to	and can be illustrated by
digitizing	converting sound or image files from an analog format (like that used in the telephone system, which consists of a nearly infinite number of states available to a signal) to a digital one, in which a signal can exist in only one of several discrete, or clearly defined, states consisting of a particular frequency	
DML	SQL-ese for Data Manipulation Language; those commands through which you query or modify data within a database	
DTD	Document Type Declaration; an SGML construct that specifies the markups to be done to a document or group of documents	
element	can be variously thought of as equivalent to an HTML tag, attribute, block, or simply as an area or component of an HTML document	

This term	refers to	and can be illustrated by
entities	what you might think, but in terms of SGML—that is, can include variables, constants, and character and format definitions; in HTML, either character or numeric data types	
event	something that happens while a program executes; in a Web context, as in all environments, can be application- or system-initiated (e.g., warning messages) or user-initiated (e.g., a mouse-over or mouse-click)	
FRAME	an HTML tag that allows you to deal with an area of a window as if it were a window unto itself	`<FRAME SRC="newfile.htm" /FRAME>`
FRAMESET	an HTML tag that allows you to define the dimensions of a frame	`<FRAMESET ROWS="100, 200, 300" /FRAMESET>`
ftp	file transfer protocol; oldie-but-goodie that allows you to log onto a server and exchange files with it in both directions	

This term	**refers to**	**and can be illustrated by**
gateway	in data communications hardware terms, a device that can connect completely dissimilar networks; in data communications software terms, a program that acts as an entry point between networks	
GIF	Graphics Interchange Format; one of the two most widely used image-file formats on the Web	
gopher	a protocol similar to http, but without the latter's strongly visual usage or hyperlink capabilities	
hexadecimal	a numbering system based on the value 16, and using the symbols 0 through 9 and A through F. In hexadecimal notation, what we would ordinarily represent as "15" becomes "F"	
hexadecimal color value	one means of representing color specifications in HTML tags	BGCOLOR="#FF FB F0" (cream)
HREF	HTML tag indicating a hyper-reference, or URL to be jumped to	

This term	refers to	and can be illustrated by
HTML	Hypertext Markup Language; can be considered a subset of the larger SGML	
http	hypertext transfer protocol; the underpinning of the Web	
hyperlink	another term for anchor or link; a point anywhere on the Web that can be jumped to directly, rather than through a linear, hierarchical path	
IETF	Internet Engineering Task Force; one of the professional bodies most responsible for developing standards for all aspects of the Internet	
IFF	Interchange File Format; image file format used in a number of environments	
image map	in effect, a menu consisting of icons or links	
IMAGEMAP	in HTML 3.0, an attribute that must be used within the FIGURE tag's delimiters, and that simply tells the browser that the figure in question has an image map associated with it	

This term	refers to	and can be illustrated by
IMG	an HTML tag that allows you to embed in a Web page, or link to from that page, an image file of a number of formats	`<IMG SRC="pic.jpg" /IMG>`
INRIA	the French National Institute for Research in Computing and Automation, or Institut de Recherche en Informatique et Systèmes Aléatoires	
instance	analogous to iteration; a single occurrence of, most frequently, a programming method	
interlaced	a technique applied to Web video transmission in which odd and even horizontal lines of fields are alternated; results in a display which largely lacks flicker and distortion	
IPX/SPX	the transport protocol native to Novell networks	
Java	the C-like programming language designed by Sun Microsystems specifically for Internet programming	

This term	refers to	and can be illustrated by
JavaScript	a scripting, that is, an interpreted (as opposed to compiled) and client-side (as opposed to server-based) language designed by Netscape Communications and Sun Microsystems to emulate Java	
JScript	Microsoft's version of JavaScript	

LANGUAGE	an HTML attribute that indicates the scripting language to be used	`<SCRIPT`
		`LANGUAGE="JAVASCRIPT"`
		`   ...   some code here   ...`
		`</SCRIPT>`

link	a non-linear, non-hierarchical connection from one HTML document to another	
LZW	a method of compression often used in GIF files	
MBONE	the multicast backbone for the entire Internet	

META	an HTML tag with which you can specify annotative information such as keywords or expiration dates for a document	`<META>`
		`HTTP.EQUIV = "expires"`
		`CONTENT = "01/01/98"`
		`</META>`

method	a generalized syntax for a programming module	

This term	refers to	and can be illustrated by
MIDI	Musical Instrument Digital Interface; file format and hardware/software that accomplishes it	
MIME	Multipurpose Internet Mail Extensions; defines data types and corresponding file name conventions for a wide variety of formats	
MPEG	Motion Picture Experts Group; file formats for both audio and video	
multicasting	the Internet equivalent of radio or television; the simultaneous transmission along a number of bandwidth ranges of multiple copies of the same audio or video item	
multimedia	in Web jargon, adding sound and high-resolution still or moving images to a page	
netcasting	Web jargon for Internet broadcasting	
NNTP	Network News Transfer Protocol	
NSSL	Netscape Secure Sockets Layer	

This term	**refers to**	**and can be illustrated by**
NTSC	video broadcast standard found in the US and Japan; mandates display of 60 fields per second, with interlaced images	
object	in object-oriented languages such as C++ and Java, any unit, such as a file, a radio box, an anchor, and so on, that can be used to carry out a task; analogous to the idea of a compound variable such as Structure in C, but with a significant difference: objects can include both data and programming instructions	
PAL	video broadcast standard found in Europe	
plug-ins	used most frequently in the context of Netscape browsers; modules created specifically to allow various versions of Navigator to play or view audio or image files	
PNG	a compression method used by GIF files	
PPP	Point-to-Point Protocol	
PPTP	Point-to-Point Tunneling Protocol	

This term	refers to	and can be illustrated by
RIFF	Microsoft's WAVE (sound) format for Windows	
s-http	secure http; a variant of the basic protocol that provides encrypting	

SCRIPT	an attribute introduced in HTML 3.0 that must be used within the bounds of the FORM tag that indicates, and allows you to incorporate, scripting commands within an HTML document	`<FORM`
		`METHOD="POST"`
		`SCRIPT="someprog.jav"`
		`... some other code ...`
		`</FORM>`

SGML	Standard Generalized markup Language	
spider	a type of Web-searching software that concerns itself with such annotative or meta-information as date of last modification (as opposed to crawlers' indexing of content); often used by push/pull-based channels	
SQL	Structured Query Language; in fact, a standard as opposed to a specific syntax	

This term	**refers to**	**and can be illustrated by**
SRC	HTML attribute, most frequently used with the IMG tag, that indicates the full path name of the source file for the image	
stylesheet	in effect, a set of directions for formatting an HTML document; somewhat analogous to, but more extensive than, macros in word processing applications	

tag	HTML formatting codes; encased in angle brackets (< >), and using a right-leaning slash (/) to indicate the end of the block formed by the tag	`<BODY>`
		`...  some other code  ...`
		`</BODY>`

TCP/IP	Transport (or Transmission in its earliest naming) Control Protocol/Internet Protocol; the family of data communication software that is the software basis for the Internet	
TIFF	Tagged Image File Format	

This term	refers to	and can be illustrated by
URL	Uniform Resource Locator; most frequently follows one of two common formats: protocol://hostname:port /path protocol://username: password@hostname: port/path	
URN	Universal Resource Name; not equivalent to URL; still being developed by the W3C	
VBScript	Visual Basic Scripting Edition; Microsoft's Visual Basic-based client scripting language	
W3C	World Wide Web Consortium; managed by the Laboratory for Computer Science at the Massachusetts Institute of Technology; a joint MIT/CERN/INRIA body, which plays a leading role in the development of standards and specifications for the World Wide Web	
WAIS	Wide Area Information Servers; most frequently house indexed text files	

This term	refers to	and can be illustrated by
XML	Extensible Markup Language; a successor to HTML and SGML that some consider the next phase in the evolution of Web publishing markup languages	

Bibliography

This Bibliography consists of two tables, the first giving print sources of additional information on the topics *Dynamic HTML in Action* has discussed, and the second giving online sources of further material on those topics.

When using the second table, bear in mind the volatility of the Web. While we checked out every URL here as this book was being written, we can't guarantee that the pages, or even the sites, referenced still exist.

Print Sources

Title	Published By	Description
Web Publishing Unleashed	sams.net	Everything you ever wanted to know and then some regarding HTML, SGML, VRML, Web scripting languages, and multimedia Web sites
Beyond HTML	Osborne/McGraw-Hill	Presents HTML alternatives and addenda such as Adobe Acrobat, database interactivity, Java, real-time audio, and multiuser environments
JavaScript Essentials: Creating Interactive Web Applications	Osborne/McGraw-Hill	An easy-to-understand guide to creating and manipulating JavaScript objects and incorporating them into Web pages
The Sound and Music Workshop	Sybex	Presents a thorough introduction to digital audio
Web Design Templates Sourcebook	New Riders	Contains a variety of Web page templates applicable to many environments, as well as instructions for implementing those templates

Online Sources

This URL	Presents
http://developer.netscape.com/library/documentation	An entry point to Netscape's searchable Developers Library
http://developer.netscape.com/library/documentation/communicator/layers/index.htm	An entry point to more complete information on layering in JavaScript
http://home.netscape.com/comprod/products/communicator/layers/layers_glossary.htm	Introductory information on layering with JavaScript
http://mbiz.co.th/tips_tricks/dyn.html	A good generalized discussion of the theory behind and various usages of the term Dynamic HTML
http://www.download.com http://www.jumbo.com http://www.shareware.com http://www.tucows.com	Shareware sites that offer a wide variety of try-it-out Web tools. But be aware that some of these tools may fail to download or install properly
http://www.hitsquad.com/smm/rta/win.html	An index of downloadable audio and video shareware and freeware tools for Windows 3.x, 95, and NT

This URL	Presents
http://www.homeworlds.com/faq/dynmdef.htm	The HomeWorlds Web site, where you can get information about a great variety of topics. Homeworlds is a Web company that offers help in building and maintaining World Web Web sites and Intranets. HomeWorlds provides a variety of standard World Wide Web Presence packages and custom Intranet packages for any size business or interested individuals. Click on the What's New link on the HomeWorlds page and you'll access a list of topics about which HomeWorlds provides info on a variety of Web technologies and topics. There's some great grounding information about Dynamic HTML here, how Microsoft and Netscape both profess to make use of the technologies, and a great overview of just how DHTML operates.
http://www.imperium.co.uk/implay1.html	The Web pages of Imperium Computing Consultants, Inc., a UK-based Web site consultants firm, that provides a wealth of info on their site, including a collection of DHTML example code and a good introduction to working with layers to build a dynamic page. Visit the site to find a variety of information about DHTML and other core Web technologies.
http://www.info.med.yale.edu/caim/manual	Solid basic Web design from the Center for Advanced Instructional Media at Yale

This URL	Presents
http://www.insideDHTML.com	A Web site that provides access to sample DHTML pages, pointers to a variety of DHTML resources and sample games, among other content.
http://www.javasoft.com	Sun Microsystems' site for everything Java-related
http://www.macromedia.com	Home of multimedia Web products like Shockwave and BackStage Development Studio
http://www.microsoft.com/ie/ie40	An entry point to Internet Explorer 4 that gives you an overview, demos, download, and more. (Be aware that to run the demos, you'll have to be browsing through Internet Explorer 4; downloading it takes several hours, even with the fastest modem.)
http://www.microsoft.com/kb (The Microsoft Technical Support Knowledge Base)	The ability to search for documents in Microsoft's collection of White Papers, FAQs, and bug reports
http://www.techweb.cmp.com/eet/823 (Electronic Engineering Times on the Web)	Latest developments in computing technology
http://www.vivo.com	Home of multimedia authoring tools like VivoActive Producer
http://www.w3.org/pub/www	An entry point to the World Wide Web Consortium's site; leads to in-depth information on W3C standards, activities, and more
http://www.webreference.com	The name pretty much says it all—a collection of information on all aspects of Web publishing

This URL	Presents
http://www.webreference.com/dhtml	Access to content from Webreference.com, one of the Web sites created by Athenia Associates, which provides information on a range of topics from webmastery to browsing and authoring, HTML and advanced site design. This URL leads to a site that features a Dynamic HTML Lab where you can view DHTML code created using IE 4 and Netscape Navigator, just for starters.

Index

N